Spies, Spin and the Fourth Estate

Anna, Ben and Arthur

Spies, Spin and the Fourth Estate

British Intelligence and the Media

PAUL LASHMAR

EDINBURGH
University Press

Edinburgh University Press is one of the leading university presses in the UK.
We publish academic books and journals in our selected subject areas across the
humanities and social sciences, combining cutting-edge scholarship with high
editorial and production values to produce academic works of lasting importance.
For more information visit our website: edinburghuniversitypress.com

Edinburgh University Press Ltd
The Tun – Holyrood Road
12(2f) Jackson's Entry
Edinburgh EH8 8PJ

Typeset in 10/13 Giovanni by
Servis Filmsetting Ltd, Stockport, Cheshire
and printed and bound by CPI Group (UK)
Ltd, Croydon, CR0 4YY

A CIP record for this book is available from the British Library

ISBN 978 1 4744 4307 4 (hardback)
ISBN 978 1 4744 4309 8 (webready PDF)
ISBN 978 1 4744 4308 1 (paperback)
ISBN 978 1 4744 4310 4 (epub)

CONTENTS

The Russian 'hit' on the spy Sergei Skripal in Britain was one of the major news stories of 2018 and ran through much of the year. The botched assassination attempt triggered an extensive UK counter-terrorism investigation to identify who had tried to kill the sixty-six-year-old Russian father and his thirty-two-year-old daughter Yulia in a nerve agent attack on a chilly Sunday afternoon in Salisbury, a medieval English city more noted for its cathedral's elegant spire than as a theatre of international intrigue.

From 1994, Sergei Skripal, a colonel in the Russian GRU intelligence agency, was bribed by British Intelligence to spy on his colleagues, allowing them to understand the GRU's post-Soviet role, objectives and capabilities.[1] Allegedly codenamed 'Forthwith' by the British, Sergei Skripal was arrested by Russia's security services in 2004, convicted, imprisoned and exchanged in a spy swop in Vienna, to be then flown to Britain and given what was presumably meant to be a new, low-key life in Salisbury. The nerve agent attack on the Skripals was another operation by the Russian secret services in Britain and caused a tense international diplomatic stand-off with President Putin's regime. The sinister GRU agency, seemingly tasked with assassinating Putin's political rivals, specialise in intimidating those who have fallen out with the regime and covertly manipulating the politics of target states.

As the murder plot commanded worldwide media interest, hundreds of journalists and TV crews descended on the city for weeks. While the media circus eventually moved on, the story remained significant, providing an example of how national security is never far from the top of the news. The Skripal story was just one of several national security stories running at the time. Only two weeks before the murder attempt, several British newspapers had alleged on their front pages that Jeremy Corbyn, the left-wing leader of the UK Labour Party, had been a paid informer of the StB, the Czechoslovakian secret service during the late Cold War. This story was based on claims by the former Czech spy Jan Sarkocy, who, working undercover as a diplomat, had met Corbyn several times in London in the 1980s. After a few days the story faded as no substantive corroboration was published, sparking claims it was just another politically inspired smear operation against a Labour Party leader.

Across the Atlantic in the USA, President Trump nominated Gina Haspel for promotion to become the Central Intelligence Agency's (CIA's) first woman director, constituting a notable gender breakthrough, but this was also a controversial appointment. Haspel had worked undercover for much of her thirty-year CIA career and while little is known about her role in covert operations, it was on the record that in the early 2000s she had taken charge of a secret 'black' CIA base in Thailand. Before she took over command, al-Qaeda leader Abu Zubaydah, among others, was rendered, detained, tortured and interrogated at this CIA base.[2]

Such national security issues had again dominated the news media across the Western world, to be replaced by more headline stories of intelligence and terrorism. The world of intelligence exudes testosterone and stimulates the audience so it rates highly in news values; as generations of journalists and editors have known, spying stories are sexy (sometimes literally with honeytraps) – and spies sell news.

Never without Strain

The worlds of spying and journalism have always been intertwined, sometimes intimate and sometimes confrontational. Sir David Omand, former director of the UK's signals intelligence agency, Government Communications Headquarters (GCHQ), has commented that the worlds of secret intelligence and journalism interact, 'but never without strain' (2009: 38). Israeli academic Professor

Shlomo Shpiro has observed the essential tension between the two professions:

> An inherent conflict exists between the open media, that wish to publish security related information as part of their responsibility toward their audience, and intelligence services, which work on the basis of secrecy and often attempt to prevent the publication of information on their activities and sources. (Shpiro 2001: 485)

The intelligence historian Richard Aldrich has observed that the relationship between secret services and the press is long-standing and remarkably close but it has not been systematically analysed: 'Despite the prolific press coverage of the intelligence services since 9/11, the interaction of this secret realm of government with the media has received little sustained analysis' (2009: 13). This book seeks to remedy this neglect.

It seeks to detail how, as part of examining the relationship between the intelligence world and the media, intelligence policy, strategy and operations have been reported. It brings together history, personal history and analysis, to give an insider's perspective on intelligence and the media. To provide context for the following chapters, it describes the origins of the official UK intelligence agencies.

Writers and journalists are there right at the creation of the modern UK intelligence services. As we will see, the way intelligence and the media interact often comes down to the relationship between individual spies and journalists, and, as in all relationships, that can vary from intimate to downright hostile. Aldrich hints at a mutual attraction between spies and journalists; 'Yet even where the relationship was prickly, there remained an underlying appreciation that journalism and espionage are cognate activities and share common professional ethics, including the diligent protection of sources' (Aldrich 2009: 14). Each side has been only too willing to take advantage of the other. Intelligence agencies have been keen to use journalism as part of their toolkit, often to give them cover when working in dangerous foreign states. In 1977 the *Pike Report* from the US House of Representatives spelt out neatly why journalistic cover is was so attractive:

Intelligence agencies have long prized journalists as informant and identity-covers. Newsmen generally enjoy great mobility, and are often admitted to areas denied to ordinary businessmen or to suspected intelligence types. Not expected to work in one fixed location, both bona fide journalists and masquerading intelligence officers can move about without arousing suspicions. They also have extraordinary access to important foreign leaders and diplomats. (Pike 1977: 223)

To build a picture of the relationship since the beginning of the twentieth century, this book explores a number of key themes. They include:

1. How spies have used the media – initially with print journalists, and later radio and TV reporters – as part of their operations, something in which journalists have sometimes knowingly and sometimes unknowingly participated.
2. Where journalists are co-opted by intelligence as propagandists.
3. Where spies have used journalistic cover and the risks that entailed.
4. Why journalists and spies are often described as 'cognate' professions that are two sides of the same coin.
5. Where journalists have brought intelligence agencies and agents to account. They may be the most effective mode of holding the secret world to account in the UK.

British Intelligence

The profession of spying is often referred to as the second oldest profession, a moniker that slyly links it with the oldest profession · prostitution – and implies a seediness and lack of morality. The British have only had a coherent intelligence operation for little over 100 years. The Secret Intelligence Service (SIS), also known as MI6, is mostly engaged in human intelligence (HUMINT). It is tasked with spying and countering Britain's enemies abroad, whether nation states or transnational terrorist groups. In Britain, the Security Service, MI5, tries to prevent intelligence gathering by other nations but it also takes on the counter-terrorism (CT) role. GCHQ conducts electronic surveillance (SIGINT – signals intelligence) across the world and supports the other two agencies. Between them, according to the 2017–18 estimates, by 2020/2021 they will employ some 16,000 staff on a £2.7bn budget.[3]

This book focuses on British Intelligence and security services and their interaction with the UK news media, but from time to time it refers to other parts of the intelligence apparatus. It also refers from time to time to the huge United States intelligence community, with its sixteen or so different agencies, and the US media. The USA is the global intelligence hegemon, with a budget estimated at $57.7 billion in 2018,[4] and is hard to ignore with its worldwide reach. The signals intelligence agencies, the National Security Agency (NSA) in the United States and Britain's GCHQ, have worked closely together for over seventy years and with the other 'Five Eyes' countries – Canada, Australia and New Zealand – and not quite so closely with another thirty-two partner countries to create a network that has global surveillance capability.

The innate and defining features of the national security apparatus – secrecy, information gathering, surveillance, intervention, arrest, imprisonment, even internment – provide the state with powerful tools to identify and act against those they define as a threat, whether internally or externally. National security is fundamental to the state and it is often in tension with other freedoms such as human rights, freedom of speech, freedom of the media, and privacy. Commentators agree that such tools need to be carefully integrated with rigorous accountability mechanisms to avoid curtailing individuals' liberties without good reason.

One aim of this book is to cut through the protective myths that surround the intelligence world. The journalist's job is not to be in awe of mystique but instead to provide challenge to the presuppositions that exist in the intelligence world as elsewhere. The eminent US intelligence academic, Loch K. Johnson, told me the media play the major role in ensuring the accountability of intelligence agencies:

> I think that (in the United States at least) the media has done much more than any other organization or group to advance intelligence accountability. Especially investigative journalists, in their drive for a good story that might lead to their professional advancement and honors (Pulitzers and

Polks, for example), have been successful in sniffing out stories and alerting elected overseers in Congress to carry out investigations. (Johnson 2015)

He has also stated that the media bring intelligence failures to the attention of the legislators in government:

> The facts and interpretations presented by the media may well be the most vital aspect of the coverage; but sustained reporting on a topic may be important, too, as a means of emphasizing its merits as a policy controversy worthy of closer attention from overseers. (Johnson 2013: 3)

This in no way suggests that journalism was or is in a perfect condition as it has many problems and failings. However, it is a pluralistic entity and within its fourth estate role the news media has a self-regulatory element, which, like everything else it does, it does imperfectly.[5]

Finally, this book is intended to give a sense of how UK journalism and British Intelligence have co-existed over the last century and, where appropriate, I use my own experience of covering intelligence as a journalist for over four decades.[6] I hope it proves to be a good read, informative, and that it provides some insight into this strange world of spies and hacks for students, academics, journalists and intelligence officers and the wider reading public alike.

Paul Lashmar
Dorchester
August 2019

Notes

1. The Directorate is Russia's largest foreign intelligence agency.
2. Abu Zubaydah was water boarded eighty-three times, and subject to all twelve of the CIA's 'enhanced interrogation techniques' – or more succinctly, torture. MI6 questioned him during this period despite knowing he had been subject to sustained torture including losing his left eye. It took until 2018 before a parliamentary committee revealed MI6 had been involved (Cobain and Doward 2018).

3. <https://assets.publishing.service.gov.uk/government/uploads/system/uploa
ds/attachment_data/file/738479/SIA_Accounts_HC1509_Web_Version.pdf>
(last accessed 16 September 2019).
4. <https://www.dni.gov/index.php/newsroom/press-releases/item/1767-dni-re
leases-budget-figure-for-fy-2018-appropriations-requested-for-the-national-inte
lligence-program> (last accessed 16 September 2019).
5. For an explanation of the development of the fourth estate concept, see Boyce
1978.
6. Some elements of this book have appeared in my books, journalism and academic papers. A detailed list appears in the References.

ACKNOWLEDGEMENTS

Richard Aldrich, Duncan Campbell, Ian Cobain, Stephen Dorril, Rob Evans, Richard Fletcher, Ivor Gaber, Peter Gill, Mark Hollingsworth, Richard Keeble, Anna Killick, David Leigh, Professor Scott Lucas, Robin Lustig, Richard Norton-Taylor, James Oliver, Professor Julian Petley, Professor Mark Phythian, Kim Sengupta and Mike Smith.

Particular gratitude goes to Professor Vian Bakir and Adrian Gatton who both gave me excellent advice along the way and some very helpful editing.

I would like to thank the *The Guardian*, *Observer* and *The Independent* newspapers for swift copyright clearance for lengthy quotes, mostly from my earlier work.

While writing this book I heard the singer-songwriter Chris Wood perform his song about Jean Charles de Menezes, who was shot dead by police at Stockwell in 2005, mistaken for one of the 7/7 bombers. It reminded me of what happens when intelligence goes wrong and why accountability is so important.

Introduction

In a democracy, a nation's intelligence agencies should play a vital role in protecting the state from any malevolent forces that pursue political change by non-democratic means. How these agencies develop and operate goes to the very the heart of democracy. The UK intelligence services are generally highly regarded, and their staff undertake what can be an extremely difficult and sometimes dangerous vocation. As former CIA officer Hayden Peake favourably noted, 'By repute, the British Secret Intelligence Service is the oldest, most experienced, and most secret in the Western world.'[1] In the global spy league, only Israel's Mossad surpasses the popular reputation of the SIS. Both the SIS and Israel's Mossad punch well above their weight and size compared with their American CIA, Russian SVR (Foreign Intelligence Service) and Chinese Ministry of State Security (MSS) counterparts.[2] Since 9/11, with the British involvement in the invasions of Afghanistan and Iraq, Britain has been a major target for Islamist terrorists. In response, the British Intelligence and security services have developed effective networks with other nations threatened by terrorist attacks and often obtain advanced warning of potential attacks in other nations.

They work in secret and usually, in Britain, we only become aware of intelligence successes when they result in arrests and court cases. In the year ending 31 December 2017, some eighty-six trials were completed by the Crown Prosecution Service for terrorism-related offences, an increase from the sixty-two trials completed in the previous year.[3] Of the eighty-six people prosecuted, seventy-seven were convicted.[4] In August 2018, a spokesperson for the British Security Service, MI5, stated they were conducting 676 'live' terrorism investigations and had foiled thirteen Islamist plots in the preceding eighteen months (Dearden 2018).[5]

Mission Creep

Intelligence academics Robert Dover and Michael Goodman say that, while intelligence has been described in the past as the missing dimension in international relations, this could not be the case today:

> It might be underexplored and under-examined by the public politicians and academics, but it is directly in front of us. In every part of society, and in all our social interactions, intelligence has a role to play in conditioning the political and social environments in which we live. (Dover and Goodman 2009: 1)

The *raison d'être* of the intelligence services is to provide the information that maintains the security of the state. This function, in part, enables the state to fulfil a political contract where the citizen surrenders certain rights to government in return for security. The concept of this contract has evolved from the Enlightenment and has been debated by philosophers such as Hobbes, Locke, Rousseau and more recently Rawls. Rawls sets the modern contract: 'Each person is to have an equal right to the most extensive total system of liberties compatible with a similar system of liberty for all' (1971: 302).

As the Intelligence community supplies information to maintain the nation state, so it needs to be understood in terms of power and its place in the state's elites. Len Scott and Peter Jackson note that 'Much of the study of intelligence concerns the relationship between power and knowledge, or rather the relationship between certain kinds of power and certain kinds of knowledge' (2004: 150). Periodically, officials within UK intelligence agencies have been accused of using the unique facilities of intelligence to further their own political, non-democratic, or bureaucratic agenda.[6] In their 2016 book, Aldrich and Cormac detail how UK intelligence agencies have often done the British prime minister's dirty work: 'For more than a century, secret wars have been waged directly from Number 10. They have staved off conflict, defeats and British decline through fancy footwork, often deceiving friend and foe alike' (2016: back cover). While in fiction there is a romantic image of Western intelligence agents, the reality can be very different, especially for those who work on the ground or undercover. The US academics Hulnick and Mattausch summarise the CIA's intelligence agent's job in its starkest terms:

> Professional standards require intelligence professionals to lie, hide information or use covert tactics to protect their 'cover,' access, sources, and responsibilities. The Central Intelligence Agency expects, teaches, encourages and controls these tactics so that the lies are consistent and supported ('backstopped'). The CIA expects intelligence officers to teach others to lie, deceive, steal, launder money, and perform a variety of other activities that would certainly be illegal if practiced in the United States. They call these tactics 'tradecraft.' And intelligence officers practice them in all the world's intelligence services. (Hulnick and Mattausch 1989: 520–1)

There is no reason to doubt that in the UK secret services have, on many an occasion, exhibited a similar ethos. The UK intelligence and security agencies have acted from time to time in the face of basic democratic principles, especially in the colonies where torture, rape and murder were part of strategies to thwart nationalists (see Lashmar and Oliver 1998b; Cobain 2013). These warnings from history of the dangers of agencies given free rein are largely ignored, especially in times of national stress. In those times, the political and popular response is to boost resources to intelligence agencies that greatly increase the agencies' power and reach, while the public have little idea of the actual efficacy or misuse. The catalogue of failures of British Intelligence is a long list. It includes: the Nazi–Soviet pact; the invasion of Norway; the Soviet A-bomb test; the Crabb Affair; the Cambridge spy ring and numerous other betrayals by our own spies; the failure to anticipate the crushing of the 'Prague Spring'; the Argentinian invasion of the Falkland Islands; the start of The Troubles in Northern Ireland; the failure to predict the collapse of the Soviet Bloc; Iraq and weapons of mass destruction; and 7/7. All are well known.

The modus operandi of the intelligence and security agencies, reinforced by popular fictional representation, has often been Utilitarian, a dispensation with tactical illegality and unethical behaviour undertaken in the over-arching pursuit of the perceived greater good. Oliver Cromwell, as the head of the British State in its brief period as a republic in the seventeenth century, put the justification neatly: 'There are great occasions in which some men are called to great services, in the doing of which they are excused from the common rule of morality' (1842: 384). Cromwell reveals himself as an antinomianist, so in his case the excuser was God – who still is cited in many of these debates.[7] Many of the spy fraternity that I have met over the years, especially those who worked in Northern Ireland during The Troubles, were manipulative, undoubting and hard and were at heart, like Cromwell, antinomianists. Some others had complex moral justifications for the unjustifiable, usually based on the exigencies of war. Some just did not bother with justification, and they seemed consumed by playing the game for the game's sake. To encapsulate the ethical justification for illegal or immoral acts in the pursuit of intelligence, Bellaby came up with the concept of *jus in intelligentia* – the intelligence equivalent of the just war argument – where you cause some harm to prevent a much greater harm (Bellaby 2012: 111).

From its early days, British Intelligence reflected the best and worst aspects of the British Empire. An example from *The Guardian* concerns a senior MI5 officer who was long serving but with opinions that would now been seen as imperialist and racist. John Percival Morton CMG OBE, better known as Jack Morton, was a former colonial police chief in India who had spied on the independence movement there. He wrote in his memoirs that, over time, 'it dawned upon me, and became deeply ingrained, that the British were the rulers of India and that the Indians were a sort of immature, backward and needy people whom it was the natural British function to govern and administer'.[8] Morton was not alone in his attitudes and was an influential figure and, by the early 1970s, the senior MI5 officer in Northern Ireland during the early stages of The Troubles.[9] His colonialist view of the Indian people, and it seems Northern Ireland's Republicans, was typical in the generations who were involved in running the British Empire and certainly not uncommon in British Intelligence and the security services. It involved a profound underlying belief that the British were a racially superior nation and viewed other races, religions and cultures as lesser.

Approval Ratings

Public support for intelligence agencies is rarely unanimous, and at different times, different sections of the population eye the intelligence community warily. If you were an active nationalist in the British colonies before independence, you would not have felt the British-run security forces were there to protect your democratic rights. If you were brought up a Catholic Republican in Northern Ireland during The Troubles, it is unlikely you would have felt your interests were being protected. How far the British state was prepared to go in Northern Ireland was revealed in recent years by the British soldiers involved in assassination squads operating against the Irish Republication Army (IRA) (Ware 2013).[10]

The problems of studying intelligence are simply a lack of recent hard facts. As a result, especially in Britain, historical accounts have always constituted the main literature. The memoirs of former intelligence officers and, increasingly, the reconstruction of past episodes from released official files are the raw material for the hitherto 'missing dimension' of historical studies (Gill and Phythian 2012: 33).

The distinguished historian Bernard Porter opened his 1989 history of political espionage in Britain with the observation that little evidence in this area is dependable and that means that even if we were able to see the official record, it might not help:

It also means that we cannot rely on the evidence we are able to see. The reason for this is that all spies and secret agents are liars, trained in techniques of deception and dissimulation, who are just as likely to fake the historical record as anything else. This is why the first rule for the reader of any book about secret services, including this one, is not to trust a word of it. It could all be lies and disinformation; not on the part of the writer necessarily, but on the part of the sources he is gullible enough to believe. (Porter 1989: viii)

Porter's word of caution is useful advice: always maintain scepticism when investigating the intelligence world.

The Fourth Estate

The other profession that this book concerns itself with is journalism, and while the latter has no claim to be as old as spying, it can be seen as just as disreputable. Despite its many failings, it does have a higher aspiration: the concept of the freedom of the press within a democracy suggests that the news media preserve the citizen's liberties from an overbearing state and corporate sector. The respected American journalist Walter Cronkite (1984) sums up the thought elegantly:

> A democracy ceases to be a democracy if its citizens do not participate in its governance. To participate intelligently, they must know what their government has done, is doing, and plans to do in their name. Whenever any hindrance, no matter what its name, is placed in the way of this information, a democracy is weakened, and its future endangered. This is the meaning of freedom of press. It is not just important to democracy, it is democracy.

The normative role played by the media in democracy is often encapsulated in the concept of the 'fourth estate' and it is particularly relevant to investigative journalism. Journalists are seen as the guardians of the public interest.[11] In the first written reference to the fourth estate concept, the philosopher Edmund Burke was quoted as having said, 'there were Three Estates in Parliament; but, in the Reporters' Gallery yonder, there sat a Fourth Estate more important far than they all' (Carlyle 1840). In this context, the other three estates are the church, the nobility and the townsmen. The fourth estate concept tasks the media to hold the errant state and powerful to account.

The fourth estate can been seen to operate in German philosopher Jürgen Habermas's concept of the 'public sphere' – a place where ordinary citizens could engage in informed discussion without fear of repression. Habermas also saw it as check on state secrecy, 'against the reliance of princely authority on secrets of state'. He located the origins of such free discussion in the coffee shops of the seventeenth century that, he suggested, created a new public and 'articulated the concept of demand for general and abstract laws and . . . came to assert itself (i.e. public opinion) as the only legitimate source of this law' (Habermas 1962; see also Melley 2012: 31). The public sphere has been subject to much debate, even by the august Habermas himself, who has revised his views from time to time and according to changes in society and technology. The question arises as to whether the internet is the new public sphere. Habermas recognises that governments and powerful corporations including large media conglomerates have the capacity to distort the public sphere. It remains an effective concept for discussion. Professor Vian Bakir has pointed out that the secrecy surrounding intelligence means that publication of intelligence is highly restricted, barring occasional whistle-blowing and sanitised official leaks: 'These characteristics mean that intelligence, if publicised, can be highly manipulated by intelligence élites, while civil society's ability to assess and verify claims is compromised by absence of independent evidence' (2018: summary).

Reporting critically on the world of intelligence is regarded as one of the most difficult specialist beats in journalism as it is, by definition, a world of secrets. The task of making sense of what spies are up to brings to mind that most appropriate catchphrase, that the secret world is a 'wilderness of mirrors'.[12] For more than a generation, the task of traversing this wilderness of misinformation to make sense of the intelligence community has largely fallen to journalists in the absence of significant public oversight. In addition, when necessary, it has been the journalists' job to bring wayward spies to account despite the emergence of an official oversight community. The UK obsession with secrecy is highlighted by how frequently what is classified top secret one day is acceptable to put into the public domain on another. I am not talking about operational matters, which are of course sensitive for a limited period; I am talking about obsessive, all-embracing secrecy. Back in 1985 David Leigh and I, then *The Observer*'s investigative team, were passed information by a highly placed source that showed that the government's budget for intelligence was already nearly £1 billion, and this was published in the paper. The government was not pleased at all that we had released this information but an editorial decision had been made that it was important the public should have an idea of how much the intelligence community was costing the nation. It is the kind of information that enables the public to make informed democratic decisions (Leigh and Lashmar 1985a). Thirty years on, this information is now so normalised it is released annually to the public by government as the Single Intelligence Account as part of the Intelligence and Security Committee annual report.

Regulation by Revelation

Academics have suggested there is a void in terms of analysing the media's role in intelligence accountability and that while scholars are increasingly paying attention to aspects of intelligence oversight, accountability and control, one under-explored dimension so far is the role of the media. The US academic and doyen of intelligence studies Loch K. Johnson's (2013) 'shock theory' of congressional accountability suggests an important role for the media in setting off the 'alarm' in case of major intelligence failures. The UK academic Dr Claudia Hillebrand notes that despite all the research into accountability, a systematic account of the media's role is missing:

> This is surprising given the numerous occasions in the post-9/11 era when controversial, and sometimes illegal, dimensions of intelligence have been revealed by the news media. Indeed the previous decade suggests that the media might have an ever-important role to play in scrutinizing the intelligence services and their work (Hillebrand 2012: 690)

Richard Aldrich neatly characterises the normative if intermittent role the media play in monitoring the spy world as 'regulation by revelation' (Aldrich 2009: 13). The investigation of the 'Spy Cops' scandal provides an example of the media acting as an effective watchdog and providing unofficial oversight of the secret world. The Special Demonstrate Squad (SOS), an offshoot of the Metropolitan Police's Special Branch, was set up as a temporary intelligence gathering operation at the height of student protests in 1968. However, it was to expand, operating against civil rights, animal rights, anti-fascist, far-right and environmental activist groups for four decades. Male and female undercover police officers not only infiltrated these groups and undertook criminal acts to maintain cover, but in some cases also had relationships with the people they were monitoring – who were unaware they were police officers – and had children with them.

There is no dispute that some of these activist groups were engaged in violence, arson and other illegal activities and that some harm was prevented. Some activists were convicted. The majority were not prosecuted. The issue of proportionality arises and there remains a lack of evidence as to the extent of useful results from this resource-heavy form of policing. As the police have been reluctant to discuss operational details, it remains an open question as to whether the SDS and the later National Public Order Intelligence Unit did more harm than good. Only persistent digging by journalists and campaigners, most notably an award-winning seven-year investigation by Rob Evans and Paul Lewis of *The Guardian*, revealed this massive policing enterprise and its moral and accountability failure (see Evans and Lewis 2013). At the time of writing, a public inquiry was taking evidence to find out what did happen within SDS. Whether this will be able to assess the divergent versions of the police and the campaigners and reconcile them into a meaningful report is yet to be seen. It is a rare example of a potential attempt to scrutinise an intelligence operation. However, the lack of concrete results has not pleased the victims and campaigners and has left the police officers involved feeling vulnerable and deserted by their former employers.

Critics have suggested that Britain has been defined by its penchant for secrecy, and that prevents citizens gaining a full understanding of the actions of the ruling elites. Aldrich has described Britain's intelligence network as 'The Empire of Secrecy':

> The British government has fought a long campaign to ensure that much
> of the history of its intelligence services remains secret. Since 1945, its

> most concerted opponents have been a motley band of memoir writers, journalists and intelligence historians. Britain's gradual retreat from absolute secrecy in the area of intelligence history enjoys some parallels with Britain's retreat from Empire. (Aldrich 2004: 922)

I would like to think I am one of the 'motley band' referred to by Aldrich. This book is written from an unusual perspective because, while it is written by an academic and published by an academic imprint, I have also reported as a journalist on intelligence for many years in the UK national news media and can bring to bear in-depth experience of the intelligence world's relationship with the media. I have investigated intelligence agencies' excesses, have reported on their successes and been an 'accredited reporter' between my newspaper and the security services.

Muckraker – A Personal Journey

I was born nine years after the end of Second World War and this is also the personal story of a son of the Empire who was brought up to believe all that was British was better – I can still recognise the distinct note of a Spitfire's Merlin engine as it flies overhead. We had just been, again, on the winning side of the second of two world wars and this had further boosted our self-belief. Of my time, I became a child of the 1960s and began to question whether what the British state did was always in the best interest of its citizens and its colonial peoples. In the 1970s, I watched the Watergate coverage unfold, sometimes on a black and white television set and sometimes in the massive broadsheet newspapers of the time. I absorbed the zeitgeist and the idea that the importance of high-quality, probing journalism in a democracy had taken hold. As a student in 1976, I started to research the ways of the intelligence brethren under the mentorship of Richard Fletcher, a lecturer at North East London Polytechnic and something of a renaissance man. I was one of his volunteer team of researchers, and we slowly uncovered the secrets of the SIS/Foreign Office Cold War propaganda organisation, the Information Research Department (see Chapter 6).[13] This investigation appeared in *The Observer* in January 1978 and was my first by-line in the national news media, a very modest one at the end of the article (Fletcher et al. 1978). We were scooped by two days by David Leigh in *The Guardian* with a similar story (Leigh 1978). I was to carry on investigating IRD for many years, often working with David Leigh – by then working for *The Observer* – or James Oliver.[14]

My first job as a journalist was on *The Observer*, and that proved to be a revelation, and brought professional satisfaction as we challenged a dysfunctional establishment. As an investigative journalist the subjects I covered ranged widely but I returned to my interest in intelligence frequently. I have worked across diverse national media platforms including newspapers and television. I joined *The Observer* in June 1978 and was to remain there until the end of 1989. I also had my first experience of reporting terrorism when I was part of the paper's team covering the Iranian Embassy Siege in 1980, an event that resulted in iconic images of a Special Air Service (SAS) team dressed in black and wearing balaclavas abseiling down the building to rescue the hostages amongst explosions and gunfire (Trelford 1980). It was a taste of how the politics of the Middle East would come to London. We produced a book for which I was the researcher. Sometimes reporting on national security got nasty, and we were criticised vociferously, not least by other Fleet Street newspapers. One of the notable periods of my career was when I was one of the journalists injuncted in 1987 by the British government in the *Spycatcher* case – as detailed in Chapter 11. In our 1990 European Court of Human Rights (ECHR) case against the British government, the judgment stated that the media has a 'vital role of public watchdog' and that we had a duty to impart information of public interest and the public had a right to receive it. The journalist reporting critically on intelligence can expect forceful counterattacks from the 'patriotic', whether in other sections of the press, the intelligence lobby or in Parliament. David Leigh and I covered the row over the *Death on the Rock* programme in the late 1980s and we received a good deal of opprobrium (see Chapter 11).

After eleven extraordinary years at *The Observer*, for eight of which David Leigh and I were the paper's investigative team, I left to join Granada TV's *World in Action* programme for over three years. I then freelanced, mostly working for the TV production company Brook

Lapping, and produced three *Timewatch* programmes, did a short stint at *Newsnight*, plus two *Dispatches* episodes. Back then, there was a lot of investigative energy and resources in television and a number of current affairs series. Newspapers also felt they needed to reinforce their investigative teams. In May 1998, I joined *The Independent* as an investigative reporter and after a highly productive three years, I resigned in summer 2001 to move out of London. Then, following a call from the deputy editor of the *Independent on Sunday*, Michael Williams, a few days after 9/11, I found myself covering the 'war on terror'.

The phrase 'war on terror' is used in the book as shorthand for a plethora of terrorism-related events from 9/11 including the 2005 London bombings and deserves to be explained. On 20 September 2001, during a televised address to a joint session of Congress, President George W. Bush proclaimed: 'Our "war on terror" begins with al-Qa'ida, but it does not end there. It will not end until every terrorist group of global reach has been found, stopped, and defeated.' From 9/11 to 7/7 I had been involved in fifty articles, some solely, most co-authored, relating to the 'war on terror'. Then, in the two years after 7/7 I was involved in a further thirteen stories. I ceased writing for the *Independent on Sunday* in autumn 2007. Since then I have carried out independent research and met whistle-blowers like the former National Security Agency senior officer Bill Binney.

I have been teaching journalism in universities since 2001 and this book is a development of my doctoral thesis, 'Investigating the "Empire of Secrecy" – Three Decades of Reporting on the Secret State' (Lashmar 2015a). Much of my work involved revealing hidden stories and now, after a long career, the material forms part of the historical record. A timeline of my writings on intelligence can be found online.[15] Interspersed through this book are a series of case studies that illustrate key moments in intelligence history, some of the more recent events that I reported on at the time.

Tradecraft

Covering intelligence as a journalist was rarely dull. During the *Spycatcher* Affair it was my task in London to regularly brief the leader of the Labour Party Neil Kinnock on progress on the court case in Australia, which my work partner David Leigh was reporting on from the antipodean court. Kinnock, as with much else during his leadership, failed to utilise the 'hot' information effectively against Margaret Thatcher's government who were making a dire mess of trying to silence the dissident former senior MI5 officer Peter Wright. Over the years, I spent an inordinate amount of time talking to intelligence sources in dingy pubs where the limited natural light served only to highlight how smoky the room was. On other occasions, it would be in the oak-panelled clubs of Whitehall. Sometimes it was a question of meeting the more discreet sources at a busy rail station.

If there was any question that we had to protect the individual as a source, we devised strategies to make sure neither they nor we were being followed. It was easier in the earlier years of my career as we did not have to deal with the closed-circuit television (CCTV) and other surveillance technology that is now so pervasive and difficult to evade. It was then possible to call intelligence people on their office phone numbers, if they had provided them, and they did not worry about the phones being tapped. Consorting with the press resulted in a slap on the wrists and not a prosecution under the Official Secrets Act or other Act as it would do now.

Meetings were held in public in busy cafes where possible since the background noise precluded being overheard, or often in the middle of a park, moving around so that conversation could not be picked up. If using a car, I would employ basic anti-surveillance techniques like driving into cul-de-sacs or going round a rounda-bout several times to check if I was being followed. We had meth-odologies for testing the bona fides of anyone who approached us. In 1982, we were approached by a very convincing cold caller to the news desk who claimed he had acted as an assassin for the SIS. It was clearly a scoop, if true. The man wanted £1,000 for the story. We almost never paid for stories at *The Observer* but this one sounded important. My partner travelled to Ventimiglia, on the border between Italy and France, with convoluted 'anti-surveillance' arrangements for meetings. Cross-checking the source's story led us to the conclusion that the source, 'Edward Christian', was none other than Joe Flynn, a conman who had fleeced a number of news organisations. Mr Flynn's most successful known operation was at the *New York National Star*, which was owned by Rupert Murdoch, and he was paid £10,000 for his story in 1975 that he had murdered the notorious Teamsters union boss Jimmy Hoffa (Leigh and Lashmar 1982). This wasted trip to Ventimiglia was a relatively early lesson that intelligence-related stories can be hard to check. The lack of openness leaves the area open to hoaxers and manipulators.

We also conducted our own surveillance operations. On one occasion, I organised a small team to follow a former SIS officer who, now in the private sector, was using his knowledge to help some very dodgy clients. Confronting people we had identified as acting against the public interest was a cardiovascular experience. Working in Northern Ireland was a tense affair when one was dealing with paramilitaries from both sides. I can recall going to confront a Royal Ulster Constabulary (RUC) Special Branch officer at his home over collusion with loyalist terrorists. Knowing there was an armed man who would not appreciate unannounced visits certainly made the walk up the path to his house seem very long. I recall on other occasions visiting the heavily fortified drinking bars in sectarian areas of Belfast where meetings with paramilitaries would take place. Information came from many directions and there were many confidential sources, some that I cannot name even now. There were good sources whom I knew only by an alias.

Bed Mates or Sparring Partners?

While our stories were often critical of the intelligence agencies, some were not. In February 1983, we revealed how an SIS asset infiltrated the Soviet trade delegation in Highgate, north London, in an operation that led to the expulsion of four suspected spies. Double glazer Bill Graham approached us a few weeks before and we were able to verify his tale of derring-do. Graham, a former prison officer, military policeman and Ministry of Defence security official, described how, after he set up a building company, he had been approached by a friend in the Special Branch. He was then asked to tender for a contract to double-glaze the Soviet trade mission, which housed 630 officials. Over two years Graham bugged the mission, stole documents and took microphotographs. The operation is believed to have led to the expulsions in 1981 and 1982 of a number of Soviet officials suspected of spying.[16] We did not know his motives but it seemed probable that Graham was encouraged to leak his story by his handlers, probably as a counter to the slew of negative stories then appearing (Leigh and Lashmar 1983; Graham 1987).

The late Philip Knightley, a journalist who knew a fair few spies in his time, joked that journalists and spies go together like Marks and Spencer. Robert Dover and Michael Goodman, in their edited collection *Spinning Intelligence*, were among the first academics to look at the relationship between intelligence and the media, asking whether journalists and spooks were twin brothers, separated at birth (2009: 7). In his chapter in Dover and Goodman's seminal book, Aldrich commented, 'Despite their frequent moments of friction, intelligence agencies and the media have many similarities' (2009: 32). That intelligence officers sometimes become journalists and writers will be no surprise to readers as they are likely to know authors like Grahame Greene, Ian Fleming and John le Carré, who were all in British Intelligence before their successful writing careers, while others, like Frederick Forsyth, assisted MI6 while working as journalists. What might come as a surprise is the extent of the interchange. After the Second World War there were many former intelligence officers demobbed and finding or returning to work in Fleet Street.[17] It was an occasional topic of conversation at *The Observer* when I worked there as a young reporter in the early 1980s, speculating how many of our colleagues had worked or might still work for British Intelligence. I know now that quite a lot had worked for the intelligence agencies (see Lashmar 2015b, 2018a).

Citizenfour

The media's watchdog role over national security was at its most controversial after the former NSA contractor, Edward Snowden, leaked a substantial archive of secret intelligence documents to journalists in summer 2013. These documents, published in the UK by *The Guardian* (see Chapter 14), revealed the capability of

Western nations to maintain a level of surveillance unsuspected by even the best-informed observers. The distinguished *Guardian* columnist Simon Jenkins wrote that any claim that 'everyone knew these things were going on' is rubbish:

> Few even within the security realm were aware that servers were being hacked, encryptions corrupted and undersea cables tagged. They did not know because the means put in place to inform them were, as Snowden clearly shows, being circumvented and disobeyed. As Lord Ashdown said today, the nerds were 'out of control'. (Jenkins 2013)

The highly critical reaction of government and intelligence agencies to the publication of the Snowden documents highlights the tensions between democratic nation states and their respective liberal news media as well as civil society over the work of intelligence agencies. In the UK the reaction against the publication of the Snowden documents was particularly hostile and *The Guardian* was condemned not only by government, politicians and the agencies but also by segments of the British media, notably the *Daily Mail*.

David Leigh, then the investigations editor of *The Guardian*, observed that understanding and discussing the relationship between intelligence and the news media is vital for journalists:

> Our first task as practitioners is to document what goes on in this very furtive field. Our second task ought to be to hold an open debate on what the proper relations between the intelligence agencies and the media ought to be. And our final task must then be to find ways of actually behaving more sensibly. (Leigh 2000)

The importance of this work is underlined in that intelligence and journalism both play significant if very different roles in the democratic process. This book focuses on the UK experience. However, I do not suggest for a moment that some other nations' intelligence and media do not behave much worse than the British have done. The suborning of journalists and the use of journalistic cover was rampant in the days of the Soviet Union and is not much better in post-Soviet Russia.

To this day, at its most contested, the relationship between intelligence agencies and the news media becomes a struggle of national security versus the freedom of speech. The intelligence agencies, by dint of the inherent need for secrecy, are the most difficult institutions of state for the news media to exercise their watchdog role over. This I have tried to do for four decades. In this book, I recall and contextualise what others and I have reported on over many years. I attempt to reveal insights into the complex relationship between intelligence and the media. If experience and history has any value, it needs to be learnt from and the obvious question is: *Can intelligence and media relations be improved?*

Notes

1. <https://www.cia.gov/library/center-for-the-study-of-intelligence/csi-publica tions/csi-studies/studies/vol.-54-no.-4/six-a-history-of-britain2019s-secret-in telligence.html> (last accessed 17 June 2019).
2. Intelligence is a broad term, which in its simplest form in this book refers to the gathering of information for the benefit of an end-user. Intelligence as discussed in intelligence studies is further distinguished from other infor- mation-gathering processes (see Gill 1996: 313; Davies 2009: 198; Warner 2009: 18). Gill and Phythian evaluated a range of different definitions that are available. They find problems with each definition and some indeed are concerned with defining intelligence in the narrower sense of information gathering. They suggest their own definition, which is adopted for this book: 'Intelligence is the umbrella term referring to the range of activities – from plan- ning and information collection to analysis and dissemination – conducted in secret, and aimed at maintaining or enhancing relative security by providing forewarning of threats and potential threats in a manner that allows for the timely implementation of a preventive policy or strategy, including, where deemed desirable, covert activities' (Gill and Phythian 2012: 11). The essence of intelligence is to identify and quantify risk to the state, and then to shift risk to reduce uncertainty for theories of risk (see Knight 1921; Gill et al. 2009: 56).
3. It is not known how many cases involved MI5 or GCHQ but increased coordi- nation between MI5 and the Met's SO15 and regional counter-terrorism units in recent years makes it likely that many cases have intelligence input.
4. See 'Operation of police powers under the Terrorism Act 2000 and subsequent legislation: arrests, outcomes, and stop and search, Great Britain, quarterly update to December 2017', Statistical Bulletin 05/18, 8 March 2018, <https:// assets.publishing.service.gov.uk/government/uploads/system/uploads/attach ment_data/file/686342/police-powers-terrorism-dec2017-hosb0518.pdf> (last accessed 17 June 2019).
5. I use the definition of terrorism in the Terrorism Act 2000, which includes not only violent offences against persons and physical damage to property. The full

definition can be found at <http://www.legislation.gov.uk/ukpga/2000/11/contents> (last accessed 17 June 2019).

6. See Leigh 1988; Schlesinger 1991; Dorril and Ramsay 1992; Keeble 1997; Lashmar and Oliver 1998b.

7. 'Antinomian' describes someone who believes that God has given them the right to ignore the normal moral law as laid out in the Ten Commandments.

8. Jack Morton CMG OBE, 'Indian Episode – A Personal Memoir', given to British Library on 27 August 1982, p. 3.

9. The Troubles were a period of civil war in Northern Ireland that ran from the 1960s to the Good Friday Agreement in 1998. On one side were the paramilitary Provisional Irish Republican Army (PIRA) who sought a united Ireland, in conflict with 'loyalist' paramilitary groups, the Royal Ulster Constabulary and the British security forces on the other side. UK intelligence worked simultaneously against Republicans and loyalists.

10. Speaking publicly for the first time, ex-members of the Military Reaction Force (MRF), which was disbanded in 1973, said they had been tasked with 'hunting down' IRA members in Belfast (Ware 2013).

11. As Allan stated, 'the emergence of a newspaper press committed to advancing "the public interest" by reporting reality in the social world in a non-partisan manner has been a fairly recent development' (2010: 32). Public interest for journalism is, as Frost puts it, is 'a poorly defined device' and it is not the same as what interests the public. There is public interest in freedom of expression itself (Frost 2011: 270). The concept is very important for journalism, as journalists will sometimes use methods, to obtain information to publish, that would be described as dubious or even illegal and can only be justified if they serve the wider public interest. The ultimate test of the public interest may occur in court and is defined by whether a judge or jury accepts that a piece of journalism is in the public interest and finds in favour of the publishers rather than the appellants. The phone-hacking scandal of the early 2000s has resulted in scrutiny of the more unseemly practices of journalists and led to calls for a much clearer definition of public interest. The editor of *The Guardian*, Alan Rusbridger, said in his 2011 Orwell Lecture: 'Why is this agreement over "the public interest" so crucial? Because, in the end, the public interest, and how we argue it, is not only crucial to the sometimes arcane subject of privacy – it is crucial to every argument about the future of the press, the public good it delivers and why, in the most testing of economic times, it deserves to survive' (Rusbridger 2011).

12. A turn of phrase attributed to one of the CIA's most controversial figures, James Jesus Angleton.

13. Propaganda is 'the deliberate attempt to influence the opinions of an audience through the transmission of ideas and values for the specific purpose, consciously designed to serve the interests of the propagandists and their political masters, either directly or indirectly' (Cull et al. 2003: 318). (Black propaganda is information released to look like it comes from an entirely different source; grey propaganda is where the source is not clear; and white propaganda is where the source is clear and open.)

14. Now a highly regarded BBC producer who has made many programmes for the *Panorama* series.
15. <https://www.preceden.com/timelines/177443-int-media> (last accessed 17 June 2019).
16. These included Victor Lazine, a second secretary at the Soviet embassy; Anatoly Zhotov, a naval attaché; Vladimir Zadneprovsky, a member of the trade delegation; and Vladimir Chernov, a translator at the International Wheat Council.
17. Fleet Street runs westwards from Ludgate Circus in the City of London. For several hundred years it was where printers and publishers set up shop, followed by the newspaper industry. 'Fleet Street' was the colloquial descriptor for the British press. Although all of the major newspaper organisations have moved out since 1985 to larger and cheaper premises elsewhere, the collective term remains in use.

ONE

Setting the Scene

For millennia, military intelligence was the dominant form of spying, although wise rulers usually had a spymaster to keep an eye on political intrigue in their court and any manipulation by foreign powers. Knowing what the enemy is intending and how they have deployed their forces has always been a central part of diplomacy and warfare. Spies are not just receptacles for information; they can rarely resist being proactive, intervening, deceiving and sometimes much, much worse.

The Art of Intelligence

As Sun Tzu, in the classic text *The Art of War* from circa fifth-century BC China, advised, 'Now the reason the enlightened prince and the wise general conquer the enemy whenever they move and their achievements surpass those of ordinary men is foreknowledge' (2007: 65). Intelligence is not necessarily a passive gathering activity but often is accompanied by proactive intervention. As Sun Tzu also observed, 'all Warfare Is Based Upon Deception' (2007: 7) and elaborated:

> Hence, when able to attack, we must seem unable;
> When using our forces, we must seem inactive;
> When we are near, we must make the enemy believe we are far away;
> When far away, we must make him believe we are near. (Tzu 2007: 7)

Sun Tzu set the tone for later intelligence textbooks. Written as a guide for members of the War Office's Intelligence Branch by one of its senior officers, Lieutenant Colonel David Henderson, in his 1904 *Field Intelligence, Its Principles and Practice* advised: 'Next to the acquisition of information, its distribution to those whom may be able to use it is the most important duty of the Intelligence Branch' (quoted in Smith 2007: 17). Good intelligence can make up for numbers and resources, as Gregory Elder notes on the CIA website:

Force and its employment are significant in driving outcomes in combat. However, it is operational and tactical intelligence, not necessarily numbers, technology, or tactics that can have the most decisive impact on how forces are employed and how success is achieved in wartime operations. History repeatedly has demonstrated that numerically inferior forces, armed with less capable technologies, can win when leaders are armed with accurate intelligence they believe they can act upon.[1]

Kings and queens have always retained individuals who delved in the dark arts of intelligence gathering and covert action. Thomas Cromwell's facility to Henry VIII was partly based on his network of informants not only in Henry's court but also in other European courts, bestowing on him frightening powers of life and death, as is well rendered in Hilary Mantel's *Wolf Hall* (2009).

Writers and journalists have frequently doubled as spies, not least because they were literate when few others were, and had access to those in power. Sir Francis Walsingham is often seen as the first great English spymaster in his role of protecting the interests of Queen Elizabeth I. Walsingham likely had in his pay as a spy the dramatist Christopher Marlowe, a contemporary of Shakespeare. The author of *Robinson Crusoe*, Daniel Defoe, was employed by British Intelligence to spy on the anti-unionist forces in Scotland before the vote on the Union in 1707 – a task made easier by the author's Presbyterianism (Lloyd 2017: 2).

Intercepting communications and deciphering those in code or secret ink had been part of the country's intelligence toolkit since time immemorial. Funded by the Secret Vote, the 'Deciphering Branch' was created in 1703.[2] This was as close as there was to a professional intelligence service before the twentieth century. The

Branch became effectively a family business under the Oxford don the Rev. Edward Willes, who had his three sons work for him. By the outset of the Victorian era, the Branch had ceased to be effective and the use of couriers rather than the post for diplomatic despatches effectively reduced the material for decryption to a trickle (Andrew 1985: 24).

The Branch was abolished after a parliamentary row in 1844 over the opening of the personal correspondence of the exiled Italian nationalist Giuseppe Mazzini. According to the academic David Vincent, Mazzini's correspondence had been opened on the instructions of the Home Secretary, Sir James Graham, at the request of the Austrian ambassador. There then followed a 'paroxysm of national anger' by the public at the thought of the government prying into someone else's letters. That it was on behalf of a foreign government exacerbated the reaction. Vincent notes that: 'A resourceful coalition of working-class radicals and Parliamentary Liberals came together to protest at the use of what they dismissed as "the spy system of foreign states"' (1991: 229). According to Vincent, *The Times* addressed the issue in a powerful editorial:

> 'The proceeding cannot be English', thundered *The Times*, 'any more than masks, poisons, sword-sticks, secret signs and associations, and other such dark ventures. Public opinion is mighty and jealous, and does not brook to hear of public ends pursued by other than public means. It considers that treason against its public self.' (Vincent 1991: 229)

Vincent believes that the episode marked the first modern crisis of public secrecy, causing the government great embarrassment and eliciting a response that spies would become accustomed to (1991: 229). The decipherer, Francis Willies, and his nephew and assistant were pensioned off with secret service money. Vincent states that Britain became the only major power bereft of the most effective weapon for spying on external enemies and despite the public refusal to change its policy, it seems to have abandoned monitoring 'enemies of the state'. Once the crisis had passed, Vincent notes, 'the state began a quarter of a century when for what may have been the first time in its history, and certainly was the last, it refrained from the surveillance of the thoughts and actions of its citizens' (1991:

230). Vincent observes that the outburst of 1844 was the first and the last full-scale debate about the extent of such practices and their justification, until well into the twentieth century (1991: 231).

The Rise of Fleet Street

In Britain during the nineteenth century, the benefits of a free press spread at the same time that public literacy increased and technology allowed for printing and mass circulation of newspapers. From the 1830s onwards, parliamentary reforms steadily abolished oppressive press taxations such as the Newspaper Stamp Duty in 1855 and Excise Duty on Paper in 1861. Tension between the government and the increasingly powerful 'press barons', the owners of the mass circulation newspapers, waxed and waned. In their seminal book on the press, Curran and Seaton observe that after the death of Lord Northcliffe in 1922, four men – Lords Beaverbrook (1879–1964), Rothermere (1868–1940), Camrose (1879–1954) and Kemsley (1883–1968) – became the dominant figures in the inter-war press:

> In 1937, for instance, they owned nearly one in every two national and local daily papers sold in Britain, as well as one in every three Sunday papers that were sold. The combined circulation of all their newspapers amounted to over thirteen million. (Curran and Seaton 2010: 39)

The press barons were interested in circulation, influence and promoting their own politics. On the one side were the press, keen to get scoops to win the circulation battles, and on the other were ministers, civil servants and an establishment who did not want the public to be informed of their failings. Such tensions had escalated in times of war where inquiring journalists were accused of lacking patriotism, for example when revealing the ramshackle conduct of the South African War (1899–1902). In some cases, the military had legitimate cause to complain. During that war, British generals were appalled that the British press printed details of troop deployments. Lord Wolseley, Commander-in-Chief of the British Army, was disgusted: 'We cannot make war as the country expects we should, whilst our enemy is kept informed by our press of everything we do' (Wilkinson 2009: 16). In 1901 the War Office cut off Northcliffe's *Daily Mail* from receiving their confidential bulletins because the paper was discovered offering 'pecuniary temptations' to government clerks willing to provide news (Wilkinson 2009: 20).

The press were great providers of political and commercial intelligence, with paid correspondents in many parts of the world, and they became a source of speedy intelligence with the arrival of the electric telegraph. The Reuters news agency was particularly important. Based in the City of London, Reuter's Telegram Company was founded by Paul Julius Reuter in 1851 and originally covered commercial news, serving banks, brokerage firms and big business. In 1858, the *London Morning Advertiser* was the first newspaper client to subscribe to the service. Already in most European countries, by 1872 Reuters began to set up bureaus in the Far East, followed by South America in 1874. Both expansions were made possible by advances in overland telegraphs and undersea cables. In 1883, Reuters began transmitting messages electronically direct to London newspapers. Reuters went some way to make up for the lack of a centralised British secret service; however, there are limitations to what journalists can do and the need for a professional secret service was increasingly apparent.

The Great Game

In the nineteenth century, British Intelligence was fragmented and mostly military in nature. It would not have been possible to run 'the greatest empire the world had ever seen' without some serious intelligence organisation:

> The long drawn out 'Great Game' with Tsarist Russia on India's North-West frontier, which reached its peak in the later nineteenth century, gave rise to an equally drawn out series of intelligence operations – conducted, however, on nothing like the sophistication suggested by Rudyard Kipling's *Kim*. (Andrew 1985: 27)

The intelligence operations paid for by the Foreign Office focused on targets overseas where the techniques of bribery and espionage were a lot less likely to be commented on domestically, and were often basic and nasty in character (see for example, Cobain 2012).

In 1873, the War Office had established an Intelligence Branch, with some twenty-seven military and civilian personnel. The art of intelligence was viewed with suspicion by many of the British military attachés posted in embassies around the world. One attaché remarked that he would never do any secret service work:

> My view is that the Military Attaché is the guest of the country in which he is accredited, and must only see and learn that which is permissible for a guest to investigate. Certainly he must keep his eyes and ears open and miss nothing, but secret service is not his business, and he should always refuse a hand in it. (Richelson 1995: 5)

When these attachés did report on military developments in their host countries, they sought to do so openly in what they considered a 'gentlemanly and honourable way' (Richelson 1995: 5).

By late-Victorian times, there was a tranche of military intelligence agencies across the world. At home, there was an urgent need to counter the 'Fenian menace', whose bombing campaign was orchestrated between 1881 and 1885. The campaign was associated with Irish revolutionary organisations, which aimed to establish an independent Irish Republic, such as the Irish Republican Brotherhood, the Fenian Brotherhood, Clan na Gael and the United Irishmen of America. The Fenian campaign was a form of asymmetrical warfare which aimed at infrastructure, government, military and police targets in Britain and in particular London. The campaign led to the establishment in March 1883 of a police unit in London's Metropolitan Police called the Special Branch that operated out of Scotland Yard, the London police headquarters. Later, Special Branch would take on other threats and develop colonial offshoots.

Invasion Fever

There is a compelling case that a single journalist was responsible for the creation of the SIS and the Security Service (MI5), as they later became. In the 1880s, William Le Queux, an Anglo-French journalist and editor, born in England, had returned to London where he edited the magazines *Piccadilly* and *Gossip*. In 1891, the mass circulation newspaper *The Globe* hired him as a parliamentary reporter. He then turned author and the most successful of his many books was *The Invasion of 1910*, which, though fiction, was written in the style of a non-fiction history book. As part of the invasion genre it complemented the more literary *The Riddle of the Sands* by Erskine Childers published in 1903. *The Invasion of 1910*, published just three years after *The Riddle*, was serialised by the *Daily Mail*. There was a delay in publication as Le Queux had detailed a specific route of the German attack in *The Invasion of 1910*, from the east coast to London. As Australian intelligence writer Phillip Knightley observes, Lord Northcliffe was not pleased:

> It was not to his lordship's liking. The line of march, it transpired, took the invading army through areas where the circulation of the *Daily Mail* was minimal. Northcliffe personally realigned the German attack to ensure that the Hun sacked those towns where chances of securing a boost to the *Daily Mail*'s circulation were strongest. Then he promoted the story by publishing, in *The Times*, the *Daily Telegraph*, the *Morning Post*, the *Daily Chronicle*, and the *Daily Mail* itself, a list of those districts the Hun would hit the next morning. (Knightley 1986: 16)

Once the novel had been rewritten, Le Queux was redeemed in the eyes of the *Daily Mail*'s proprietor as its serialisations boosted his paper's circulation and fitted in with Northcliffe's business plan based on the canny Northcliffe's observation that the average Briton 'liked a good hate' (Andrew 1985: 74).

The *Daily Mail*, then as now, liked to inspire tingling fear in its readers.

The plot consists of a sneak German invasion of Britain with Teutonic spies infiltrating across the country in advance of the invasion force, sowing confusion and preventing the British Army from defeating the Germans now sweeping across the Home Counties. The Germans defeat the British on the edge of London. At the last minute, a resistance movement called 'The League of Defenders' coalesces and liberates the country. It is a masterpiece in provoking fear, ranking alongside the idea that Napoleon Bonaparte, 'the bogey man', would come and steal children from their warm English beds. Le Queux's sensationalist book was a great success, and was translated into twenty-seven different languages and sold over one million copies.

The tone of *The Invasion of 1910* was foreboding, warning that those in power were asleep at the reins at the time of maximum danger. The British public at large, it intimated, were complacent. The notion that Britain was as unprepared as portrayed by these spy mania authors became an *idée fixe* resonating with the public, despite the whole genre being lampooned by P. G. Wodehouse in his 1909 book *Swoop*, where he had Britain invaded by nine different countries at once. As the SIS historian Keith Jeffery notes, the invasion genre authors might have been playing off public fears, 'Yet they seemed to hit the Zeitgeist in Britain where generalised (and well-founded) concerns about growing *relative* international weaknesses readily fuelled fevered speculation about foreign agents flooding the country and working towards its destruction' (Jeffery 2010: 5, emphasis original).

Enter the Secret Service Bureau

As Britain entered the twentieth century, its intelligence community was a patchwork of agencies with most located in the army and navy. The lack of a central secret service bureau had been a recognised problem in Whitehall and War Office circles long before, notably by the legendary Field Marshal Earl Roberts, a hero of the Boer War. However, until Le Queux's *The Invasion of 1910* came along, Roberts and others had failed to persuade the government to create one. There had been official pressure for a modern counter-espionage unit since April 1907 when a joint conference of naval and military officials had met to consider 'the Powers Possessed by the Executive in Time of Emergency'. Le Queux and Roberts joined forces and spymania filled the newspapers. Britain's first mass circulation newspaper, the *Daily Mail*, supported Roberts in his demands (Andrew 1985: 76). In February 1909, the *Weekly News* appointed a 'Spy Editor' – perhaps the first national security reporter. It ran the headlines 'Foreign Spies in Britain', '£10 given for information' and 'Have you seen a Spy?' There was a climate of public anxiety, which was exacerbated by journalists and authors hugely exaggerating the level of the threat.

Such was the strength of public paranoia that in March 1909 Prime Minister Herbert Asquith, of the Liberal Party, responded by appointing a high-powered subcommittee of the eminent Committee of Imperial Defence to consider 'the question of foreign espionage in the United Kingdom'. A month later they recommended that an independent 'secret service bureau' should be established which 'must at the same time be in close touch with the Admiralty, the War Office and the Home Office' (Jeffery 2010: 6). It fell under the control of the Military Operations 5 (MO5) Directorate of Military Operations of the War Office. The first head of the Bureau was the Admiralty's nominee, Mansfield Cumming (born 1859), an officer with surprisingly little experience of intelligence. He was, however, a workaholic and he took up his duties in October 1909, a week early (Jeffery 2010: 15).

The first Bureau office was at Ashley Mansions in Vauxhall Bridge Road in London, and early in 1910 Cumming set up a bogus address with the Post Office – Messrs Rasen, Falcon Limited, a firm of 'shippers and exporters'. Cumming had been joined shortly after the Bureau's creation by the War Office's nominee, an army officer, Captain Vernon Kell (born 1873), who was a linguist and had experience of intelligence gathering. While he was on the intelligence staff in Tientsin in Northern China, he was also the foreign correspondent for the *Daily Telegraph*. He had seen his first action during the Boxer Rebellion. Ill health had led to his return to the War Office and his being available for this curious new posting.

Cumming and Kell settled into a somewhat fraught working relationship and by 1910 they had separate bureaus. Cumming took charge of what was to become the SIS, focusing on foreign intelligence, and Kell was to become head of the Security Service, concerned with domestic issues (though responsibility for counter-subversion and counter-espionage did not become solely MI5's until 1931). From the outset, both sections were subject to the bureaucracy of the War Office. Colonel George Macdonogh, who had overall charge of MO5, made it very clear there was a very limited budget. As revealed by his progress reports, now in the National Archives, Kell had spent much of his first eighteen months with the Bureau cultivating good working relations with chief constables, many of whom were retired army officers and sympathetic to the Secret Service Bureau's (SSB's) overtures (Northcott 2015: 294). After six months, Kell concluded that SSB had 'justified its institution'. Meanwhile the War Office had to hand over their complete German intelligence network, including their prized 'Agent B', to Cumming (Jeffery 2010: 16). Even with the creation of the Secret Service Bureau, Le Queux kept the pressure up with a new blockbuster in 1909, *The Spies of the Kaiser*, which claimed that Britain was being overrun by German spies.

In those fevered pre-war years, and lobbied persistently by Vernon Kell at the Home Section of the Secret Service Bureau, the government passed a new, much more catch-all, Official Secrets Act in 1911. The 1911 Act – which Kell said was necessary if he was to do his job properly – went through Parliament in one day with minimal debate but supported by vocal politician Winston Churchill. Even then the news media were concerned about the additional powers the Act provided compared with the 1889 Act. The *Daily Mail* reported that the Newspaper Proprietors' Association protested about the 'far reaching liabilities which the Bill imposes upon the public and the Press'. The new Act had a much wider scope, it complained: 'It affects anyone and everyone, and not officials alone.'[3]

Ripping Yarns

The Secret Service Bureau staff were conscious of how little they knew of the domestic German military build-up. Captain Cumming set to work with gusto and described spying as 'capital sport'. He was a gung-ho character who carried a swordstick, wore a gold-rimmed monocle and had a liking for driving his Rolls-Royce at great speed. Cumming's part-time assistant, Cyrus 'Roy' Regnart, a Royal Marine officer, was even more enthusiastic than his chief, a trait that was to prove problematic. He decided to recruit various military officers to go to the north of Germany on 'duck shooting' holidays while in fact spying on German military installations and warship construction. In summer 1910, without telling Cumming, Regnart started to dispatch his new intelligence agents. Royal Marine officer Captain Bernard Trench and his friend, Royal Navy Lieutenant Vivian Brandon, went 'on holiday' in August 1910 to assess northern German military sites like Kiel dockyard and a whole range of islands in an adventure that was more than reminiscent of *The Riddle of the Sands*.

Unfortunately for the gung-ho Trench and Brandon, the German authorities became suspicious and arrested the pair, and found a good number of incriminating notes and photos poorly hidden in their hotel. The *Daily Mail*'s report of their arrest took the best possible interpretation of events from a British point of view and indeed expressed some outrage. The *Mail*'s 'Special Correspondent' reported: 'I am told that both prisoners are undergraduates at Cambridge. They describe themselves of no definite occupation and say they are without funds. Mr Trench has been staying near Copenhagen studying Scandinavian languages.'[4] He dismissed the worth of the German authorities' case and added that the photographs the two men had taken of the forts on the island of Waneroog were 'harmless'.

With equal and opposite momentum to the *Daily Mail*, the German press made great play of the spy case. The *Berliner Neueste Nachrichten* demanded the prisoners 'be made incapable of reporting what they may have seen by means of appropriate mental treatment so that they may not retain too clear a memory of what they have seen' (Smith 2010: 23). The two men effectively used an 'open source' defence that everything they had seen was in full public view and not hidden; however, it was an unsuccessful ploy. Their trial took place at the Leipzig Supreme Court on 22 December 1910 and they were found guilty of espionage and sentenced to four years in prison. A series of other arrests of SSB agents followed in Germany with further embarrassing trials.

Cumming was apparently none too happy about Regnart's *Boy's Own* activities and the bad publicity as they made the Bureau look amateurish. Later in 1911, Cumming managed to get a spy operating in Germany who was competent, by hiring Hector Bywater, a journalist based in Dresden, who in his day job reported on naval matters for a range of British and American newspapers and journals. Given the code name 'H_2O', he turned out to be one of the best pre-war agents, producing a series of regular reports between

1913 and 1914. Captain Jackson of the Admiralty remarked that H_2O 'sent a lot of good stuff. He mostly reported on naval and aero-nautical developments' (Jeffery 2010: 34). It was good intelligence work and Bywater was paid, appearing in the Bureau's accounts as 'fixed agent abroad'. Spying can be a lucrative, if precarious, occupation.

Notes

1. <https://www.cia.gov/library/center-for-the-study-of-intelligence/csi-publicati ons/csi-studies/studies/vol50no2/html_files/Intelligence_War_2.htm> (last accessed 17 June 2019).
2. The Secret Vote is the amount of money provided for funding the intelligence services. It has often been publicly discussed. In 1853, for example, there was a row in Parliament over the amount of money it was costing, which was covered by the newspapers of the time. Before the twentieth century, the Secret Vote was often diverted for nefarious use.
3. 'Official secrets', *Daily Mail*, 5 May 1908, p. 8.
4. 'Arrested Englishmen', *Daily Mail*, 25 August 1910.

TWO

The Great War

Despite the pre-war blundering, Cumming and Kell had developed a viable intelligence and counter-intelligence operation just in time for the coming conflict and they had some early successes once war was declared. In November 1914, Karl Krüger, a former German naval officer, approached British Intelligence officers in the Netherlands. He had access to a wide range of information on naval construction and fleet dispositions and was willing to sell these secrets at a price. Krüger provided vital intelligence for the rest of the war, including crucial revelations regarding German losses at the Battle of Jutland in 1916.[1]

As the war progressed, the Bureau managed to run spy operations in the captured territories. Most impressive was 'La Dame Blanche', a network of local spies in German-occupied Belgium that provided significant information on German troop movements. Its two leaders, Walthère Dewé and Herman Chauvin, began work for the British in 1917. Cumming's organisation took over responsibility for the network, and by the end of the war 'La Dame Blanche' had expanded to almost 800 members (Jeffery 2010: 78–84). By watching German trains passing through Belgium, they provided important data to British Intelligence in the Netherlands. By the end of the war, intelligence from 'La Dame Blanche' provided the British with details of German troop movements through occupied Belgium on almost a daily basis.

MO5(g) (MI5)

There are different views of Vernon Kell as the first head of the Home Section of the Bureau. One is that he was an effective leader and organiser, the masterful intelligence chief. Kell's grandson Jamie Robertson summed up the preferred view:

> I think in those days, you know, Britain, certainly 1909–1920 which is the period we are talking about, we were a great power, a great empire and really, the values were different compared to nowadays. He embodied all those values. He was a gentleman and was the perfect officer and gentleman, with that classic upper-middle-class lifestyle. He was a great patriot, very religious and family was very important. He was for doing his bit for King and Country and that too was important. (Robertson 1997)

The story of a sweep clearing out all Germany's spies in Britain in the first day of war is the MI5 foundation story, as the moment of validation for the Home Section of the Bureau. The story took hold; for example, in 1920 the *Manchester Guardian*, quoting from a new publication by Sidney Felsted, the semi-official historian of espionage, detailed the destruction of the pre-war German spy system in the UK. Noting that the outbreak of the great European war found Germany without a spy system in Britain, Felsted explained:

> The reason for this did not lie at the door of the notorious Steinhauer, head of the German secret service, but rather at that of a certain far seeing English gentleman. Acting on the assumption that it is easier to deal with a known peril than an unknown one, we forbore to arrest numerous spies in this country, but contented ourselves with keeping in touch with their numerous activities and manifesting personal interest in their correspondence.[2]

The claim for this success dated back to the afternoon of 5 August 1914, when, within hours of the declaration of hostilities, Home Secretary Reginald McKenna stood in the House of Commons to report that 'within the last twenty-four hours no fewer than twenty-one spies, or suspected spies, have been arrested in various places all over the country' (Hiley 2006: 51). There was a great deal of sensational coverage by Fleet Street as much of their read-ership were convinced the country was riddled with German spies and fifth columnists. Kell had told McKenna they had rounded up all the agents of any note working for German naval intelli-gence. The head of the British section of German naval intelligence, Gustav Steinhauer, later acknowledged that the Kaiser had been beside himself with fury when told of the wholesale round-up of Germany's secret service agents:

> Apparently unable to believe his ears, [he] raved and stormed for the better part of two hours about the incompetence of his so-called intelli-gence officers, bellowing: 'Am I surrounded by dolts? Why was I not told? Who is responsible?' and more in the same vein. (Northcott 2015: 75)

The foundation story is to be found on MI5's website today but is it a myth? Here is an early case study that reveals the recurring difficulties in telling the story of intelligence and trying to penetrate the secretive world of intelligence. It is also an early example of the politicisation of intelligence, a theme that would recur all the way through to the 2003 Iraq War and beyond. There is the fasci-nation of the news media, in this early case the newspapers of Fleet Street and the regions, with all aspects of the 'shadow underworld' of spying. Unfortunately for McKenna, the press were taking too much interest in his bravado claims and Ralph Blumenfeld, the editor of the paper taking the most, the *Daily Express*, pressed the Home Secretary to provide some concrete evidence.

Unpicking the Spin

Seventy years on, forensic work on MI5 files by the intelligence his-torian Nick Hiley in the National Archives painted a very different picture from McKenna's boasts: 'The event is still celebrated by MI5, but a careful study of the recently-opened records shows it to be a complete fabrication', he notes. When McKenna asked for more detail there followed, as Hiley puts it, 'a desperate trawling of police reports' (2006: 46–8). Under pressure from McKenna, Kell and his team had to cobble something together that appeared to conform to a round-up of spies. Inconveniently, Kell's actual targets were not spies but suspected potential saboteurs, and the arrests and prosecutions did not fit the story told to Parliament. The facts had been twisted to fit the Home Secretary's claims.

In September 1914, the *Daily Express* editor, Blumenfeld, criticised the Home Office for its lack of vigour over what appeared to the editor (and public) to be a continuing flood of German espionage agents. Consequently, McKenna allowed him to see 'a great chart crossed and dotted' (Hiley 2006: 51) compiled by MI5 and that apparently showed the place of arrest of each German agent. The Home Secretary told Blumenfeld:

> This shows what became of the spies about whom you were crying out. The very moment that war was declared they were all put under lock and key, all at one swoop, and the next morning the whole German spy system . . . was smashed to smithereens. (Hiley 2006: 51)

Hiley examined the six surviving lists of suspects to show how and why MI5 created and perpetuated this 'remarkable lie', observing that this story is neither internally consistent nor supported by contemporary documentary evidence:

> Over almost a century MI5 has made five separate attempts – in 1914, 1921, 1931, 2004 and 2009 – to support its foundation myth with supposed facts, all of which have failed miserably. Five attempts to revive a corpse are surely enough, and it is time that MI5 pronounced it dead and moved on to a better understanding of what really happened in August 1914, when Kell mobilized his unit against a non-existent army of German saboteurs. (Hiley 2010: 452)

Hiley has little time for Kell's portrayal as a hero in the history books. He argues that Vernon Kell gained a reputation that was to keep him in office for thirty years, yet there is little enduring reason to praise the work of MI5 in the Great War.

To be fair to MI5 – which became its designation in 1916 – it had to some extent been doing its job, catching eleven real German spies in the period before war began, and on the outbreak of hostilities it picked up Berlin's main 'spymaster' in Britain, an Islington barber called Karl Gustav Ernst (Smith 2006). He was more the ring's postmaster than spymaster, channelling hundreds of letters between the German agents and the German secret service. As one of those arrested at the time, who rather oddly was not on the list of twenty-one, Ernst pushed for a public trial on the basis of being a British citizen and was tried for spying in 1914 (he had been active since 1910). He was jailed for seven years. The secretive Home Section was not mentioned in the press reports.

Ungentlemanly Acts

With most German spies in Britain neutralised by the middle of the war, MI5 shifted its focus to perceived threats from communist subversion within the armed forces and to prevent sabotage to military installations. By 1917, the registry – where all incoming intelligence was collated and stored – consisted of 250,000 cards and 27,000 personal files on suspects which allowed MI5 to determine quickly whether persons or organisations had come to their attention (Andrew 2009: 58). In the course of the war, MI5's staff increased by a factor of nearly fifty to a total of 844. German archives reveal that at least 120 spies were sent to Britain at some point during the First World War. According to Christopher Andrew, the official MI5 historian, some sixty-five German agents were caught. There is no evidence that any of the remainder sent back significant intelligence to Germany (Andrew 2009: 75).

A post-war MI5 report based on the experiences of the Great War concluded: 'It is apparently a paradox, but it is none the less true, and a most important truth, that the efficiency of a counter espionage service is not to be measured chiefly by the number of spies caught by it.'[3] Though MI5 did catch a record number of spies in 1915, it was probably less successful then than in 1918, when it caught none. As the MI5 website currently notes, good 'protective security' and the deterrent effect of the executions of some captured spies had by then made it difficult for Germany to recruit any spies for work in Britain. Nor were they able to carry out sabotage operations as effective as those in the USA that included blowing up a huge arms dump in New Jersey in which 900 tonnes of explosive was detonated, killing seven people and damaging the Statue of Liberty.[4]

Cabinet Noir

In the run-up to the First World War, Rear Admiral Henry Oliver was appointed Director of Naval Intelligence (DNI) division at the Admiralty. As Britain was a naval power, naval intelligence was the most substantial of the British military intelligence organisations. At the outbreak of war, intercepted coded messages began to arrive at the division, but no one knew what to do with them. In August 1914, Oliver's team were fully occupied with other war issues and lacked experience of code breaking. Instead, the perceptive Oliver recruited Sir Alfred Ewing, the Director of Naval Education (DNE), who he knew had an interest in ciphers, and asked him to set up a group for decoding messages. This became known as Room 40 – from its location in the Admiralty.

In late 1914, 'Blinker' Hall took over as DNI and grasped the potential of Room 40, setting out to recruit able civilians and military to staff it. Room 40 broke German naval codes and played an important role in several naval engagements during the war, detecting major German ventures into the North Sea that led to the battles of Dogger Bank and Jutland when the British fleet was sent out to engage them. Andrew observes that Room 40 contained probably the oddest collection of people ever to work in the Admiralty but that together they provided better intelligence than ever before in British history. He believes their greatest achievement was to make surprise attack by the German Navy impossible (Andrew 1985: 145).

Probably the most important contribution of Room 40 to the war was decrypting the Zimmermann Telegram, a cable from the German Foreign Office sent via Washington to its ambassador Heinrich von Eckardt in Mexico which played a major part in bringing the USA into the war. Room 40 watched the increasingly aggressive Bolshevik agitation of British communists. Decrypts showed the Russian delegations establishing secret links with the embryonic British Communist Party and subsidising the sympathetic newspaper the *Daily Herald* by using smuggled diamonds. Room 40 was monitoring Bolshevik telegrams and even Lenin's personal messages (Aldrich and Cormac 2016: 37–43). During the Great War a development occurred that was going to be of increasing importance. In 1917, Gilbert Vernam proposed a teleprinter cipher, for which a previously prepared key, kept on paper tape, would be combined character by character with the plaintext message to produce the cipher text. This led to the development of electromechanical devices such as cipher machines.

In 1919, Room 40 merged with the British Army's intelligence unit MI1b to form the Government Code and Cypher School (GC&CS), moving from Watergate House near Charing Cross in London to Queen's Gate, Kensington in 1921. It was placed under the remit of the head of SIS. As at every war's end, the contractions of manpower started nasty bureaucratic wars between agencies fighting for survival (see Smith 2007).

Blurred Lines: Spies and Journalists

It was an American liberal Senator, Hiram Johnson, who is said to have coined the expression 'The first casualty when war comes is truth', over the United States' entry into the First World War. As historian Sheila Fitzpatrick has explained accurately and with some irony, there are rules for writing about the enemy in wartime:

> You must never forget that your side and his are at war, and that your side is right and his is wrong. Your writing must not give aid or comfort to the enemy. It should never humanise the other side but rather emphasise its essential, evil otherness. Overt partisanship is not just allowed in time of war but required. Even-handedness, if you choose to write about the enemy, would amount to treason. (Fitzpatrick 2019: 13)

The British press rarely reported the actions of their intelligence services, especially in wartime as it would been seen as unpatriotic and would have undoubtedly brought a clash with the wartime censors.

With the Official Secrets Act of 1911 in force and the imposition of wartime restrictions, official policy sought to discourage even peacetime disclosures (Jeffreys-Jones 2018: 19). There was, in theory, no reason for the British press to know about the secret services or have contact with them under the exigencies of war. They were, after all, secret organisations. However, the documentary record shows that by the First World War, close links between intelligence and journalism were commonplace. The British

MI1c (SIS) station chief in Geneva, William George Middleton Edwards, was accredited by *The Times* to provide cover for his spying. In addition, an agent, Jim de Teux, codenamed 'Walfisch', was sent to Athens with the cover of being a journalist for the *Daily Mail*, after getting Lord Northcliffe's permission. The point of this operation is not known but the *Daily Mail* paid de Teux a £15 a month 'salary' to help maintain the cover (Smith 2010: 182–3).

If you look at the two professions[5] of journalism and intelligence, there are similarities in the way they gather and analyse information. Journalists and spies are two quite distinct kinds of knowledge producers – both often investigate without the consent of the people they are seeking information about and then produce knowledge for distinct purposes (Dover and Goodman 2009: 9). One of the similarities of journalists and intelligence officers is that they get often get information from personal sources. The typology in Table 2.1 compares the way the two professions work.

Intelligence	Journalism
Identifying requirements	Initial facts or clues
Consulting organisational memory – 'the files' and open sources	Cuttings review
Specific targeting	Determination of specific research questions
Possible source identification and management	Possible source identification and management
Collection of information	Data collection
Processing of information	Verification
Analysis of information	Analysis and interpretation of information
Evaluation by managers	Evaluation of story with editors and lawyers
Dissemination of analytic product, that is, 'intelligence'	Dissemination
Feedback from customer and policy makers	Feedback from targets and audience

The great difference is that journalists seek to publish what they find. Intelligence agencies provide secret reports to a very select group of 'clients' in government, Whitehall or law enforcement.

From its beginning, the Secret Service Bureau and then MI5 and SIS had seen the benefits of recruiting journalists and disguising their agents as newspaper correspondents. Recruiting journalists to intelligence work made a lot of sense to the first generation of British Intelligence chiefs. Many journalists already had excellent high-level contacts in countries of great interest. If they did not, they could get access in foreign lands without drawing too much suspicion. Some journalists would willingly put information out through their newspapers that suited their intelligence and propaganda employers. Editors were often complicit in these arrangements.

Another significant recruit for the SSB was Arthur Ransome, who is now best remembered as the avuncular author of the tale of youngsters and boats in the Lake District in *Swallows and Amazons*. Before that, he had been a journalist and for a time an agent for MI1c. In 1914, Ransome became a foreign correspondent for a radical newspaper, the *Daily News*, and covered the war on the Eastern Front and then the Russian Revolution of 1917. He was sympathetic to the Bolsheviks and became close to its leaders, including Vladimir Lenin, Karl Radek and Leon Trotsky. In Russia, he met Trotsky's personal secretary, who would become Trotsky's mistress and then Ransome's second wife, Evgenia Petrovna Shelepina (Smith 2010: 260). The ostensibly left-wing journalist Clifford Sharp, a Fabian and the first editor of the *New Statesman*, recruited Ransome to MI1c. During the war, Ransome ran the British Propaganda Bureau (BPB) in Stockholm, which was part of the SIS and tasked with penetrating Russian revolutionary groups.

According to the archive files, Ransome was given the codename S.76 (Jeffery 2010: 174). His SIS controller was a Major Scale, who appeared on the Diplomatic List as the assistant British military attaché in Stockholm. In a similar vein was the journalist W. T. Goode of the *Manchester Guardian*[6] who published a famous interview with Lenin and also happened to be an MI1c agent (Jeffery 2010: 255–6). *The Times* correspondent in Petrograd, Robert Wilton, was an SIS agent. On leave in London, he told both Cumming and his editor that the Bolsheviks were not a serious group, a view shared by many of Cumming's agents in Russia (Knightley 1986: 56).

Cumming's nephew, Professor Bernard Pares, worked as a MI1c officer close to the front line in Russia. As the War Office did not give him a salary, he asked Cumming whether he could write for the *Daily Telegraph* to subsidise his costs. Cumming approved the request. Pares was also involved in running the *International News Agency*, an MI1c propaganda operation, and was later knighted for his intelligence work (Smith 2010: 207). The agency was tasked with placing pro-Russian stories into British newspapers and vice versa. The *éminence grise* of this operation was the ubiquitous Ransome, aided by other journalists that included Hamilton Fyfe of the *Daily*

Mail, Guy Berenger of the Reuters news agency and Morgan Philips Price of the *Manchester Guardian* (Smith 2010: 256). It was not a great success, but intelligence chiefs could already see the potential of news agencies as means of propaganda distribution and to provide cover to their spies.

MI5 also hired indigenous journalists as agents and propagandists in many countries. A recruitment by British Intelligence of a foreign journalist that now seems unfortunate is that of Benito Mussolini, later the Italian fascist dictator. In 2009, newly released MI5 archive documents revealed that Mussolini got his start in politics in 1917, with the help of a £100 weekly wage from MI5. In return, Mussolini, an editor, published propaganda in his newspaper encouraging Italians to remain in the war alongside the Allies. As part of his arrangement with MI5, he also had his henchmen attack peace protesters. Mussolini's payments were authorised by Sir Samuel Hoare, a Member of Parliament (MP) and MI5's man in Rome (Kington 2009).

The SIS or MI5 were not shy of making best use of journalists and journalism cover. While discouraging coverage of many of their nefarious activities, the intelligence services have always leaked information to selected members of the media. As early as 1916, the DNI Admiral Hall leaked details about Sir Roger Casement. In the early years of the century, Casement, a diplomat, had made his reputation uncovering the appalling human rights abuses in the Congo and Peru, and was knighted for his work. In 1913, disillusioned with British imperialism, he resigned and threw in his lot with the cause of Irish nationalism. He was involved in the events around the 1916 Easter Rising, including arranging for a shipment of arms from Germany.

The eavesdroppers in Room 40 picked up worrying messages between Casement and the Germans as he travelled. Casement was looking for a mutually beneficial alliance for the Irish and the Germans against the British. Room 40 tracked his movements through his messages, and on his return to Ireland Casement was arrested by the British authorities. He was found guilty of treason and sentenced to death. Casement was still popular in some British circles. To prevent calls for clemency, Hall secretly provided the media with excerpts of Casement's private journals, which included numerous explicit accounts of homosexual activity (Aldrich and Cormac 2016: 31). Casement was hanged in Pentonville Prison in August 1916. Whether Casement's diaries were forgeries would be debated for nearly eighty years. In 2001, I reported that an effort was being made to resolve the matter for once and for all: 'Forensic tests were to be carried out to solve one of the 20th century's most bitter political controversies surrounding the execution of Sir Roger

Casement, the Irish patriot and human rights crusader, who was hanged for treason' (Lashmar 2001). A year later, the tests showed the diaries to be genuine.

Notes

1. From the SIS website, <https://www.sis.gov.uk/our-history.html> (last accessed 17 June 2019).
2. *Manchester Guardian*, 2 February 1920, p. 12.
3. Christopher Andrew, 'MI5 in World War I', Security Service MI5, <https://www.mi5.gov.uk/mi5-in-world-war-i> (last accessed 17 June 2019).
4. Christopher Andrew, 'MI5 in World War I', Security Service MI5, <https://www.mi5.gov.uk/mi5-in-world-war-i> (last accessed 17 June 2019).
5. I use the term 'profession' lightly here. Whether you can call journalism or being an intelligence officer a profession is open to debate. Some journalists rail against journalism being called a profession and prefer to call it a trade.
6. Later to become *The Guardian* newspaper.

THREE

The Interwar Years and the Dark Arts

That military intelligence was still the most important part of British Intelligence remit in the interwar years is shown by the wartime designations of MI5 and MI6, where MI stands for military intelligence; those acronyms remain the common shorthand for the agencies a century later. With deep peacetime cutbacks, MI5 was in a turf war with both the Special Branch and the SIS for political supremacy and funds. Mansfield Cumming died shortly before he was due to retire in 1923, and a former Director of Naval Intelligence, Rear Admiral Hugh 'Quex' Sinclair, was appointed the new head of SIS.

In the early 1920s, members of the British establishment thought they had much to be proud of: a strong innovative economy, a burgeoning financial centre that offset declining trade, an efficient military and parliamentary democracy. However, in the wake of the Great War and the Russian Revolution, capitalism was to enter an early period of crisis with the General Strike of 1926, the stock market crash of 1929, and then the Great Depression that left the decade forever recalled as a period of mass unemployment, failing industries and volatile governments. It is hard in the modern world to grasp how politics polarised in countries profoundly disturbed by war and inequality and the battle to extend the right to vote from the few to the many. At the one extreme was communism and at the other fascism, with MI5's old operative Mussolini in Italy and Hitler's seizure of power in Germany.

That the vanguardist, extremely repressive Bolsheviks won out in the communist power struggles in 1917 in Russia did not help. The British royal family and establishment took the murder of the Tsar and the Russian royal family as a very clear warning. As the First World War ended, the British shifted military resources to assist the White Russians in the war with the Reds, including sending troops and agents to counter the Bolsheviks. Mark Phythian has noted that the intelligence agencies did not fade away in the Great War's aftermath, but dug in, developing deeper bureaucratic roots, and expanding their personnel base as their expertise was deployed against the emerging threats represented by the Communist Party of Great Britain (CPGB) and the extreme right in the shape of the British Union of Fascists (BUF): 'Legends of its preventive powers grew, but at times masked a reality of surveillance so rudimentary that its objects realized they were under surveillance and adapted their activities accordingly' (Phythian 2005: 654).

From Kell's time onwards, MI5 was to be staffed by public school educated men, returnees from the colonial police forces and former police or military officers, and was solidly pale in complexion and attitude. Their counter-Bolshevik game was upped when a senior secret service officer, Desmond Morton, recruited Maxwell Knight, a fervent anti-communist, mildly eccentric jazz musician and keen naturalist. MI5's activities were to become murky and the distinction between anti-Bolshevism, anti-communism and anti-trade unionism was blurred.

According to Morton, 'when required to for his previous masters', Knight 'and two friends burgled, three nights running', the offices of Communist and Labour Party organisations in Scotland. Knight was taken on, initially for a three-month trial, as a sub-contractor, running M division, the agent handling. Morton had sent him around the country to gather information on Communist organisations. He reported that 'with every passing month Knight has got his agents nearer and nearer the centre of affairs' and Sinclair therefore approved his continued employment (Jeffery 2010: 233).

Keeping the Lid On

The Scottish journalist and writer Compton Mackenzie had had a good war and produced a series of memoirs of his adventures.

Mackenzie had served as an intelligence officer in the Eastern Mediterranean, and that provided the material for his third memoir, *Greek Memories*. For authenticity the memoir contained some wartime Foreign Office telegrams, and disclosed that the first chief of SIS had been known as 'C' after the first letter of his surname and a range of other insignificant classified information. The reaction by the newspapers to *Greek Memories* is instructive: 'Mystery Chief of the Secret Service, Capt "C's" identity disclosed' announced the headline in the *Daily Telegraph* on the day of the book's publication. One Hector Bywater, Cumming's very effective agent in Germany before the war, reported the story. Bywater did not mention his previous career in his reporting. Now, as the paper's naval correspondent wrote of 'C', 'the identity of this remarkable man, who before and during the war probed the naval and military secrets of the Central Powers, had been revealed in print for the first time' (Jeffery 2010: 240).

Compton Mackenzie was charged under the Official Secrets Act 1911 for communicating to unauthorised persons 'information which he had obtained while holding office under His Majesty' (Moran 2013: 65). It was thought that, at least in part, the prosecution of Mackenzie was instigated to intimidate former Prime Minister David Lloyd George who was proposing to publish a warts and all memoir (Moran 2013: 68). In the end, there was a plea bargain where Mackenzie admitted guilt on the understanding he would get a small fine of £100 and pay £100 towards costs. He got his own back by writing the satirical novel *Water on the Brain*, which lampooned the SIS disguised under the name MQ9 (E), 'The Directorate of Extraordinary Intelligence'.[1] As intelligence historian Christopher Moran has pointed out, in the first half of the twentieth century, the worst offenders for releasing state secrets were former ministers writing their memoirs, often for substantial royalties: 'Preventing ministers from revealing too much proved a difficult task for which no easy solution was found' (Moran 2013: 54). A great deal of effort was put into keeping the secrets of Room 40 during the First World War so potential enemies would not be aware of Britain's codebreaking capability.

Like Maxwell Knight, former intelligence officers became active on the right, often involving themselves in private covert operations against left-wing activists. Admiral 'Blinker' Hall, the former head of Room 40, had become a senior figure in the Conservative Central Office, the Tory MP for Eastbourne and a senior figure in the Economic League. The League was an anti-trade union organisation that covertly blacklisted many thousands of working-class trade unionists over many decades.[2] Another member of this right-wing cabal was John Baker White who was to become the Director General of the Economic League for the best part of half a century.[3] The League shared information with the Special Branch and the right-wing news media. On the other hand, the Soviet Union was supporting international agitation and propaganda to encourage communist revolution across the world. There is no doubt that many members of the CPGB owed their loyalty to the Party and not to the nation. The Soviets used a range of organisations driven by the Comintern to spread the revolution, and the NKVD (Soviet Intelligence Service) efficiently suborned pro-communist individuals to be spies – and that included many journalists.

Peacetime Cuts

By 1925, though MI5 had secured its survival, it had only thir-ty-five staff. Kell told Whitehall's Secret Service Committee that, because of lack of resources, 'he had no "agents" in the accepted sense of the word, but only informants, though he might employ an agent for a specific purpose'.[4] Morton recruited agents from industry and journalism. He claimed to have recruited *The Times* correspondent in Rome as SIS network controller for the Italian capital. This would likely have been Colin Coote, who later became editor of the *Daily Telegraph*.

What MI5 did have from early on was a surveillance system that monitored thousands of suspects, sometimes obtaining informa-tion by illegal means. In 1929, a Deputy Assistant Commissioner of the Metropolitan Police, J. F. C. Carter, discovered that Desmond Morton and Maxwell Knight were behind the burglary of the offices of Communist and Labour Party organisations in Scotland. Historian Keith Jeffery explains:

Carter . . . was understandably aggrieved at SIS muscling in on his territory. Indeed, if a report by Knight of a meeting over lunch with the DAC on 23 July 1930, as passed on by Morton, is anything to go by, Carter was incandescent with fury about the development. (Jeffery 2010: 233)

Carter argued that Maxwell Knight and Morton were 'doing the whole of this thing for the Conservative Party' and added that Ramsay MacDonald, the prime minister, was 'against this sort of work' (Jeffery 2010: 233).

The Zinoviev Letter

The 'Zinoviev Letter' was an inflammatory document published in the British press – the *Daily Mail* on 24 October 1924 – four days before the general election. It appeared to be a directive from the Soviet leader Grigori Zinoviev of the Communist International in Moscow to the Communist Party of Great Britain dated 15 September 1924, ordering the intensification of agitation against British democracy in advance of armed insurrection and class war. It played to fears of the Soviet threat.[5] Although well known, the story of the Zinoviev Letter is significant as it is an early example of the subterranean networks linking intelligence officers and journalists. Many believed publication of the letter led to the failure of Labour's 1924 bid for power under Ramsay MacDonald, though this view is now rejected on the basis that the election would have been lost anyway. The letter seemed authentic at the time but historians now believe it was a forgery. Suspicion remains that British right-wing activists, with the connivance of allies in the security and intelligence services, deliberately used the letter to engineer a Labour defeat. According to Jeffery, 'SIS was certainly involved, as the letter had been obtained by the Riga station, who had forwarded an English text to Head Office on 2 October' (2010: 216).

The SIS also had a politicised role in the affair (see Jeffery 2010: 216–22). Historian Christopher Andrew argued that MI5 had little to do with the official handling of the Zinoviev Letter, apart from distributing copies to army commands on 22 October 1924, no doubt to alert them to its call for subversion in the armed forces:

... Security Service archives shed little light. Other sources, however, provide some clues. A wartime MI5 officer, Donald Im Thurn ('recreations: golf, football, cricket, hockey, fencing'), who had served in MI5 from December 1917 to June 1919, made strenuous attempts to ensure the publication of the Zinoviev letter and may well have alerted the *Mail* and Conservative Central Office to its existence. (Andrew 2009: 150).

The new Conservative Party government set up a Cabinet committee to look into the claims around the publication of the letter. On 19 November 1924, the Foreign Secretary, Austen Chamberlain, reported that members of the committee were 'unanimously of opinion that there was no doubt as to the authenticity of the Letter' (Andrew 2009: 151).

The conspirators were protected by their elite network, the historian Gill Bennett observed, 'Feeling themselves part of a special and closed community, they exchanged confidences secure in the knowledge, as they thought, that they were protected by that community from indiscretion' (Bennett 1999: 28).

A review of the surviving evidence, commissioned in 1998 by then British Foreign Secretary Robin Cook, concluded that the letter was almost certainly a forgery, although its precise authorship cannot be determined. Bennett notes, 'It also concluded that the idea of the forgery as part of an institutional campaign, directed by British Intelligence to discredit the Labour Government, is inherently improbable' (2006: 80). Phythian notes:

> A 1999 investigation confirmed what had been an article of faith for generations of Labour Party supporters, that the document was a forgery, and that SIS officers were involved in passing it to the *Daily Mail*, where it was published . . . Hence, suspicions of intelligence interventions in domestic British politics stretch back to the earliest days of the agencies, and have been shown to have some foundation. (Phythian 2005: 654–5)

Examples of unethical activity, as well as activity of the highest ethical standards, by the intelligence services are frequent in the historical record.

Whether or not MI5 or SIS officially played a part in the Zinoviev Letter, it reinforced the notion that they were politically to the right, a notion that has stuck and continued into the twenty-first century.

'An orgy of government indiscretion'

Early on, agencies learnt how to control selected journalists. Prior to the 1960s, there was relatively little direct reporting of the intelligence services and their activities in the UK, USA or, for that matter, elsewhere. There was some opaque coverage of their successes and failures but detailed coverage of the agencies was discouraged at every level. The scant coverage that did appear was largely supportive and there was little in the way of criticism in the media. Of the agencies, the eavesdroppers – the people who intercepted communications and if necessary decrypted them – got the least press. Probably most journalists had no idea they even existed because GC&CS, from their Queen's Gate base, went to great efforts to keep their activities secret. It was government policy to neither confirm nor deny the existence of such agencies. The remarkable exceptions came in the 1920s. After the Russian Revolution, British Intelligence had successfully intercepted a large number of Soviet government communications. In 1923, Lord Curzon, the Leader of the House of Lords, angered at Soviet efforts to destabilise Britain, decided to make it clear to the Soviets that the UK knew what they were up to. He both revealed details of intercepts in a protest note and further taunted the Soviets that Britain was able to read their secret correspondence. Consequently, the Soviet regime knew the British intercepted communications, but this was not shared with British public.

Then in May 1927, the Home Secretary, Sir William Joynson-Hicks (popularly known as Jix), ordered a raid on the All-Russian Co-operative Society (Arcos), the Soviet trading company in London. Unfortunately, it did not reveal much evidence of subversion. To demonstrate the decision to raid Arcos was legitimate, the Cabinet decided to release details of Soviet intercepted cables. This was all made public in a Commons Statement and then a debate. As Christopher Andrew later commented, this debate on 26 May, 'developed into an orgy of government indiscretion about the Secret Service for which there is no parallel in modern parliamentary history' (Andrew 1985: 470)

The press seized upon on the Prime Minister's statement. In those days, there was an extensive regional press, as well as national press, and they reported Parliament in detail. The *Devon and Exeter Gazette* of 25 May under the headline 'Break with Soviet Union: Momentous Declaration by the British Premier. Damning disclosures' on page eight notes the premier had read from one secret Soviet telegram and then 'Mr Baldwin quoted from other documents which revealed that Soviet representatives had solicited information for the purposes of a political campaign in this country.' The result of these breaches was that the Soviet Union swiftly adopted new codes and ciphers that defeated the British codebreakers, who were unable to decrypt any further Soviet communications until after 1939.

The Usual Suspects

Alongside hundreds of left-wing trade unionists and communists throughout the interwar years, MI5 had kept a close eye on a considerable number of prominent authors and poets. I do not go into any detail about MI5 monitoring writers as James Smith explores this in his book specifically on this topic (Smith 2012). These writers did also undertake journalism from time to time but they were essentially authors or poets. W. H. Auden and George Orwell were just two of the many writers who because of the political polarisation of the time had engaged with political groupings that were being kept under surveillance by MI5. The extra powers given to MI5 in 1931 meant the service watched and kept detailed files on many of the authors we still recognise as major figures. MI5 monitored many of the left-wing groups at the time of the Spanish Civil War in which British citizens were banned from engaging. Nevertheless, many ignored the edict. The poet, author and essayist Stephen Spender was watched by MI5 as he went to Spain as a journalist for the *Daily Worker* (Smith 2012: 40–1). Like many authors, he dipped in and out of journalism for ideological and financial reasons.

The Rise of the Far Right

Following Hitler's rise to power, the attention of the Service, once very focused on communists, turned to investigate the threat of subversion from the far right. Sir Oswald Mosley's British Union of Fascists was of particular concern, with pitched battles fought between fascists and communists on the streets of some of the larger cities. MI5's leading agent runner, Maxwell Knight, who had once personally been closely involved with the far right and was close to William Joyce, had considerable success in penetrating British fascist movements. Several of his sub-agents were journalists, and the communist newspaper the *Daily Worker* employed others. Maxwell Knight nurtured the media; his assistant and girlfriend, Joan Miller, wrote in her memoirs that Fleet Street editors were frequent visitors to Knight's dinner parties (1986: 76). The relationships between intelligence and the media developed apace into a tangled web.

MI5's most striking pre-war success was the penetration of the London embassy of Nazi Germany through the anti-Nazi German diplomat, Wolfgang zu Putlitz, whose constant message was that the British policy of trying to appease Hitler by making concessions to him made war more, not less, likely. Putlitz came close to despair in September 1938 when Prime Minister Neville Chamberlain returned from the Munich conference claiming that an agreement pressuring the Czechs to surrender the Sudetenland on their western border to Germany meant not only peace with honour but 'peace for our time'.[6]

The *Red Book*

It felt strange, almost eerie, to be the first member of the public to hold and read the notorious *Red Book* when it was finally released into the public domain in January 2000. Its thick pages have a totemic significance and its blood-red leather is a symbol of the fascism and anti-Semitism that once was far more powerful in the British establishment than their successors care to admit. It was seized at the behest of MI5 in the early days of the war as part of a significant counter-intelligence operation, and its caretaker was arrested by the British police and later convicted of spying for Germany. For many years, this sinister tome had been locked up in the Wiener Library, a private collection in central London. It was there, among the dusty shelves devoted to the Holocaust and Jewish history, that I was given permission to view it (Lashmar 2000a).

The *Red Book* is the membership list of the Right Club, a secret organisation founded in May 1939 by Captain Archibald Ramsay MP. During the Spanish Civil War (1936–9), Ramsay was swept up by the tide of fascism and came out as a pro-Franco and virulent anti-Semite and a devoted enemy of international communism. He toured the UK fulminating on the 'Judaeo-Bolshevik Plot' (Lashmar 2000a). He became closely associated with pro-Nazi circles in Britain and, by 1938, was a leading figure in the Nordic League. He was unfazed by the 1938 Kristallnacht pogrom, when the Nazis blatantly showed the violence they could inflict on the Jewish community. As the war loomed over Europe, Ramsay became further convinced that Jews were orchestrating a confrontation between Britain and Germany. In response, he set up the Right Club. 'Our first objective', he later wrote, 'was to clear the Conservative Party of Jewish influence' (Lashmar 2000a).

Unlike the populist BUF, the Right Club was secret and exclusive. Its members were aristocrats and Members of Parliament, academics, clerics, civil servants, journalists and wealthy dilettantes. Some were old enough to have fought and even distinguished themselves in the 1914–18 war, and undoubtedly saw themselves as British patriots. However, they were pro-Nazis who supported Hitler's treatment of Germany's Jewish population. From King Edward VIII to the first Viscount Rothermere's *Daily Mail* and downwards, there was a widespread view that only a powerful Germany could hold back the threat of Bolshevism, and that Britain should be supporting Hitler, not preparing to fight him. The existence of the *Red Book* had been first revealed during a tense wartime debate in Parliament. By then, it had already been seized by MI5 at the home of the American pro-Nazi spy Tyler Kent. For forty years, the ledger was believed to have been lost and its whereabouts was much speculated upon.

The *Red Book* was divided into male and female membership lists with notes as to whether they had paid their dues, made donations or received their club badge – which featured an eagle killing a snake. However, if the badge seems mildly comic now, the vehemence with which these establishment figures hated Jews was chilling (Lashmar 2000a).

Reading down the list, written with a fountain pen by Ramsay, some of the names still resonate as prominent members of the establishment: Arthur Wellesley the 5th Duke of Wellington, the 2nd Baron Redesdale, the Earl of Galloway, Lord Ronald Graham, Princess Blücher, Sir Ernest Bennett, Prince Turka Galitzine and Britain's most notorious Second World War traitor, William Joyce. Later known as Lord Haw-Haw, Joyce broadcast propaganda from Germany and paid for it with his life when the British hanged him after the war. There is Commander E. H. Cole, who was the Chancellor of the White Knights, a British version of the Ku Klux Klan. MPs included Sir James Edmondson, Colonel Charles I. Kerr and John M'Kie. The book also lists donations. Sir Alexander Walker, then the head of the Johnnie Walker whisky dynasty, is shown to have donated £100.

Inevitably, there were journalists in this unsavoury coterie. A well-known anti-Semitic member was A. K. Chesterton, a First World War military hero, who, though married to a Fabian, became close to Sir Oswald Mosley and on joining the BUF became its director of publicity and propaganda as well as chief organiser for the Midlands.[7] Another, Imperial College graduate, Norman Hay, worked with fellow member Lancelot Lawton to set up a BUF journal called *Information and Policy*. Lawton was described by MI5 asset in the Right Club Geoff Mandeville Roe as being 'one of Lord Northcliffe's young men' who had been groomed at *The Times*. He had been the editor at the School of Slavonic and East European Studies of *East Europe and Contemporary Russia* (Griffith 2010: 140).[8] When war broke out, Ramsay was undeterred. He nominally dissolved the Right Club but continued work with a ten-strong inner circle, including his assistant Anna Wolkoff. Early in the war, his protégé Lawton was a frequent speaker at Nordic Club meetings, another Ramsay offshoot. Lawton's theme was that Nazis should annexe Ukraine for Germany's economic good and necessary expansion – *Lebensraum*.

Professor Richard Griffith details how these individuals continued to support Germany even into the Phoney War: 'As various "patriotic" movements tried to hammer out a common anti-war policy in October 1939, Hay for instance had a "productive" private meeting with Sir Oswald Mosley and Admiral Domville on the 13th of that month' (2010: 220). Further secret meetings followed but ultimately to no avail as the country's mood turned further anti-Nazi (Griffith 2010: 220). While there is evidence that many Right Club members dropped out of view at the beginning of the war, others continued to share his pro-Nazi enthusiasm (Lashmar and Mullins 1998).

MI5 was concerned the Right Club could form a focus for a wartime pro-Nazi resistance so it sent in three penetration agents. One was Joan Miller, the girlfriend of MI5's agent runner Maxwell Knight. They monitored the Club's activities over the next months. Miller detailed her role in her 1986 book.

In April 1940, attempting to keep the membership list secret, Ramsay took the precious *Red Book* to Tyler Kent for safekeeping. As a cipher clerk at the

US Embassy Kent had diplomatic immunity. A month later, with diplomatic immunity removed by the US ambassador, the police raided Kent's flat. He and Wolkoff were charged with supplying the Germans with secret cables between Churchill and the US President. The other members of the inner circle, including Ramsay, were rounded up and detained under Defence Regulation 18B, an anti-fifth-column clause. Ramsay, the only serving MP detained under this law, was released from detention in 1944. He lost his seat in 1945 and died a decade later (Lashmar 2000a).

What happened to the *Red Book*? According to Griffith, its existence was publicly revealed in the 1941 trial involving Ramsay, and the police had it until October 1944; however, it seems likely that it was returned to Ramsay after his release that year. Nothing was seen of it until the late 1980s, when it was discovered at the bottom of an old safe in a solicitor's office. Luckily, the finder was familiar with Griffith's work and passed it to him. He used it as a primary source for his book, *Patriotism Perverted*, then deposited it at the Wiener Library.

Churchill's Insurance

Under the erratic leadership of Hugh Sinclair, the SIS had moved into Broadway House in 1926, an oppressive warren of an office block near Parliament that looked from the outside like a French château gone to seed. SIS officers had operated from British embassies using the diplomatic cover that was devised after the Great War as 'Passport Control Officers', a suitably anodyne title making them look unimportant in the embassy hierarchy. Everyone knew passport control was the local SIS officers, including the local taxi drivers. After the great economic crash of the late 1920s, the Treasury reduced funding to the secret service so the number of Passport Control Officers dropped to just nineteen across Europe in early 1931. While key bureaus covering the Soviet Union and Germany were retained, there were great gaps in SIS coverage.

Worse, the quality of the field officers in the SIS, despite coming from the upper reaches of British society, was poor according to contemporaries (Knightley 1986: 86–9). To compensate, the SIS recruited patriotic businessmen who often travelled or lived abroad. The intelligence historian Michael Smith suggests: 'It developed good relationships with a number of British firms, such as Vickers,

Shell, British American Tobacco, the Hudson's Bay Company and APOC [the Anglo-Persian Oil Company], under which the companies' employers would be encouraged to collect intelligence' (Smith 2010: 338). It was good improvisation but while these volunteers could produce political and economic briefings, they were unlikely to produce high-grade diplomatic intelligence.

There were those who realised that a much more extensive intelligence organisation was desperately needed. Under the patronage of Churchill, whom he had met in France on front-line tours during the First World War and struck up respect and a friendship with, Desmond Morton became head of the newly founded Industrial Intelligence Centre in 1931, and was responsible for providing intelligence on the plans and capabilities for manufacturing munitions in other countries. Jeffery contends that 'It had a wide sphere of interest, though the principal focus was on industrial capacity for war' (2010: 313).

Morton was Churchill's close adviser. With the rise of Hitler, the British government did not want to see a new threat looming on the horizon and the SIS paid too little attention to Germany and Italy. As the legend correctly has it, Churchill was alive to the threat but out of government and starved of intelligence so he set up his own informal intelligence network with the help of Morton. Churchill was still a powerful political figure. In 1932, Morton obtained the permission of Prime Minister Ramsay MacDonald to provide Churchill with certain confidential reports and information. This arrangement was endorsed and continued by the two succeeding Prime Ministers (Baldwin and Chamberlain), and was of considerable value to Churchill's campaign for British rearmament. When Churchill was made Prime Minister in 1940, he made Morton his special adviser. Both Morton and Dick Ellis, a former soldier who joined the SIS in 1923 and rose to a senior rank within the agency, had contact with William Stephenson, a Canadian businessman who was quiet but impressive and later to play a vital role in the USA during the Second World War.[9]

At this point, an officer by the name of Claude Dansey became significant. He had moved from MI5 to the SIS after the First World War and was effective at recruiting and running agents. According to *The Guardian*, 'on at least two occasions, assets he developed within the Irish nationalist movement were able to warn British Intelligence about plans to dynamite Buckingham Palace' (Norton-Taylor 2001). Many of Dansey's sources included American industrialists, who would eventually make up much of his extensive contact list. After working for intelligence during the First World War, he went into business. After losing his money in the Wall Street crash, Dansey rejoined the SIS in Italy to monitor Mussolini's Fascist movement. Noted for being acerbic and a cynic, Dansey was appalled at the state of the SIS, which he believed to be incompetent. He set up a sub-department called the Z-organisation, an intelligence network completely separate from the SIS one. Operating under business cover from Bush House in London, the Z-organisation drew on Dansey's own business and industrial contacts for agents including volunteers who would help for patriotic motives or just for the thrill (Jeffery 2010: 317–19).

Journalistic cover for Z-organisation was regularly provided by the Kemsley Newspaper Group and later by the *Daily Herald*, *The Times*, the *Daily Telegraph* and *The Observer*, among others. Journalism was an excellent cover for intelligence agents in the field; ideal cover came from professions where asking questions in high places did not cause concern. Dansey even funded the creation of what became a highly successful film production company, Alexander Korda's London Films, as cover for agents travelling around pre-war Europe. It is likely that the Bertram Mills Circus was also used in much the same way, particularly as Mills's son, Cyril, was a senior MI5 officer in the Doublecross Committee during the Second World War and remained an 'asset' long after that (Mahl 1998: 67).

In the late 1930s, the SIS recruited a number of journalists including Frederick Voigt from *The Guardian*, Geoffrey Cox from the *Daily Express*, and from the *Daily Mirror*, David Walker. Walker described his recruitment: 'I was asked to lunch at a West End restaurant by a naval commander I knew. He said I might be interested in a job of national importance that I could do while continuing to work for the *Mirror*.' Asked what the pay was at the *Mirror*, he was offered the same to work for the SIS. He never told the *Mirror* of his second job (Knightley 1986: 91).

Even as it became clear at the end of the 1930s that a war was inevitable, Britain's intelligence services were far from war ready and demonstrated that strange British characteristic of relying on a mix of amateur and professional individuals to conduct their business. Journalists were also increasingly moving into the secret world both as propagandists for the new covert 'news' organisations and into the mainstream spy organisations, as their existing skill sets saved time since they did not need the same level of training as raw recruits.

Notes

1. Compton Mackenzie went on to write many books including *Whisky Galore* (1947), which was turned into a popular post-war comedy film. He was a founder of the Scottish National Party and was eventually knighted by Queen Elizabeth in 1952 for services to literature.
2. I was one of the journalists who uncovered the blacklisting operation of the Economic League (see Leigh and Lashmar 1988b). This, I must admit, was run rather like an MI5 operation with the cultivation of inside sources and monitoring of staff movement.
3. Baker White had worked for a private sector spy agency. He became a propagandist in the Political Warfare Executive (PWE) during the Second World War and then the Conservative MP for Canterbury from 1945 to 1953.
4. See the MI5 website's history section, <https://www.mi5.gov.uk/history> (last accessed 17 June 2019).
5. The contents and context of the letter can be found in the National Archives, <http://webarchive.nationalarchives.gov.uk/+/http://yourarchives.national archives.gov.uk/index.php?title=The_Zinoviev_Letter> (last accessed 17 June 2019).
6. <http://www.MI5.gov.uk> (last accessed 17 June 2019).
7. Chesterton re-enlisted in the army early in the war but was later invalided out. After the war he remained a journalist, right wing and an advocate for the Empire. In the mid-1950s, Chesterton was appointed by Lord Beaverbrook to his papers as a literary adviser, contributing to the *Daily Mail* and the *Sunday Express*. He ghost wrote Beaverbrook's autobiography, *Don't Trust to Luck*.
8. Roe's reports detailed the ingrained anti-Semitism that prevailed in a wide swathe of British society at the time.
9. Stephenson was to make a major input in America's entry into the war; see the section 'The Quiet Canadian' in Chapter 4.

FOUR

The Second World War

Claude Dansey would be proven right about SIS's weaknesses, but his Chinese wall between the SIS and the Z-organisation was to be demolished. Shortly after the declaration of war, the SIS suffered a catastrophic loss: the 'Venlo Incident'. This was essentially a successful covert German *Sicherheitsdienst* (SD, Security Service) operation, in the course of which two British Intelligence officers were abducted on the outskirts of the border town of Venlo, in the Netherlands, on 9 November 1939. The SIS resident at The Hague, Major Richard Stevens, and The Hague resident of the parallel Z-organisation, Captain Sigismund Payne Best, were tricked into believing a high-level anti-Nazi Wehrmacht general wished to hold secret talks in London. The SD agents held out the possibility of a military coup and Hitler's arrest.

Instead, the two officers were dramatically kidnapped and taken to Germany for interrogation. 'Under duress, Best and Stevens described in great detail the internal workings of SIS – which, at the very least, served to confirmed information the Abwehr [the German foreign intelligence service] may have extracted from another SIS officer' (Richelson 1995: 129).

The first damage limitation action by the British was to close The Hague SIS station, but as Richelson notes the damage to the network was enormous:

> SIS . . . had withdrawn all its personnel from Prague, Warsaw, Bucharest, and Berlin once war had begun. In addition, the Wehrmacht's May 1940

Blitzkrieg forced closure of the stations in Paris and Brussels. . . . The remaining stations on the continent – Stockholm, Lisbon, and Berne – produced little of value. (1995: 129)

Obtaining useful intelligence in much of Europe, now largely occupied by the German Army, was risky. Some neutral cities like Lisbon and Casablanca attracted networks of rival spies. With the transparent 'Passport Control Officer' diplomatic cover clearly redundant, British Intelligence officers and agents used a wide range of covers in the field, frequently posing as journalists, during the Second World War. There were also networks of 'front' news agencies engaged in covert propaganda. The most successful were in the USA, manipulating American public opinion in favour of entering the war (Montgomery Hyde 1989; Mahl 1998). Early on, Sir William Stephenson, a contact of Desmond Morton's, had been recruited into the intelligence world and was the key British Intelligence representative in New York. He persuaded the New York-based Overseas News Agency to provide cover for British agents abroad (Lashmar and Oliver 1998b: 13).

MI5 and the Double Cross System

At the start of 1939, MI5 had only thirty-six officers, assisted by 103 secretarial and Registry staff (Andrew 2009: 220). When war was declared, a flood of reports, vetting requests and inquiries overwhelmed the Security Service. They were also trying to deal with an IRA bombing campaign with some seventy-two attacks and had to contend with fears of a 'fifth column' of Nazi sympathisers in Britain working to prepare the ground for a German invasion. This resulted in thousands of reports of suspected enemy activity, each of which had to be investigated. Following the embarrassment of the torpedoing of the battleship HMS *Royal Oak* at anchor in the supposedly secure harbour at Scapa Flow and a number of other incidents, which were all put down to the activities of 'undiscovered Nazi spies', an underwhelmed Churchill forced Kell to resign towards the end of May 1940. In late 1940, most staff evacuated to Blenheim Palace and in March 1941, Sir David Petrie was appointed the first

Director General of the Security Service with a remit for massive expansion.

Under Sir David, the Service underwent major reforms that greatly improved its ability to deal with the demands of wartime, and its major successes against German espionage followed. Internment for enemy nationals, instigated at the outbreak of the war, effectively isolated the Germans from most of their British-based agents. Some were 'turned' by the Service. Some became double agents, feeding misleading information to the Germans on military and diplomatic strategy throughout the war. This was the famous 'double cross' system run by the 20 Committee. Cyril Mills of the circus family was the controller for Pujol.[1] Howard Campbell, a well-known journalist and SIS officer during the Second World War, summed up Cyril Mills as 'an enterprising, perceptive, obstinate, opinionated, cheerful, loyal, delightful and wholly lovable man'.[2] Being nice is not necessarily a good qualification for those involved in intelligence. The opposition, as British Intelligence was about to discover, did not play by a set of rules.

Meanwhile, MI5 had grown from a small, ramshackle counterespionage section in 1939 to a large security service by 1945. Its reach extended across the old Empire and through offshoots such as Security Intelligence Middle East (SIME) in the Middle East as well. While MI5 was never as ruthless as the Gestapo, it was not afraid to use violence and the threat of being shot to persuade its captives, whether German prisoners of war (POWs), German agents or members of the British Union of Fascists, to talk (see Cobain 2012). Its colonial offshoots were even less restrained when dealing with nationalists and communists they had apprehended. The new Labour government of Clement Attlee, suspicious of the right-wing ethos of the Security Service, imposed an 'honest copper' as its new chief in 1946, Sir Percy Sillitoe, a former Chief Constable of Kent.

GC&CS

In the secret but competitive world of cryptography, electromechanical cipher machines were coming into wide use. Great advances in both cipher design and cryptanalysis were happening. In the 1930s, the Germans made heavy use, in several variants, of an electrome-chanical rotor machine known as Enigma. As the Second World War loomed codebreakers and their support staff were recruited, trained and assembled in requisitioned facilities at Bletchley Park, a stately home an hour's train journey north of London. One of the primary objectives of the organisation was to break the Enigma codes. Their first success came in January 1940 when they decrypted Luftwaffe messages. (For a more detailed account see Aldrich 2010.) This produced vital intelligence in support of Allied military operations on land, at sea and in the air of the type Sun Tzu had recommended 3,000 years earlier. Bletchley Park saw the birth of the information age with the industrialisation of the codebreaking processes ena-bled by machines such as the Turing/Welchman Bombe, and the world's first electronic computer, Colossus (Aldrich 2010: 28).

Special Operations Executive

Spying is best performed discreetly and not by drawing attention to oneself. If you combine spying with bombing and assassination, it draws attention to your proximity. It can be a hard distinction to make because covert action needs intelligence to be effective, and intelligence is often collected by those undertaking covert opera-tions. Churchill understood these problems well and so while the SIS repaired after the Venlo Incident, he ordered a new organisation to be created. As historian Ted Cookridge notes, 'A few strokes of the pen, and a body was created "to coordinate all action by way of subversion and sabotage against the enemy overseas" or as Churchill put it, "to set Europe ablaze"' (Cookridge 1965: 3).[3] The new organisation was called the Special Operations Executive (SOE) and was established under the Minister of Economic Warfare, Dr Hugh Dalton. Consequently, the Ministry of Economic Warfare was known in Whitehall as the 'Ministry of Ungentlemanly Warfare'. One of Dalton's assistants there was Christopher Mayhew, then a twenty-five-year-old Oxford tutor, who organised the SOE training schools before going on to serve with Special Forces. He was later to play an important part in post-war propaganda.

Churchill pressed for an immediate counter-offensive against the German occupation of the Continent. SOE's main focus over the following years, and its *raison d'être*, was its work with the resistance groups that sprang up across Europe and the Far East. Indeed, as the official historian of SOE, M. R. D. Foot, wrote, 'SOE was a world-wide body. There was no continent; there was hardly any country, where it did not do something' (Foot 1984: 172).

Pen as Sword – The War of the Propagandists

At the end of the 1970s, I spent a great deal of time in archives researching Britain's wartime propaganda operation and interviewing those who had been involved. It was clear that from 1940 onwards one key figure was Leslie Sheridan, by then, unfortunately, deceased. 'Sherry', as he had been known to his friends, apparently urbane, clubbable and energetic, was to become a major figure in British covert propaganda for over two decades. Before the Second World War, Leslie Sheridan had been a news editor at the *Daily Mirror*.

Under Nazi politician Joseph Goebbels, the German propaganda machine had been in full swing since the early 1930s, and films like Leni Riefenstahl's *Triumph of the Will* and *Olympia* were widely circulated. They are considered two of the most effective and technically innovative propaganda films ever made. Shortly before the outbreak of war, tentative steps had been taken to develop a British propaganda capability, which included a Foreign Office organisation called Electra House (EH); a research branch of the War Office, Military Intelligence (Research) (MIR); and Section D of the SIS.

When Churchill set up the SOE 'to set Europe ablaze', it was handed the controlling remit for covert propaganda, which it put under a department called SO1. This was to have a major role in propaganda by bringing together all recently created propaganda-based departments. Sheridan was the joint personal assistant to the SOE head, Sir Charles Hambro (of the banking family), and eventually held the rank of lieutenant colonel. Starting in the Balkans and using his contact book of Fleet Street journalists and foreign correspondents, by 1941 Sheridan's network covered the main neutral capitals of the world. In 1940, he notably recruited journalist Kim Philby – perhaps the most effective British traitor of all time – then working for *The Times*, who wheedled his way into the SIS in 1941 where ultimately he was able to wreak havoc on British Intelligence operations by passing on inside information to the Soviet KGB (Philby 1969: 29).

If the confusing plethora of propaganda units reads like a recipe for disaster, it was. It was not until two years into the war that a serious effort was made to organise effectively. The minister in charge of the Ministry of Information, Alfred Duff Cooper, who had a remit covering domestic propaganda as well as the neutral countries, was agitating to control SO1. SO1 was detached from SOE to become a separate entity, the Political Warfare Executive (PWE), run by a director general under Foreign Office supervision. Robert Bruce Lockhart – who was sentenced to death *in absentia* in Russia in 1919 for assisting the anti-Bolshevik forces – had been appointed a deputy Under-Secretary of State at the Foreign Office to coordinate propaganda. He later complained that, 'For twelve months the energy of whole propaganda effort, which should have been directed against the enemy, has largely been dissipated in interdepartmental intrigues and strife' (Cruickshank 1981: 25–6).

Meanwhile, the affable 'Sherry' set to and brought in journalists to help with the intended covert propaganda operation. His then wife Doris, whom he had met at the *Daily Mirror*, was assigned to the Britanova news agency in New York. Lionel Hale, a dramatist, broadcaster and journalist, was recruited to assist Sheridan. (Later, Hale was the first host of the long-running Radio 4 *Round Britain Quiz*.) Hale's SOE personal file records that he was 'altogether a most efficient and attractive man whose sense of fun and humour enhances and is partially responsible for his exceptional capability in many branches of journalism'.[4] Hale's deputy was Colin Wintle who was to become the liaison officer between PWE and SOE. The son of a Bristol general practitioner, Wintle worked on a local Bristol newspaper and then went on to Fleet Street as a correspondent on the *Daily Mirror* and the *News Chronicle*.

Eventually promoted to the rank of major, Wintle worked a lot with another significant journalist who became involved in propaganda, Sefton 'Tom' Delmer, a Berlin-born linguist with perfect German. Delmer had become friendly with Hitler's aide, Ernst Röhm, who arranged for him to interview Adolf Hitler in 1931. In 1933, Delmer was posted to France as the head of the *Daily Express* Paris Bureau.[5] He then covered important stories including the Spanish Civil War and the invasion of Poland in 1939. He also reported on the German western offensive into Belgium and France in 1940. Delmer returned to Britain and worked for a time as an announcer for the German Service of the BBC. In September 1940, he was recruited by PWE to organise black propaganda broadcasts to Nazi Germany as part of a psychological warfare campaign. The idea was that the radio station would undermine Hitler by pretending to be a fervent Hitler–Nazi supporter. Delmer's most notable success was a shortwave station 'Gustav Siegfried Eins 1' (GS1). It purported to be organised by the 'Der Chef', a hard line Nazi, who despised both Winston Churchill ('that flatfooted son of a drunken Jew') and the Nazi Party traitors who had undermined National Socialism's glorious aims. GS1 went on the air on 23 May 1941. The part of Der Chef was played adroitly by Peter Secklemann, a former Berlin journalist (Lashmar and Oliver 1998b: 14–15). Journalists and writers gravitated towards propaganda work and, for some, the twilight world of special operations.

Black Propaganda

It was not until 1942 that the British covert propaganda operation had really coalesced. The 'country headquarters' – the designation of the stately home Woburn Abbey – was where the PWE's most covert activities were organised. By 1941, it housed some 458 propagandists drawn mostly from Fleet Street, the publishing world and universities, including figures who became senior politicians like Patrick Gordon Walker and Richard Crossman. As Phillip Knightley was to note, 'Many journalists thought they could best help defeat Hitler by writing propaganda for one of the information offices or by serving in one of the secret services' (2006: 7). One of the most effective methods was the use of rumours or 'sibs' (from the Latin *sibilaire*). Cruickshank records that the formation of sibs was a serious business:

> An Underground Propaganda Committee, the existence of which was known to only a few, met weekly at Woburn to examine whispers put forward by the Joint Intelligence Committee, the Foreign Office, the Service Departments, and PWE Regional Directors and to arrange for those which were approved to be put into their final shape. (Cruickshank 1981: 109)

The number of sibs slipped out was in the thousands. All were filed and referenced and can be found in a file in the National Archives. A vivid example is sib R/669, designed to demoralise the German Wehrmacht on the Eastern Front. This invented but plausible rumour attributed to a Swiss doctor the statement that '200 German soldiers had to be castrated due to the severity of the Russian winter'. This one found its way into an American news agency's service under the heading 'The eunuchs of the Eastern Front' (Nichols 1978: 1).'[6]

Sheridan had assembled and led a diverse team. However, those who knew him said the real power behind the throne was the remarkable SOE secretary Adelaide Maturin, who proved professionally highly capable. Then thirty-one years old, Adelaide had been born in Lymington on the south coast of England. Those who knew her told the author that she had natural authority. Sometime in the middle years of the war, Sheridan divorced Doris and married Maturin. Another significant recruit in personal terms for Maturin and Sheridan was, as we shall later see, Johann Leopold Welser, known as 'Hans' and listed as being from Geneva but likely a refugee from the Nazis. All were involved in secret propaganda work.

In the months leading up to 6 June 1944, PWE had run a major campaign of strategic deception. The propagandists were often in tension with the BBC, which they viewed as the ideal propaganda tool. The early BBC had come slowly to news, and bulletins from the time (as now can be heard in the archives) were delivered by men with Received Pronunciation and were very dull. In 1940 the BBC only had two staff reporters, one of which was Richard Dimbleby. The Dunkirk evacuation was minimally covered at the time as only three reporters saw any of the actual events and the BBC did not report the battle until four days after it started. A BBC staff member who worked in Broadcasting House during the war, Penelope Fitzgerald, was later to record that they were 'improbably dedicated to putting out the truth' (Jack 2018: 6).

Throughout the war, the BBC was struggling with notions of balance and objectivity while under constant pressure to support the government position. Now considered Britain's greatest socialist writer, George Orwell worked as a talks producer in the BBC's Indian section and was unhappy about bias. On one occasion, he was required to produce a story about British promises to the Indian Congress to give independence if India assisted in a British victory. This item misrepresented some of the more critical Indian politicians. Orwell weighed up this ethical issue later in *Partisan Review*:

'As to the ethics of broadcasting and in general letting oneself be used by the British governing class,' . . . 'it's of little value to argue about it, it is chiefly a question of whether one considers it more important to down the Nazis first or whether one believes doing this is meaningless unless one achieves one's own [socialist] revolution first'. (Jack 2018: 3)

Compared with Axis propaganda, Orwell 'felt he had kept "our little corner fairly clean"' (Jack 2018: 3). Richard Crossman, later a Labour government minister, worked at PWE and recalled:

> meetings between the PWE and the officials of the BBC took the form of long bitter fights. Quite properly, the BBC officials were determined to do nothing beyond reporting the straight news . . . Our job was to inject the highest percentage of propaganda content we could into the news service of the BBC. (Lashmar and Oliver 1998b: 18)

He notes that the BBC largely won. The BBC principle was to report the news even if it was bad, and that gave the BBC authority. The BBC's reputation was useful because when an inaccurate piece of information was smuggled in, it was more likely to be believed. As Sir Arthur Dodds-Parker[7] later observes, 'I've always found, as a principle, that truth is much more valuable and effective than trying to concoct a load of falsities and black propaganda. Sooner or later people find out and they never trust you' (Dodds-Parker 1997).

The Quiet Canadian

A week after President Roosevelt returned from signing the Atlantic Charter with Churchill, a series of British Intelligence reports on Vichy France were sanitised and deliberately leaked to the *New York Herald Tribune*. The exposés accused the French Embassy in Washington of conspiracies against America's well-being and in support of Nazi Germany's ambitions. They roused a nation-wide furore: 'Vichy agents sought plans – tried to get blueprints of weapon defending Britain from invasion' was one headline that ran in a September 1941 edition of the *Herald Tribune*. The Vichy Ambassador to Washington, DC, Gaston Henry-Haye, was angered into claiming that the whole affair was a 'de Gaullist-Jewish-FBI-British intrigue' (Stevenson 1976: 330). It was part of a British covert operation to change public opinion and encourage the USA to join in the war against Germany and the other Axis nations.

Until the middle of 1940, the majority of US media editorial positions on the European war were strongly isolationist. The British strategic objective propagated by Churchill – with Roosevelt's secret agreement – was to bring the USA into the war with Germany. The coordinator for this momentous task was a Canadian, William Stephenson, who had been a fighter pilot during the First World War and an outlier of Churchill's personal pre-war intelligence network. The head of SIS, the aristocratic Sir Stewart Menzies, sent Stephenson to the USA on 21 June 1940, to be the Passport Control Officer in New York City. He set up the cover office – British Security Coordination (BSC) – on various floors of the Rockefeller Center (the Rockefellers were sympathetic to the British cause).

To undermine American isolationists, who did not want their country drawn into the European war, the British targeted the group which the pioneering sociologist C. Wright Mills later classified in his book *The Power Elite* (first published in 1956). Wright had noted that the USA was not controlled collectively by its citizens but rather by a wealthy Anglo-Saxon elite from Ivy League schools. In his book on BSC, Thomas Mahl expands on this approach: 'Most of the members of this establishment were middle- or upper-class Protestants of Northern European, often English, descent' (1998: 6). Other than those of German descent, they tended to believe that America needed to side with the British against the Axis.

From July 1940, Stephenson played a major but discreet part in setting up the Council for Democracy, recruiting anglophiles including Henry Luce, Lew Douglas, C. D. Jackson, Freda Kirchwey, Raymond Gram Swing, Robert Sherwood, John Gunther and Leonard Lyons, Ernest Angell and Carl Joachim Friedrich. According to the American author Kai Bird, the organisation 'became an effective and highly visible counterweight to the isolation rhetoric' of the America First Committee led by Charles Lindbergh and Robert E. Wood: 'With financial support from Douglas and Luce, Jackson, a consummate propagandist, soon had a media operation going which was placing anti-Hitler editorials and articles in eleven hundred newspapers a week around the country' (1992: 109). This was to be just one of many front organisations set up at the behest of BSC.

BSC became an umbrella organisation, coordinating all British Intelligence operations in the USA and seeking to avoid turf disputes between agencies. Overall, the purpose of BSC was to investigate enemy activities, prevent sabotage against British interests in the Americas, and mobilise pro-British opinion in the Americas. Part of that was a 'huge secret agency of nationwide news manipulation and black propaganda' (Mahl 1998: 13). BSC had influence in the *Herald Tribune*, the *New York Post*, the *Baltimore Sun* and *Radio New York Worldwide* (Montgomery Hyde 2001: 66). It also secretly subsidised the Boston-based shortwave radio station WRUL that broadcast in twenty-two different languages and, being on a shortwave frequency, it could broadcast over great distances and reach millions of listeners. BSC recruited a huge number of journalists and editors as agents and sympathisers, and their impact on American public opinion was enormous. The influential thinker and columnist, Walter Lippmann was among those who 'rendered service of particular value' (Mahl 1998: 13). Each agent was given a code number with the prefix G. Journalist Walter Lucas, who worked for BSC black propaganda section SO1, was given the code number G.124. He planted stories in publications including the *Christian Science Monitor* (Mahl 1998: 13).

BSC staffing expanded mostly by recruiting British journalists and writers. Grace Garner, Stephenson's secretary, said he recruited many journalists including Sydney Morrell from the *Daily Express* and, as already noted, Doris Sheridan from the *Daily Mirror*.[8] Sheridan liaised with the Arab sections in New York, keeping in touch with foreign nationals. University professor Bill Deakin worked for the office, as did the philosopher A. J. Ayer. Other recruits included Cedric Belfrage of the *Daily Express*, who during the Second World War was also passing information about British spying methods to the Soviet Union. He later co-founded the radical US weekly newspaper the *National Guardian*. Also on board were the glamorous Spitfire pilot and later children's author Roald Dahl, after he was transferred to Washington, DC, as Assistant Air Attaché; Ian Fleming, Intelligence Corps officer; and H. Montgomery Hyde, a counter-espionage Intelligence Corps officer who later became a Unionist MP.

BSC was effective, and while claiming to maintain US neutrality, President Roosevelt helped the British with the Lend-Lease deal. This followed on from the 1940 Destroyers for Bases Agreement, whereby fifty old US Navy destroyers were transferred to the Royal Navy and the Royal Canadian Navy in exchange for base rights in the Caribbean. Churchill also gave the USA base rights in Bermuda and Newfoundland at no cost, allowing British military assets to be redeployed. Lend-Lease was a programme by which the USA supplied Free France, the United Kingdom, the Republic of China, and later the Soviet Union and other Allied nations with food, oil and materiel between 1941 and August 1945. This included warships and warplanes, along with other weaponry. After the Japanese launched a surprise and damaging attack on the US military at Pearl Harbor on 7 December 1941, the USA joined the war. From then onwards BSC acted as an administrative headquarters more than an operational one for the SIS and the SOE and was a channel for communications and liaison between US and British security and intelligence organisations.

BSC may have represented the largest single covert operation in British Intelligence history. Ian Fleming himself once wrote, that 'James Bond is a highly romanticized version of a true spy'[9] and then pointed to William Stephenson as the real thing.[10] At the height of its operations in late 1941, there were many hundreds of agents and many hundreds of discrete supporters. Its power was sufficient that it finally stirred the suspicions of the head of the FBI, J. Edgar Hoover. America's embryonic intelligence community was heavily influenced by BSC; many years later, CIA Executive Director David W. Carey confirmed that Sir William Stephenson had played a key role in the creation of the CIA.[11]

The attorney Ernest Cuneo was the American liaison between British Intelligence, the White House, the FBI, the Treasury and the embryonic US intelligence services. He later noted that:

Given the time, the situation, and the mood, it is not surprising however, that BSC also went beyond the legal, the ethical, and the proper.
Throughout the neutral Americas, and especially in the U.S., it ran
espionage agents, tampered with the mails, tapped telephones, smuggled propaganda into the country, disrupted public gatherings, covertly
subsidized newspapers, radios, and organizations, perpetrated forgeries –
even palming one off on the President of the United States – violated the
aliens registration act, shanghaied sailors numerous times, and possibly
murdered one or more persons in this country. (Ernest Cuneo, quoted in
Mahl 1998: 126)

Many other unofficial biographies and histories of BSC followed. William Stevenson's 1976 account of his former chief, William Stephenson, has been repeatedly challenged for accuracy and stands charged with helping create a myth. The biography by H. Montgomery Hyde (1989) is considered more accurate. (For other more rounded views, see Naftali 1993; Cull 1995; Mahl 1998; Calder 2004; Conant 2009; Stafford 1986.)

Notes

1. The false information Pujol supplied helped to persuade the Germans that the main D-Day attack would be in the Pas-de-Calais, so that they kept large forces there before and even after the invasion.
2. See <http://www.circopedia.org/Cyril_Mills> (last accessed 18 September 2019).
3. Ted Cookridge was an author with a deep knowledge of the intelligence world and I had the pleasure of visiting him from time to time in his central London *fin de siècle* apartment with its astonishing and comprehensive library and his voluminous card index – this was in the days before personal computers.
4. TNA HS 9/645/4, SOE personal file of Lionel Ramsay Hale.
5. Delmer wrote a two-volume autobiography, *Trail Sinister* (1961) and *Black Boomerang* (1962).
6. <https://sites.durham.ac.uk/writersandpropaganda/tag/siboftheweek/> (last accessed 18 September 2019).
7. Arthur Dodds-Parker was a colonial administrator and then head of SOE in various wartime theatres. He was later a junior Foreign Office minister from November 1953 to 1954 as a Parliamentary Under-Secretary of State for Foreign Affairs, then a Parliamentary Under-Secretary of State in the Commonwealth Relations Office from 1954 to 1955, before resuming his junior ministerial position at the Foreign Office in December 1955.
8. <https://spartacus-educational.com/2WWstephensonW.htm> (last accessed 18 September 2019).
9. This quote appears in the foreword, written by Ian Fleming, to *Room 3603* by H. Montgomery Hyde. This is the title that *The Quiet Canadian* (1989) was published as in the USA. The UK version did not have the foreword.
10. The intersection between spy fact and fiction has become of academic interest recently. Professor James Der Derian has written a number of papers; see especially Der Derian 2000. McCrisken and Moran (2018) discuss how real spies were influenced by their fictional counterparts.
11. In late 1983, Sir William Stephenson, by then eighty-eight years old and frail, made a rare venture from his home in Bermuda to New York to attend a dinner held in his honour attended by 750 people, many of them ex-intelligence agents. The Veterans of Office of Strategic Services (OSS) awarded him their William J. Donovan Award, given to 'an individual who has rendered distin-

guished service to the United States of America. The purpose of the award is to recognize someone who has exemplified the distinguishing features that characterized General Donovan's lifetime of public service to the United of States of America as a citizen and a soldier' <https://www.osssociety.org/award.html> (last accessed 18 October 2019).

FIVE

The 'Era of Trust'

At the end of the war, many British journalists returned to 'Civvy Street' or, more precisely, to Fleet Street. The area had been badly bombed during the war, especially around St Paul's Cathedral. But newspapers were still printing and reconstruction of the area began in earnest. These journalists now had intelligence contacts but were also skilled in arts of black propaganda, having worked for the PWE or Ministry of Information (MOI). They were also unlikely to break the implicit understanding that the British press would avoid reporting on the intelligence services. In the post-war years, those journalists favoured with inside information from the world of spying tended to have worked for major intelligence agencies or have shared values that made them 'one of us'. Many senior national media journalists, especially in the first half of the century, had worked in intelligence at some point in their careers, often during wartime. When it came to the credibility of the intelligence services, 1945–74 was as much an 'era of trust' in Britain as it was in the USA. Yet, after the war, reporting on national security increased. Those reports were often favourable, if oblique, and often did not name agencies. There was, though, a gradual increase in the level of scepticism expressed by the news media, especially at times when incompetence or malpractice by the intelligence agencies had become blatant. Leaks from the world of intelligence became more frequent.

Perhaps one of the most remarkable leaks came from the newly reinstated D-Notice Committee itself. In the UK, the Defence Notice

(D-Notice) has existed since 1912 as a method used by Whitehall to persuade editors not to publish stories the state believes are harmful to national security.[1] The objective of the system is to prevent inadvertent public disclosure of information by the media that would compromise UK military and intelligence operations and methods, or would put at risk the safety of those involved in such operations. In 1945, the wartime Chief Press Censor, Admiral George Thomson, had become secretary of the Committee. Although Thomson's job was to keep the nation's secrets out of the press, in 1947 he wrote eight articles for the *Sunday Dispatch* and then published a book called the *Blue Pencil Admiral*. In these writings, he refused to delete references to telephone tapping and referred at length to MI5's success in running double agents – then still unknown outside Whitehall – and disclosed a number of other sensitive details. This infuriated the intelligence services but Thomson was not prosecuted, probably out of fear of embarrassment.

Government embarrassment was also to feature in the 1950 case of the British atomic scientist Klaus Fuchs, who had been providing the Russian GRU intelligence agency with atomic secrets from as early as 1943.[2] In 1949, the Soviets were able to test their first atomic bomb, 'First Lightning', much to the surprise of the West. It was not until after his arrest in January 1950 that Fuchs confessed to spying and was jailed for fourteen years. MI5 withheld embarrassing information about the mishandling of the Fuchs investigation from then Prime Minister Clement Attlee at briefings (Aldrich and Cormac 2016: 148). The news media, led by Chapman Pincher at the *Daily Express*, questioned MI5's effectiveness for failing to detect Fuchs earlier.[3]

Two Sides of the Same Coin?

Even within my first newspaper, the liberal *Observer*, there were a number of journalists who had worked in intelligence. In more recent years, as more evidence came to light, I was able to track down a considerable number of *Observer* journalists who worked for or worked with the SIS or other intelligence organisations (see Lashmar 2015b, 2018b). It was not very different in other newspapers, though the relationship was much, much closer in some.

There is a well-worn cliché, 'Once a spy always a spy', and a journalist who has had intimacy with the intelligence service is usually regarded with caution by other journalists. For example, the late Phillip Knightley, an expert on national security, was convinced from his own experience that intelligence agencies had penetrated the mainstream media extensively and claimed that MI5 'has agents in most newspaper offices' (Knightley 2006: 9). His writings provided a great deal of evidence of the collusion between British journalists and the SIS.

In a 2006 article Knightley identified the continuing close links between the SIS and journalists after the Second World War. One of the most important hubs was part of the Kemsley newspaper empire – the international news agency, the Kemsley Imperial and Foreign Service. Better known by its cable address, Mercury, the agency provided journalistic cover to MI6 officers working abroad. The Thomson Newspapers company which owned *The Sunday Times* did likewise. The former naval intelligence officer, journalist and creator of James Bond, Ian Fleming, was the editor at Mercury. He ran a network of journalists working across the world, many of whom had been (and might still have been) intelligence officers (Knightley 2006: 8). Fleming instructed his reporters to produce regular 'situation reports', or 'sitreps', providing insight – not for publication – about activities in their parts of the world (Lycett 1996: 170). Knightley notes:

> Fleming sent Cedric Salter of Special Operations Executive (Second World War secret army) to Barcelona, Ian Colvin (who had close links to the SIS) to Berlin and Henry Brandon, an 'SIS asset' from central Europe, to Washington. Donald McCormick, formerly of Naval Intelligence, became Mercury's stringer in Tangier and later foreign manager of The Sunday Times. The link between journalism and spying was largely 'old boy' and informal but sometimes Mercury produced important 'scoops' for British intelligence. (2006: 8)

Another key SIS asset in Mercury was Richard Hughes, *The Sunday Times* correspondent in the Far East, the journalist who persuaded Moscow to parade the British traitors Guy Burgess and Donald Maclean for a press conference after their defection to Moscow.

Anthony Terry, later *The Sunday Times* bureau chief in Bonn, had also worked as a Mercury correspondent and before that as an officer of British Intelligence in Berlin and Vienna. (Knightley 2006: 8).

Anthony Cavendish, a former SIS officer, whom I met a number of times in the 1980s when he was fighting a battle with the government to get his autobiographical book *Inside Intelligence* (1997) published, said:

> At the end of the war a number of SIS agents were sent abroad under the cover of newspapermen. Indeed, the Kemsley press allowed many of their correspondents to co-operate with SIS and even took on SIS operatives as foreign correspondents. (Knightley 2006: 8)

Cavendish was an interesting character who had worked for military intelligence from the war to 1948 and then the SIS from 1948 to 1953 serving in Germany and Austria. He went on to work for British United Press International for many years as a journalist and witnessed the Soviet invasion of Hungary in 1956. Cavendish had been drummed out of the SIS for an affair in Vienna with the American ambassador's daughter.

Philby and *The Observer*

When Kim Philby came under suspicion for being a Soviet spy he was asked to leave the SIS, though many of his colleagues refused to believe there was any truth to the allegations. To soften the blow, the old boys' network came into play and he was found alternative employment as a journalist. A briefing document for Prime Minister Harold Macmillan, now in the National Archives, summarised the arrangement:

> The then Head of MI6 considered it bad security for a former member of the Secret Service to be destitute and, bearing in mind that an injustice might have been done him, agreed to give him help in finding a journalistic appointment on the 'Observer'.[4]

An officer of the SIS had made the approach to the editor and Philby took up his new assignment as *The Observer*'s Middle East correspondent in 1956, resident in Beirut. He was employed in a similar capacity by *The Economist* magazine.[5] Subsequent British governments denied that Philby had continued working for the SIS but the writer Michael Smith notes that the briefing document in full is as close as we have come to confirmation of the widely believed position that he was working for both British Intelligence and the press in Beirut. The Philby case remains fascinating but atypical. He eventually defected to the Soviet Union when it became clear the case against him was building.

There is a famous comment made by *The Observer*'s editor, David Astor, rebuffing Soviet claims in 1968 of the extensive penetration of Fleet Street by the SIS (see Dorril 2015; Lashmar 2015b), and then repeated by his successor Donald Trelford over allegations that the newspaper had journalists who also worked for the SIS on its staff:[6] 'The only spy we have had working for *The Observer* – and that without our knowledge – was one of theirs, Kim Philby' (Dorril 2015: 206). However, in just one of a number of episodes revealing the close proximity of intelligence contacts around the paper, Trelford recalls in his autobiographical book a revealing meeting, as editor of *The Observer*, with the then head of SIS. He was having lunch as usual at the Garrick Club when the 'owlish' head of SIS, Sir Maurice Oldfield, 'padded' up to his table and asked whether *The Observer* had any news of their foreign correspondent, Gavin Young. 'We heard he was swept overboard in a storm off the Celebes. If you get any news, you'll know where to find me.' Trelford was not yet aware of this latest Gavin Young drama, which had taken place in the tempest-prone seas off Sulawesi. He says of Oldfield's request: 'I could only assume that by "we" he meant the Secret Intelligence Service and that Gavin belonged to it, or was at least well enough known to it for "C" to care about his whereabouts.' On his return to the office, *The Observer* editor was told that the paper had just had a telex to say that Gavin was shipwrecked but was okay. 'I duly passed on the message to what I had to assume was his other employer that "our" man was apparently safe' (Trelford 2018: 122).

Given that so many of the post-war generation of journalists who had worked for intelligence were rather secretive about it, it was hard to shift the notion that there were still mutually beneficial connections between them and their intelligence contacts. Trelford also identified other colleagues of the period who had served in the SIS. He related his own experience as a young editor of a paper in East Africa of travelling to the then Rhodesia (now Zimbabwe) several times during the period of Ian Smith's Unilateral Declaration of Independence (UDI) from the UK in the early 1960s and how he reported back to his regional SIS station officer, Ronnie Bloom, what he had found there (Trelford 2018: 56–8).

The Soviets assumed that pretty well all British foreign correspondents in Moscow were SIS spies and tried to 'turn' them. Phillip Knightley tells the story of Jeremy Wolfenden who was assigned to Moscow in 1962 as a *Daily Telegraph* correspondent. The KGB set Wolfenden up with a homosexual 'honeytrap', took compromising photographs of him and then proceeded to blackmail him by threatening to send the photographs to his paper. Wolfenden reported the whole story to the British Embassy, but on his next visit to London he was called to see an SIS officer who told him to 'pretend to co-operate with the Russians but report everything to us' (Knightley 1986: 386). Trying to get out of this mire, Wolfenden asked for a new posting in Washington, but he was again contacted by his SIS controller who wanted to resume their spying relationship. According to Knightley, a few months later Wolfenden was found dead in his bathroom, apparently having fallen and cracked his head on the washbasin. He was only thirty-one years old (1986: 387).

Smiley's People

The post-war SIS continued working behind the scenes to mould events to the perceived British national interest, and their numerous covert operations were, unsurprisingly, not reported at the time. Many years later, David Leigh and I revealed in *The Observer* that British secret service officers had blown up as many as a dozen ships in which Jewish concentration camp survivors were to be smuggled to Palestine in 1947 (Leigh and Lashmar 1988a). We were told the story by a high-level Whitehall source and it was then confirmed by those close to the action at the time.

Described by one retired officer as, 'the blackest page in MI6's post-war history', 'Operation Embarrass' had been hitherto a very well-kept secret and the attacks on Zionist ships a part of the campaign to deter emigration to Palestine (Dorril 2000: 549). The government was concerned that if too many Jews from Europe reached Palestine, it could trigger further violence in the unstable region (Dorril 2000: 549). Operation Embarrass had been launched on the order of Ernest Bevin, the Labour Foreign Secretary. The order for a campaign to stop the flow of emigrants was marked 'Top Secret' and sent round the corner to SIS headquarters at 60 Broadway.

The order to block the flow of Jewish refugee ships went down the line of command to Colonel Harold 'Perks' Perkins, a pre-war mill owner in Poland who had been in the Polish Section of SOE through the war. Perks planned the operation. Assigned to conduct actual attacks in the Mediterranean was veteran Special Forces officer Lieutenant Colonel David Smiley, the son of a baronet and an extremely colourful character. To assist him he had another SIS man, Wing Commander Derek Verschoyle, the former literary editor of the *Spectator*. With hundreds of thousands of displaced Jews scattered across camps in Europe, the Zionist underground bought barely seaworthy tramp steamers to transport the refugees, mostly with funds donated by Jewish organisations in the USA. The rust-bucket ships used Italian ports as key refuelling and provisioning points on their way to Palestine. Under the control of the 'Bricha' escape organisation, these ships had already been used to ship more than 85,000 refugees to Palestine. They would have transported a lot more had Smiley and the SIS team not intervened. They suborned a Greek shipbroker, from whom they obtained details of ships that had been purchased and their captains' intended voyages. Posing as Adriatic cigarette smugglers, Smiley and Verschoyle used a small boat to move discreetly around the Italian ports identifying these ships.

Leigh and I were told in 1988 that details of this operation were so secret the file was locked in a safe in the Cabinet Office with a number of other major intelligence secrets that the government did not want in the public domain. By that time Smiley, British former Special Forces soldier and adventurer, was one of the most celebrated British cloak-and-dagger agents. During the Second World War, he had served behind enemy lines in Albania, Greece, Abyssinia and Japanese-controlled eastern Thailand. In his memoirs Smiley (1984) notes he was 'seconded to MI6' throughout 1947 without saying what he was doing.

We were to learn a lot more about Smiley who, in the phrase, had 'had a good war'. After Sandhurst he had been in the Blues Calvary regiment from 1936 to 1939. In search of action, in 1940 Smiley joined the Somaliland Camel Corps, but was to arrive at Berbera the same day it was decided to evacuate. He returned itching for action to Egypt where he convinced a family friend, the Commander in the Western Desert, General Wavell, to recommend him for the newly formed commandos. Smiley was appointed a company commander with the rank of captain to 52 Commando. He then fought against Vichy French forces in Syria until he was recruited by the SOE in 1943 and undertook his first operation with them in Palestine that same year. Smiley and Lieutenant Colonel Neil 'Billy' McLean parachuted into Albania, carrying out guerrilla operations, for which Smiley was awarded a Bar to the Military Cross in 1944.

After the war, Smiley often worked for the SIS. What his Embarrass team did was to attach limpet mines to the hulls of the refugee ships. Instructed not kill anyone or sink ships after they had left port, Smiley's team fitted their targets with timing devices so that, by the time the mines exploded, the SIS team had left Italian waters. On at least one occasion, the timer malfunctioned. Those involved have claimed they did not risk refugees' lives as there were only 'caretakers' on the ships in harbour.

In the official SIS history, Jeffery says five ships in Italian ports were sunk (2010: 692). It is possible a dozen ships were sunk across the Mediterranean, including a ship called the *Struma*. Intelligence historian Stephen Dorril writes: 'there have been persistent rumours that one unidentified ship packed with refugees may have been blown up at sea, whether by accident or design' (2000: 548). Aldrich and Cormac claim: 'MI6 even considered blowing up the Baltimore steamship *President Warfield* – later hailed as the "Exodus" ship that launched the Israeli nation – at its anchorage in France' (2016: 153).

After Operation Embarrass, Smiley organised secret operations against the Russians and their allies in Albania and Poland. Smiley, Julian Amery, Billy McLean and David Stirling were to become the key figures in post-war British Special Forces operations around the world. In 1958, the British were determined to preserve control over the Gulf state of Oman. Britain was trying to prop up the despotic ruler (Cobain 2016: 77–8) against his rebellious subjects, mostly tribesmen in the mountains. On the day it was released under the thirty-year rule in 1989, Leigh and I got hold of the heavily redacted file on British operations in Oman. The Cabinet documents spelt out the reasons that Britain wanted to maintain use of the air base at Masirah and that oil might be discovered in the kingdom. However, it showed the government was very keen to avoid publicity for any British operations and did not want to have civilian deaths (Leigh 1989).

The Sultan accepted an 'annual subsidy' of £371,000 (Leigh 1989) and twenty-three British officers for his army including a commander, and the nucleus of 'a small airforce' to put down the rebels. In return he handed over the airbase on lease for ninety-nine years. The new commander of the Sultan's army was David Smiley. Instead of regular troops, the British government covertly sent in two squadrons of the SAS. The cover story was that a 100-man SAS squadron was training the Sultan's army.

The Cabinet document notes: 'There was a reasonable chance its move to Oman would be unnoticed' (Leigh 1989). The SAS went in, fresh from the jungles of Malaya, and the rebels were routed (Leigh 1989). Oil was found but the despotic Sultan (Cobain 2016: 77–8) became such a problem that in 1970 the British helped his son overthrow his father. His right-hand aide in this mission was Lieutenant Colonel Timothy Landon whom he knew from Sandhurst – the elite British officer training establishment. The only confirmed casualty in this coup was the elder Sultan's foot when he inadvertently shot himself. With British help Sultan Quboos has ruled autocratically ever since. Landon stayed on to advise Quboos for many years. When he died in 2007, by then Brigadier Sir James Timothy Landon, KCVO, he left an estate worth £200 million[7] from his work with the Sultan. Britain continues to retain close links with Oman; for example, in the 2000s, I met British helicopter pilots who were being seconded to Oman.[8]

The Oman success was only one aspect of Britain's problems with its imperial possessions in the region. In the British Crown colony of the port of Aden, Macmillan and the Cabinet reluctantly ordered air attacks on Yemeni villages, as cross-border shelling 'undermined our authority in the area', although the Chiefs of Staff wondered 'whether it was expedient to embark on a policy which was liable to cause civilian casualties' (Leigh 1989: 4). After his assignment in Oman, Smiley organised, with SIS blessing, royalist guerrilla resistance against a Soviet-backed Nasserite regime in Yemen. Smiley's efforts helped to force the eventual withdrawal of the Egyptians and their Soviet advisers, paved the way for the emergence of a less anti-Western Yemeni government, and confirmed his reputation as one of Britain's leading post-war military Arabists.

Even then, Smiley was not the type of chap to settle back into civilian life. In June 1963, an SIS asset, the then foreign editor, S. R. 'Pop' Pawley, provided Smiley with deep cover as a *Daily Telegraph* journalist.[9] He flew with his old SOE sidekick Billy McLean, now another SIS asset and Conservative MP, to Saudi Arabia.[10] McLean was there to report back to British Prime Minister Harold Macmillan. Smiley was there to wage a guerrilla war against nationalists in Yemen.[11] With the proclamation of a Yemen Republic, riots in support broke out in Aden against the British. The British government and the SIS sought to help the Saudis and bolster royalist forces in Yemen. Liaising with King Faisal of Saudi Arabia and the SIS, who arranged for former SAS and other mercenaries to accompany him, Smiley made thirteen trips to Yemen between 1963 and 1968. According to his obituary in the *Daily Telegraph* (which did not mention that the paper had provided him with cover):

> Often disguised as a local, Smiley travelled on foot or by donkey for weeks at a time across Arabia's most rugged terrain. He won the admiration of his colleagues, both Arab and British, for his toughness, bluntness, and shrewdness as an adviser. King Faisal, whom Smiley greatly admired, personally expressed his appreciation. (*Daily Telegraph* 2009)

Smiley and other British adventurers ended up working for or with pro-British potentates around the Middle East from the Second World War until the 1990s. According to the *Daily Telegraph*

> Smiley's exploits led some to suggest that he was, along with several other candidates, a model for James Bond. It was also widely mooted that John le Carré, albeit unconsciously, had taken the name of his hero from the real-life Smiley. (2009)

David Smiley died in 2009 aged ninety-two.

Into a Cold War

The case of Foreign Office officials Guy Burgess and Donald Maclean, in particular, began to reveal how effective the NKVD had been before 1939 in recruiting and placing ideologically motivated agents in key Whitehall posts in Britain. The atomic spies and traitors within MI5, SIS, SOE and the Diplomatic Service had failed to attract the full attention of a service lacking leadership and riven with internal dissension. When, in May 1951, Burgess[12] and Maclean disappeared from Britain, the press extensively speculated on what had happened. Their whereabouts was something of a mystery until they appeared at a press conference in Moscow in 1956 during which they confirmed they had defected.

As early as 1954, the London *Evening News* (then the other main London tabloid evening paper alongside the *Evening Standard*), recognising the sexiness of the secret world, planned to run a series of articles on the up-to-date secrets of MI5 in which it would detail the handling of the Fuchs case by MI5. However, the *Evening News* editor was convinced by Admiral Thomson (who was still at the D-Notice Committee despite his earlier indiscretions) to take a more 'patriotic' stance and concentrate on MI5's wartime successes instead (Moran 2013: 114).

In the 1960s, the successful identification of a number of spies – including the Portland spy ring: George Blake, an SIS officer; and John Vassall, an official at the Admiralty who was 'honeytrapped' by the KGB (the NKVD's successor) in Moscow – demonstrated the need for more focused counter-espionage methods. Lord Denning's report into the Profumo Affair in 1963 revealed publicly for the first time details of MI5's role and responsibilities, but must be described as one of the most misleading and ineffective reports in British modern history.

During the 1960s and 1970s, MI5 was once again internally riven by questions about the loyalty of senior officers and the rivalry with the SIS for supremacy for counter-terrorism in Northern Ireland. In particular, the accusations that a group of MI5 officers had deliberately set out to undermine British Prime Minister Harold Wilson were so persistent that they are even addressed on MI5's own website where the Service deny there was any substance to the allegations (see also Leigh 1988). MI5 was working against the Soviets and this resulted in the mass expulsion from the UK in 1971 of 105 Soviet personnel that severely weakened KGB and GRU intelligence operations in London following the defection of a Soviet intelligence officer.

As Knightley explained to the academic Justin Schlosberg,

Those very few journalists who do have some sort of access or privilege are so jealous and guard it so clearly that it's almost worthless. They're in the pocket of the person who's providing them with what information they can get. (Schlosberg 2013: 138)

Most news reports of the UK intelligence agencies would be confined to the outcomes of their successes, for instance the arrest of spies or pure speculation on the world of 'cloak and dagger'. The little that appeared was supportive and not inquisitive. It was not until the 1970s, some three decades after the end of the Second World War, that the story of Ultra codebreaking and Bletchley Park was made public. Aldrich notes that, thereafter, much of the strategic and operational history of the Second World War had to be rewritten: 'Before the 1970s, one of the most important aspects of the Second World War, the fact that many of the operational intentions of the Axis had been transparent to the Allies, had been methodically airbrushed from historical writing' (2004: 925).

The Legacy

By July 1946, SOE had been disbanded, with some of its officers, agents, some whole sections and a number of operations being transferred to the SIS. Senior officer Bickham Sweet-Escott, who later wrote a very readable account of SOE titled *Baker Street Irregular* (1965), was tasked with winding up the loose ends of SOE around the world. He did so, but he told Richard Fletcher that he had left 'a skeleton in cupboard in every country' for potential later British use (Fletcher 1982: 103). Britain's wartime excellence in deception was much praised when it was finally admitted. Phythian observes that the performance of the intelligence agencies in the Second World War provided their greatest legitimating successes from the Enigma codes, to the work of the Special Operations Executive, the use of double agents and the various successful deception operations: 'Although many of these could not be revealed until later, some popular accounts appeared in book form and, as with *The Man Who Never Was*, by the 1950s were being immortalized in film' (2005: 655).

However, exposure to the dark arts of intelligence left its mark on many of those who had worked for the SIS such as the late Malcolm Muggeridge, a famous journalist and commentator, who said he had learned from his years there that:

Nothing should ever be done simply if there are devious ways of doing it . . . Secrecy is as essential to intelligence as vestments to a Mass, or darkness to a spiritualist séance, and must at all costs be maintained, quite irrespective of whether or not it serves any purpose. (Muggeridge 1973: 122–3)

Not long after the end of the Second World War, Bickham Sweet-Escott's skeletons – an enormous intelligence complex that stretched across the world and operated in many countries and colonies – were to be resurrected and redirected in a new, undeclared war.

Notes

1. For a history of the D-Notice system, see the organisation's website at <http://dsma.uk/history/> (last accessed 17 June 2019).
2. Another British nuclear scientist, Alan Nunn May, had also been spying for the Soviet Union and was caught.
3. This was an early appearance in print of the journalist Chapman Pincher, who would later style himself as Britain's first investigative journalist and was one of the first to have the national security beat, covering the world of spying in depth, mostly for the *Daily Express*. The ubiquitous Pincher's journalism was to become controversial. He was later the target of historian E. P. Thompson's famous caustic observation that Pincher was the urinal where Ministers and officials queued up to leak their official secrets, scandals and innuendo (Thompson 1980: 113, 116). It was an insult in which Pincher took perverse pride. In 2009, he wrote: 'It is satisfying, at the age of 94, to look back on a career in investigative reporting spanning more than sixty years – in various media – and to know that I would choose to repeat it in preference to any other profession' (Pincher 2009: 149).
4. PREM 11/4457.
5. PREM 11/4457.
6. For a fascinating account of the 1968 Soviet claims about Fleet Street–MI6 links, see Dorril 2015.
7. <https://www.telegraph.co.uk/news/obituaries/1557161/Brigadier-Tim-Landon.html> (last accessed 18 October 2019).
8. In 1981, then Prime Minister Margaret Thatcher made an official visit to Oman to meet with Sultan Quboos. In early 1984, David Leigh and I broke the story of how the Prime Minister's son, Mark Thatcher, acted as middleman on behalf of a major British construction group that was attempting to win a £300 million construction contract to build a university in the kingdom. The information was provided to us by a very senior Whitehall source who was appalled that Mark was allowed to tag along on the visit and that he stood to gain personally from an official visit (Leigh and Lashmar 1984a).
9. Smiley was just one of the many MI6 spies that Pop Pawley and the *Daily Telegraph* had given cover to.

10. Smiley and McLean had worked together in Albania as SOE liaison officers with Enver Hoxha. Hoxha was then the political commissar of the Albanian partisans fighting the occupying Italian forces. When the Italian government had signed an Armistice with the Allies in 1943, the German military then occupied the strategically important Albania. Hoxha's partisans, still advised by Smiley and McLean, now fought the Germans. In 1944, as the German occupiers were driven out, Hoxha became the head of state of Albania, which he remained until his death in 1985.

11. For a detailed account of Smiley and MI6 in Yemen, see Dorril 2000: 677–700; for more on Pawley, see Dorril 2015.

12. Old Etonian Burgess had worked in the BBC in the early war years as a producer while freelancing with MI5 and MI6. In October 1941, Burgess took charge of the flagship political programme *The Week in Westminster*, which gave the Soviet spy almost unlimited access to Parliament.

SIX

Cold War Warriors

In 2007, faced with the rise of Islamist terrorism, the British government set up a shadowy Whitehall unit to be at the heart of its counter-terrorism strategic communications aimed at Muslims, in both Britain and the Middle East.[1] The British-based element of the covert campaign was part of the controversial Prevent counter-radicalisation programme and was run by the Home Office's Research, Information and Communications Unit, or RICU. A former SIS officer, set up the unit shortly after arriving at the Home Office. RICU, it is reliably reported, had a Cold War model – the Information Research Department (IRD) – the propaganda unit established in 1948 within the Foreign Office by the Labour government (Cobain et al. 2016). Documents obtained by *The Guardian* show RICU outputs some material that is government branded, but its main focus is send out counter-radicalisation messages that are disseminated by 'discreet campaigns supported by RICU without any acknowledgment of UK government support' (Cobain et al. 2016). Shying away from the word propaganda, RICU prefers the bland post-Cold War phrase 'strategic communications', but their methods are similar.[2] RICU use what Bakir defines as strategic political communication, a more subtle term than propaganda (Bakir 2013).[3]

The creation of RICU shows how the British government seeks to repeat what it sees as its more successful ventures. Closely aligned with the SIS and secret for its lifetime, IRD's decades long, taxpayer funded operations were revealed in detail in *The Observer* and *The*

Guardian in early 1978.[4] I was part of the team whose IRD story made it into *The Observer* (Fletcher et al. 1978). The project had a curious start, as in the early 1970s, my lecturer, investigative journalist Richard Fletcher, who specialised in exposing covert operations by intelligence agencies, noticed an odd advertisement in *The Guardian* that raised his suspicions. The advert was for a bibliography, *Books on Communism*, written by R. N. Carew Hunt of St Anthony's College, Oxford. As Fletcher knew, St Anthony's academics then had close links to the SIS. 'I also knew that it was not financially viable to publish books on such a boring subject as Communism. I suspected the book was subsidised in some way', Fletcher later reflected (Lashmar and Oliver 1998b: xiii). Checking the Companies House accounts of the publisher, Ampersand Ltd, revealed someone called Leslie Sheridan had set it up in 1947. Fletcher thought initially Ampersand was a CIA front as at the time he knew nothing of Sheridan or his wartime background.[5]

A little later Fletcher, reading William Stevenson's (1976) hagiography of Sir William Stephenson, *A Man Called Intrepid*, noticed a footnote on page 329 referring to a wartime news agency called Britanova. The importance of Britanova was confirmed to Fletcher by a former colleague of Leslie Sheridan's. Set up in 1940, Britanova was the first of what became a global network of British Intelligence media fronts spanning nearly forty years (Lashmar and Oliver 1998b: 173–4). As detailed in Chapter 4, Stephenson had been tasked by the SIS to go to the USA to help bring them into the Second World War by any means possible (his biographer with the strikingly similar name was his deputy and a professional journalist). Part of the campaign involved propaganda and covert action against Germans based in America. Britanova had been set up and used for that purpose in support of Stephenson's covert operation, the 'British Security Coordination' office run out of the Rockefeller Center.

Curiosity prompted Fletcher to check Britanova's accounts and they interconnected to a network of news agencies that spanned the world and of which a number featured the wartime propagandist Leslie Sheridan as a director. This was before the internet and Google so every document had to be searched for and located physically. Companies House, the National Archives and libraries spread across cities and universities all provided clues to this operation. Over the next eighteen months, the research team were able to piece together a vast covert network of journalists, news agencies and publishers. Following a hiatus after the Second World War the network had restarted afresh as an anti-communist operation. Now based in the Foreign Office, as the Information Research Department, it had been hugely successful in its own terms but we saw it as a massive 'spin' operation.[6]

To attack capitalism, imperialism and communism

In 1947, the Soviets set up the Cominform, an aggressive well-funded agitprop (agitation and propaganda) body tasked by the Kremlin to promote communism across the world. Western nations felt they should respond to the onslaught of pro-communist anti-Western propaganda. The former SOE trainer Christopher Mayhew, by then a Labour government cabinet minister, proposed the creation of a counter-propaganda department. He saw it as a response to the Cominform and as a driver for social democracy. Mayhew argued that Britain 'shouldn't appear as defenders of the status quo, but should attack Capitalism and Imperialism along with Russian Communism' (Smith 1980: 68).

Another person who supported the creation of an organisation to counter the Cominform was Norman Reddaway. He had risen to the rank of lieutenant colonel during the war and joined the Foreign Office in 1946 where he was to be Christopher Mayhew's principle civil servant. He energetically helped to create IRD, where he served for several postings during his career at the Foreign Office.

The first Foreign Office mandarin to run IRD was Ralph Murray, a linguist with six languages. Murray was an interesting character who had moved from being a journalist to a propagandist and had an impressive career in the Foreign Office. He had started as a reporter in newspapers working in Bristol. He then joined the BBC as a journalist before the Second World War. After the outbreak of war, he worked in the secret world, sometimes with SOE, sometimes with PWE and sometimes with the codebreakers at Bletchley Park. He had been involved with supporting the Yugoslavian partisans and at one point met their leader, Tito.

Murray decided that Leslie Sheridan was the person to call in and Sheridan was able to utilise some of the old wartime news agencies, including the Cairo-based Arab News Agency (ANA), and set up some new 'fronts'.[7] If Murray, a senior Foreign Office official, had been given overall charge of the department, it was actually the affable Sheridan who was in day-to-day control. He was in his element. He was able to call on the establishment and apparently independent figures, many of whom were in the media, and who were made directors of IRD's growing number of front companies.

Not everyone was impressed by IRD's Leslie Sheridan. Fleet Street's man about town and commentator, Malcolm Muggeridge, icily commented in his diary for 13 November 1950, that Sherry was 'Rather a sad piece of debris, former news editor of the Mirror, now publicity consultant, and black propaganda specialist for the Government, SOE in the war – the whole bag of tricks' (Jenks 2006: 64). IRD colleague Norman Reddaway later said Sheridan 'tended to go back to the era of dirty tricks' as he created the modus operandi for the new outfit (Jenks 2006: 64). IRD portrayed itself to its 'clients' – journalists, trade unionists, politicians and Cold War warriors – as a sort of benign private press office. The line between public relations (PR) and propaganda can be opaque. Walter Lippmann, the journalist and theorist, expressed a cynical view of PR in the early years of the twentieth century in his ground-breaking book *Public Opinion*:

> it follows that the picture which the publicity man makes for the reporter
> is the one he wishes for the public to see. He is censor and propagandist,
> responsible only to his employers, and to the whole truth responsible,
> only as it accords with the employers' conceptions of his own interest.
> (Lippmann 1922)

This was a very effective characterisation of IRD's work.

Early on, IRD was involved in Operation Valuable, SIS's attempts to liberate Albania from the Soviet bloc in 1949–50. British-trained refugees were smuggled into the country to organise a coup. Psychological warfare was conducted by IRD-aided 'black' (unidentifiable) radio stations. The Albanian operation failed, partly because Soviet spy Kim Philby fed SIS's plan back to

Moscow resulting in the capture and execution of most of the émi-grés. Another early recruit had been the dissolute Soviet spy Guy Burgess (Lownie 2015: 175). He had moved from the BBC to the Foreign Office, and by the end of 1946, he was a personal assistant to Foreign Office Minister, Hector McNeil. After a few months, McNeil seems to have tired of the erratic Burgess and when the new Information Research Department launched, McNeil suggested that Burgess join. Burgess had an appropriate skill set with stints as a journalist and propagandist. After just two months, Christopher Mayhew had him removed. 'Burgess', he said, 'is dirty, drunk and idle' (Jenks 2006: 64).

Aldrich has described IRD as a 'covert political warfare section', as successor to the wartime PWE (2001: 128). As Mayhew proposed, IRD was set up and largely financed from the 'Secret Vote', the same undisclosed budget as the intelligence services. The National Archives have been releasing IRD files since 1996 and they continue to be slowly released. Deery examined the first batch for 1948 and 1949 and noted that their diversity exemplifies the wide front on which the Cold War was fought. They covered Soviet labour camps, support for anti-communist activity behind the Iron Curtain and encouraged Red Army defectors. IRD established a Singapore office to counter communist activity in Malaya. The Department spon-sored an anti-communist trade union paper, *Freedom First*. Its team compiled confidential lists of politicians and BBC employees to whom 'non-attributable' IRD propaganda could be sent for use in speeches and broadcasts (Deery 1997: 219). One of the first sets of articles commissioned by IRD was by the former communist Norman Ewer who wrote critically about life in Russia (Purvis and Hulbert 2013: 56). Ewer continued with his work for the *Daily Herald* and worked closely with the Cold War warrior and later Cabinet Minister Denis Healey.

A Family Affair

By the time of Churchill's post-war Conservative government in 1951, IRD had dropped its founding concept of promoting social democracy. It had shifted direction and was now an anti-communist propaganda and pro-Empire unit. It was tasked to complement the hugely better-funded CIA cultural warfare operations. Expansion followed, and recruits from Fleet Street and elsewhere were brought in to good salaries. Leslie Sheridan tried to recruit a young Tony Benn in 1950, tempting him with an offer of a very generous £1,100 annual salary, on top of his pay as an MP. In his diaries, Benn said that his dad told him to turn it down as both he and Sheridan knew it was illegal for an MP to take an 'office of profit' (Lashmar and Oliver 1998b: 118). Sheridan brought many of the SOE old team back together including the now naturalised Hans Welser.

Adelaide Maturin, who was to became Sheridan's second wife, played a major role in IRD, and took her many secrets to the grave despite Richard Fletcher and other researchers' later attempts to talk to her. Former colleagues told us that she was capable of great attention to detail, and was the adroit manager of SIS's large, delicate long-term 'front' operations. She worked with the lawyer and former SOE bureaucrat Victor Cannon Brookes through his family practice, Cannon Brookes & Odgers, to make the various IRD fronts look like normal companies. All these characters, Maturin, Sheridan, Brookes and many more, were involved in secret work. Like the others, Sheridan had a low public profile. Despite all his years working for the Foreign Office, only once did he appear in the Foreign Office yearbook, that for 1961, which listed him as assistant head of IRD. About the same time, Adelaide and Sherry's marriage ended. In a remarkable change of partners in spring of 1962 Adelaide married Hans Welser in Westminster and, on the same page of the register index, it can be seen that Sheridan married Margaret Welser, Hans's former wife. While the personal affairs of IRD personnel are not really a point of interest to this book, these interchanging relationships do give a sense of how incestuous this world was. For his IRD work, Hans was awarded an OBE in the Birthday Honours of 1960 when he is described as a Grade 7 Officer, Branch A, Foreign Office. He was likely an SIS officer. Adelaide followed her former husband Sheridan into the Foreign Office yearbook, in her case for the 1962 edition, where she was described as a Chief Executive Officer, Foreign Office. She too had close connections with the SIS.

At its peak in the late 1960s IRD was a substantial department employing 400 staff based at Riverwalk House on Millbank Pimlico, with an annual budget of over £1 million (Lashmar and Oliver 1998b: 138). IRD was officially a straightforward information operation distributing foreign affairs analyses. Material for use in this anti-communist propaganda was procured from a variety of sources including other departments within the Foreign Office. There were also British missions overseas; 'informal committees' within the Service ministries chaired by the deputy directors of intelligence; and a loose network of sympathetic individuals based in the Labour Party, the trade unions, and various other organisations and institutions (Wilford 1998: 358). Much of the routine work consisted of producing briefings of two types: 'Category A', classified analyses of intelligence material distributed to cabinet ministers and some MPs and civil servants; and 'Category B', with intelligence references removed, disseminated to individuals in the media, academia and trade unions and to many foreign officials. The prominent writer and journalist

Neal Ascherson, then a young reporter at *The Observer* newspaper, was introduced to the IRD in 1960 by his colleague Edward Crankshaw, a more senior Soviet specialist. 'I was taken to a London club and we had a nice lunch with Edward and myself and this gentleman', Ascherson recalls. 'After I'd been looked over and tested . . . I was allowed to receive the news bulletin of eastern European "product"' (Berg 2019). The IRD information was delivered by hand and treated as secret – but Ascherson says he 'very rapidly discovered it was completely useless', since it contained 'stale, out of date' news (Berg 2019). Ascherson may have dismissed the products of IRD's industry but many lazier journalists were happy to publish IRD material.

Meanwhile IRD was expanding in all directions with its anti-communist propaganda. It has been suggested that the IRD's discreet propaganda could not compete with the din of the CIA's 'Mighty Wurlitzer' as its propaganda machine was dubbed (see Wilford 2008). Academic Andrew Defty claims that US and UK cooperation in this area was much greater than previously believed (2002: 125). He notes that although Britain and America adopted different methods, they often combined to good effect. However, the scale of the US output did not guarantee its impact, and there were benefits in both approaches. Britain's discreet approach was more appropriate for countering Communism in the free world (2002: 125). Like all government organisations without proper account-ability IRD was subject to mission creep. IRD was involving itself in various covert operations attempting to influence the choice of leadership in the former colonial countries, interfering in domestic trade unions and mounting other black propaganda exercises that could not be described as anti-communist.

The BBC and IRD

At the beginning of 1949, the BBC Russian Service transmitted a series of talks by Grigor Tokaev, a colonel with the Red Army, and a specialist in long-range rocketry who had defected to the SIS towards the end of 1947.[8] The Foreign Office had encouraged the broadcasts. Historian Alban Webb observes: 'This was the first time the BBC had put a defector on air and in doing so broke what until then had been somewhat of a taboo in the External Services over the ethical value of such a move' (2014: 53). The first released files that IRD records show that the Foreign Office held an almost pro-prietorial attitude towards the BBC's Overseas Services as revealed by the new head of IRD.

Hugh Wilford notes that in February 1948 Ralph Murray declared his belief that 'the BBC might be geared into the new policy much more than it is at present' and then listed a scale of broadcasting 'target priorities'. This was, he admitted, 'very thorny ground', but the new publicity policy nonetheless required IRD to induce the BBC, 'by persuasion if possible, to undertake such programme development as might help us'. Murray was optimistic that the Corporation would accept such an approach (Wilford 1998: 364). The BBC complied and a long-term relationship was established.

Later organograms in the National Archives of the IRD show a section devoted to liaising with the BBC. IRD material poured into the BBC and was directed to news desks, talks writers and different specialist correspondents. The programming of the BBC's Overseas Service (which would change its name to the World Service in 1965) was refined in close consultation with the Foreign Office and its information departments.

The BBC kept close links with the intelligence community. An operation run by the experimental joint MI5/SIS 'London Station' had snared a defector in 1971. Oleg Lyalin, a KGB officer working undercover at the Soviet's London trade mission, was recruited as a British agent before eventually defecting. The government wanted to make the most of this publicity opportunity and gave a great deal of information to the press after his defection. A BBC team under director Graham Carr was given special assistance to produce an hour-long documentary that included MI5 footage of KGB agents collecting from dead drops in a London park (Aldrich and Cormac 2016: 296–301). However, just how close the BBC and MI5 were I was not going to discover until 1985 (see Chapter 10).

'The Friends' and IRD

There was a part of IRD that was very much a creature of the SIS. Going back to SOE, it was noted the covert action should be supported by propaganda.[9] That was part of IRD's remit, with Hans Welser running the 'Special Operations' desk which seems to have been the SIS liaison.[10] Who did IRD account to? It was not always clear. Supposedly through the Foreign Office hierarchy to the Foreign Secretary. However, like the closely related SIS, it sometimes evaded political control. As with the Khokhlov case, IRD appeared motivated by hubris against their political masters. In April 1954 a KGB officer Nikolai Khokhlov was ordered to assassinate Georgi Okolovich, a leading Russian dissident living in West Germany. The SIS picked Khokhlov up after he lost heart on Okolovich's doorstep and confessed his mission to Okolovich (Aldrich and Cormac 2016: 169–70).

Khokhlov had with him an array of secret assassination weapons including a poison dart hidden in a cigarette butt and two miniaturised KGB pistols. The SIS and IRD thought this was manna from heaven and planned to hold a press conference for Khokhlov to tell his strange story and show his arsenal. The SIS and IRD, including John Rennie, the head of IRD and later head of SIS, went to ask permission from Prime Minister Winston Churchill who turned out to be 'totally opposed' because it would make a hero out of a traitor. According to Aldrich and Cormac, the SIS and IRD carried out their own deception against Churchill. 'They passed Khokhlov onto the Americans, who presented him as a defector to the CIA' and ran a press conference with the defector hugging his intended victim. Back home press had a field day and the *Illustrated London News* devoted a full page to the story (2016: 169–70).

By the early 1950s, IRD was involved on numerous fronts. In the Middle East, it tried to persuade Arabs that communism was anti-Islamic; in Europe it set up émigré news agencies to cause disruption in the communist bloc; and in Malaya it launched an anti-communist campaign jointly with MI5 and the SIS. IRD also intervened in India, which was resolutely neutral during the Korean War (1950–3) to try to get the Indians to join the international forces fighting the Northern Koreans and Chinese. It is a well-practised trope that the British had learnt from the Second World War that the truth was the most effective propaganda weapon. This was based on the proposition that the BBC had reported Britain's defeats as well as its victories, which gave its broadcasts enormous credibility. Such objectivity might have been the aspiration that was not always fulfilled. Propaganda was dropped into BBC broadcasts. Objective reporting was not IRD's intention; in its day-to-day supply of information to journalists it used selective facts usually highlighting Communism's failings or any perceived nationalist weakness while ignoring successes on the path to self-determination and democracy. IRD did like to slip its material in to flows of more objective reporting to enhance the credibility of their reports.

News in the Middle East

One of the most important fronts used for the propaganda was the Arab News Agency (ANA) with its head office on the first floor of the Immobilia Building in Sharia Sherif Pasha in the centre of Cairo. The highly regarded journalist and Middle East expert Tom Little was the director of ANA, a news agency that supplied the worldwide Reuters' news wire service to a huge number of newspapers in the Middle East and beyond. On the wall of the general manager's office hung framed copies of three famous Reuters dispatches, announcing respectively the end of the Franco-Prussian War in 1871, the armistice on the Western Front in 1918 and the unconditional surrender of the German armies in May 1945. By 1956, ANA serviced much of the media in the region and mostly delivered agency news copy in the same way its rivals did. However, unlike its rivals, it also provided other, secret functions for the British State.

ANA had thirty-five staff members in Egypt and fifty-nine in other countries. Richard Fletcher concluded that

> ANA operated the most comprehensive service in English and Arabic available in the Middle East with branch offices in Damascus, Beirut, Baghdad, Jerusalem and Amman, and representatives in some 15 other cities, including Paris and New York. It was taken by nearly every Arabic newspaper, as well a *Sharq al Adna*, *All-India Radio* and the BBC. (1982: 103)

The covert propaganda operations ran behind the news media fronts.

When IRD joined forces with the SIS they reverted to SOE/PWE style covert black propaganda disseminating rumours and what we would now call fake news and spin. The propagandists used a wide range of anti-Nasser stories including portraying him – a long time nationalist – as a Hitler like figure. *Sharq al Adna* posed as a legitimate Arab radio station while secretly being owned and run by the SIS. After the Second World War *Sharq al Adna* had quietly moved to a British base on Cyprus and alongside its usually open broadcasts was operating a separate covert broadcast propaganda operation six hours a day against the Nasser government. Britain tried to keep these operations secret even from the Americans.

However, the CIA picked up its transmissions. As Cormac notes:

> On top of familiar lines about Nasser the CIA spotted coded messages within broadcasts, including 'wait until the dawn breaks'; 'do not move until you hear the birds sing'; 'watch the even numbers at full moon' and 'the lighthouse flashes for the third time'. (2018: 125)

The CIA thought this was part of the British efforts to work with rebel factions in Egypt. 'Unsurprisingly, the CIA traced these transmissions back to Cyprus and its monitors reported having recognised the voices of two *Sharq-al-Adna* announcers, when a microphone was inadvertently left live' (Cormac 2018: 125).

During the run-up to the Suez Crisis, the SIS had all but taken over the regional MI5 SIME,

> with four times as many staff working there as MI5's paltry twelve. From SIME's offices they launched covert operations across the region – much to the concern of MI5, which was conducting a much more defensive type of action by developing security relationships with local governments. (Cormac 2018: 126)

IRD was involved in covert operations of a more sinister nature including conspiring with dissidents for regime change. Eden wanted the SIS to assassinate Nasser and there were, as Cormac writes, rumours of SIS plans to do exactly that – none of which was committed to any available public record. 'Candidates for the latter supposedly included Nasser's doctor, the Muslim Brotherhood, a group of dissident military officers, a German mercenary and even the SAS' (Cormac 2018: 123). According to the former senior MI5 officer, Peter Wright, in *Spycatcher*:

> At the beginning of the Suez Crisis MI6 developed a plan through the London station, to assassinate Nasser using nerve gas. Eden [then prime minister] initially gave his approval to the operation but later rescinded it when he got agreement from the French and Israelis to engage in joint military action. (Wright 1987: 16)[11]

The SIS was not geared up for assassination, as Aldrich and Cormac observed: 'The problem was that MI6 did not kill people very often' (2016: 200). Peter 'Spycatcher' Wright alleged the nerve agent was tested on sheep. When the Suez invasion failed, the assassination plan was resurrected, but according to Wright then failed 'lamentably' (1987: 16). As was often the case, basic concepts of morality went out the window when the British Empire's interests, no matter how ill conceived, were concerned. As the Egyptian leader took control of the Suez Canal, the British stepped up their counter-Nasser operations. The ANA spy ring was a 'triple function' operation (cover for spying, propaganda and covert operations): it provided a convenient base for British anti-Nasser undercover operations and extra staff were dispatched by Whitehall into the agency to help.

The memoirs of Selwyn Lloyd, the former Conservative Foreign Secretary, record that, as the Suez Crisis worsened in the summer of 1956, the British Cabinet's plan for toppling Nasser called for several months of psychological warfare to be followed by military intervention if this did not work. Temporary additions to the office included Sefton Delmer, who had been in charge of a strand of British black propaganda during the Second World War, and William Stevenson, who was the biographer of William Stephenson. Delmer was once again working for the *Daily Express*, who supported his secondment back into secret government work. Delmer and Stevenson's propaganda objective was to equate Nasser with Hitler, which was Prime Minister Eden's simplistic view.[12] Delmer and Stevenson had much more success with this line in London, especially with Delmer's own employers, who could see a xenophobic allusion that would resonate with their readers.

The Suez Spy Ring

Although a regular at the bar of the Cairo Yacht club in the mid-1950s, Captain John Thornton Stanley MC was not a well-known figure in Cairo except among those who shared his enthusiasm for sailing (he was treasurer of the Yacht Club). The forty-year-old insurance salesman was a portly chap who featured heavy glasses and a thick moustache and a taste for tweed jackets and baggy trousers. He and his wife lived a low-key life as expatriates and he had every reason to keep a low profile.

Captain Stanley had a distinguished war record as, among other things, an SIS radio operator who served in the underground movement in Crete, where he lived for a year disguised as a Cretan shepherd. After the war, Stanley worked briefly for the Intelligence Corps in Athens and Thessaloniki during the early stages of the civil war in Greece, before apparently taking up his old pre-war job with the Prudential. The Egyptian authorities certainly thought 'The Man from the Prudential', living quietly in Cairo, was a British agent.

On the cusp of September 1956, five weeks after Nasser's government had seized the Suez Canal, the Egyptian secret police, the Mukhabarat, started a series of raids and in the early hours arrested their targets, often in their Cairo homes. Thirty people were eventually rounded up and taken to a nearby prison to be interrogated. The Egyptian authorities said they were all part of a network spreading out from the ANA.

All those arrested were accused of being members of a spy ring, of which James Swinburn, a former teacher turned secretary of the ANA, was the head. Others, according to the newspapers of the time, included Charles Pittuck, of the Marconi Radio Telegraph Company of Egypt, who had been Swinburn's stand-in when he was away; and James Zarb, described as a businessman.

At a press conference the night after the first arrests the Director General of the Egyptian Information Service claimed that the two men charged with espionage, James Swinburn and Charles Pittuck, had confessed to being members of a spy ring, and to passing information to John Gove and James Bernard Flux, diplomats at the British Embassy. A representative for the British Embassy denied categorically that it was in any way involved in the alleged plot.

Tensions were high and the Mukhabarat's spy hunt was not over. At 2.30 am on 3 September 1956, Captain Stanley was awakened in his flat in the residential quarter of Zamalek by a dozen armed police officers bursting into his room. He was taken to his office under escort at four o'clock in the morning. The office was searched and he was taken to prison and interrogated for four days and nights. Perhaps fortunately, his Greek wife and their two-month-old child were in Crete, where Mrs Stanley's family lived. According to local reports at the time, his neighbours thought he was an unlikely spy.

As can be seen with John Stanley, some of the arrested men had prior connections with British Intelligence and special operations. James Zarb, the Maltese owner of a porcelain factory, had served with SOE in Yugoslavia during the Second World War. He was described as a former Royal Air Force (RAF) serviceman who had risen to the rank of flight sergeant during the war. Following the war, he spent a year in Belgrade with the Military Mission, before moving to Alexandra, Egypt, where he married, started a family and established a business apparently as cover.

A few days after the arrests, the ANA office in Beirut was dynamited by assailants who left a message calling on 'British spies to get out of the Lebanon' (Guardian correspondent 1956: 1). The two officials of the British Embassy, Gove, head of the visa section and Flux, a first secretary in the commercial section, were declared *persona non grata* by the Egyptian government. Flux had been in Egypt since 1919. A group of journalists including Delmer, Stevenson, Ann Sharpley of the *Evening Standard* and Eileen Travis, an American working for the *Daily Mail*, were expelled too. However, on 8 February the following year the *Daily Telegraph* reported President Nasser's demand for four British 'plotters' to hang, under the headline 'Egypt Demands Death for 'Spies'. The trial lasted until the end of May, and the panel of judges gave their verdicts three weeks later. Zarb and Swinburn were found guilty and sentenced to ten years and five years hard labour respectively. Stanley and Pittuck were acquitted and left Egypt after nearly ten months in prison. According to Reuters' reports of the trial, Swinburn confessed, for which he received a lighter five-year sentence, and was released in 1959. He had been in possession of secret Egyptian naval papers including an assessment of naval defences around Alexandria (Dorril 2000: 632). The Egyptian authorities had been tipped about the British network several years earlier by the Soviets, most likely on information provided by SIS double agent George Blake (Bloch and Fitzgerald 1983: 122).

An Egyptian, fifty-one-year-old Sayed Amin Mahmoud, a headmaster said to be the main British agent, was executed. His son, naval Captain Ahmed Amin and a number of other Egyptians were given long prison sentences (Lashmar and Oliver 1998b: 70). Also accused *in absentia* were: Alexander Reynolds, George Thomas Sweet, John Reed McGlashan and George Arthur Roe. As the *Daily Telegraph* noted in his 2010 obituary, exactly how John McGlashan, an SIS officer listed as a third secretary in the Embassy, came to be seized in Cairo remains a mystery.

Equally mysterious was the manner in which McGlashan was released and with the other three spirited out of Cairo to safety. Eleven Egyptians and one Yugoslav were charged with spying. Details of the ANA Cairo spy ring that emerged painted the SIS as barely competent, allowing agents to run networks of fictitious informants so they could claim their pay. Following a lengthy campaign to clear him, James Zarb was released after from Cairo's Turah Jail after four and half years in 1961. The media heavily covered his arrival at Heathrow Airport by a BOAC Comet. A short Pathé news sequence now on YouTube shows Zarb, a balding, diffident man, evading questions politely. In a somewhat strange moment shortly after his return he was the subject of a 'This is Your Life' TV show in 1961 hosted by Eamonn Andrews.

Captain Stanley was held for months in solitary confinement, even as the British–French–Israeli invasion was underway about, which he had no knowledge, and amused himself with growing a huge handlebar moustache. Egyptian authorities' suspicions were aroused by his meticulous gramophone record indexing system but there was little evidence against him, except his wartime record, and he was eventually released.

Second Strike

The ANA spy ring had been part of a much more substantial SIS anti-Nasser operation. Julian Amery, a famous Special Forces interventionist, Conservative MP and former wartime SOE officer, had made contact with a cabal of rebel Egyptian officers outside the country. If the British government arranged the overthrow of Nasser, these officers were lined up to take power.

With all its field officers and agents in Egypt neutralised, the SIS scrambled around for help with its assassination plans for Nasser. James Mossman had worked for SIS during the war, but by 1956, was working for the *Daily Telegraph* as a correspondent. He was posted to Egypt for the paper. In Cairo, he was approached by John McGlashan on behalf of the SIS with a request to help. Apparently Mossman claimed he had finished with intelligence work; the officer appealed to his patriotism, telling him that 'you must do this because we are about to go to war with Egypt' (Dorril 2002: 633). After agreeing to cooperate Mossman was asked to drop off a package from the boot of his Morris Minor at the twelve-mile post outside Cairo. He had been given a telephone number on which to confirm safe delivery. Upon calling, Mossman discovered he had contacted the wrong man. 'The package had contained £20,000 in English banknotes which was intended as a bribe to Nasser's doctor to poison Nasser' (Dorril 2000: 633).[13] The crisis came to a head with an invasion of Egypt in late 1956 by Israel, followed by Britain and France. The aims were to regain Western control of the Suez Canal and to remove Nasser. After the fighting had started, political pressure from the USA, the Soviet Union and the United Nations led to a withdrawal of their forces by the three nations. The episode humiliated Great Britain and France and strengthened Nasser. There is probably a file still locked up in the SIS that tells the full unexpurgated story and, for instance, how McGlashan was spirited out of Cairo and then out of the country.[14] The bungling led to the slow decline of ANA as a viable 'independent' news agency. It functioned from its Beirut and Aden offices but was the company was eventually dissolved in 1972.

Forgery and Fake News

In 2019 the National Archives released some 2,000 files of IRD material, nearly double the number that had been released in the preceding twenty years. I worked with the BBC Radio 4 reporter Sanchia Berg to examine some of the files. There was for the first time confirmation that IRD had forged documents and circulated what we would now call fake news. One complicated scheme involved faking a press release from the World Federation of Democratic Youth (WFYD), a Communist-backed organisation based in Budapest. In 1963, African students in Bulgaria made international news. Scores had left the country, claiming racial discrimination, and the IRD decided to use this to 'intensify indignation ... against Bloc countries' (Berg 2019[15]). On forged headed notepaper, the IRD team circulated a press release to hundreds of newspapers and opinion formers. The press release was reprinted, for example, in full by a news agency in Zanzibar – and it included the racist statement that the Africans 'emerging from the jungle darkness of want, were not equipped to understand that food, fuel and clothes were not freely attainable ...' (Berg 2019[16]). The African students who saw it were disgusted by the 'Bulgarian' letter. The student union of Nigeria complained this was a declaration of 'white superiority' (Berg 2019[17]). Meanwhile IRD staff gleefully wrote to each other about the success of their forgery. Some weeks later, rather behind the curve, WFYD insisted it had been a fake release (Berg 2019).

The IRD files show they printed and distributed statements purporting to come from the International Institute for Peace in Vienna on a number of occasions. They also faked posters from the International Union of Students, replacing the acronym 'US' with Chinese characters, to turn an anti-US nuclear campaign into an anti-Chinese one. The newly released files also confirmed that IRD's biggest operation was against Egypt and its leader Colonel

Nasser in the build-up to, during and after the Suez Crisis in 1956 (Berg 2019). What we have learnt about IRD is that it propagated selected facts and in some cases fabrications while deliberately suppressing equally important facts that did not suit its agenda.

Notes

1. As Cormac pointed out, the Research, Information and Communications Unit were taking advantage of developments in information communications technology to monitor behaviour by examining the internet activity of individual targets (2018: 279).
2. Cobain to author 2018.
3. Bakir defines strategic political communication as: 'Comprising of political communication that is manipulative in intent, that uses social scientific techniques and heuristic devices to understand human motivation, human behaviour and the media environment, to inform effectively what should be communicated – encompassing its detail and overall direction – and what should be withheld, with the aim of taking into account what influences public opinion and creating strategic alliances and an enabling environment for government policies – both at home and abroad' (2013: 3).
4. IRD had been mentioned in passing in Page et al.'s 1968 book on Kim Philby (p. 203).
5. It was only later during our research that we on Fletcher's team discovered Sheridan's earlier role in SOE and PWE.
6. This was years before the term 'spin' was coined to express selective use of the truth and to be misleading.
7. After the war, the demobbed Lieutenant Colonel Sheridan set himself up as a public relations consultant with his former SOE colleague Colin Wintle.
8. The Russian Service started broadcasting in March 1946.
9. For a comprehensive history of British covert action see Cormac 2018.
10. Some of their staff spent time as intelligence officers. John Ogilvy Rennie, head of IRD from 1953 to 1958, later became head of SIS. IRD operations in Malaya during the crisis of the 1950s were run by Maurice Oldfield, then SIS station chief in Singapore, later the chief of SIS. The last head of IRD was Ray Whitney, who had done time in the SIS, and who later became a very right wing Tory. (Within a few months of leaving Whitehall, Whitney was attacking the West's 'sell out to Marxists in southern Africa' in an article in *Free Nation*, the newspaper of the far-right National Association for Freedom.)
11. Pincher had made reference to the assassination plot in 1981 but probably as a result of talking to Wright (1981: 173).
12. <http://news.bbc.co.uk/1/hi/uk_politics/5193202.stm> (last accessed 20 October 2019).
13. Further evidence exists of Eden's orders to kill Nasser: see Aldrich 2001: 479; Bower 1995; and Corera 2017a.

104 / Spies, Spin and the Fourth Estate

14. Keith Jeffery's (2010) official history only took MI6 up to 1949 so there is no mention of the Arab News Agency fiasco.
15. National Archives FO168/958/959/960.
16. National Archives FO168/958/959/960.
17. National Archives FO168/958/959/960.

SEVEN

Agitprop

The Suez Crisis, presided over by the Prime Minister Anthony Eden, whose judgment was impaired due to long-term illness, is one of the markers of the decline of British Empire. If the Empire and Britain's influence was waning, IRD pressed ahead with portraying the nation as a redoubt against the insidious onslaught of communism. IRD was expanded and better resourced during Wilson's Labour government of 1966, with efforts made to extend anti-communist pro-British coverage in Latin America (see Lashmar and Oliver 1998b: 79–80). IRD had its fingers in an increasing range of political concerns.

Bookworms

This opaque Foreign Office department was also secretly sponsored book publishing on a substantial scale, with reputable publishers, just as the CIA did with the American firm of Frederick A Praeger. Again, with Leslie Sheridan as a prime mover, IRD covertly published more than 120 titles in two decades with taxpayer's money (Lashmar and Oliver 1998b: 101). Sheridan set the covert operation running with a 'front' publishing company called Ampersand. The first titles, a dozen books on various anti-communist themes, were published between 1952 and 1955. Noted Labour Party Cold War warrior Denis Healey wrote one, *Neutralism*, which argued that neutralism was akin to communism.

Following on from Ampersand, a range of publishers were

subsidised to put out books including Batchworth Press (1951–4), Phoenix House (1955–9) and then Bodley Head (1960–71) published the Background Books series. These were all readily supplied free to journalists and other opinion formers. With the Batchworth Press, the first title to be published was, *Why Communism Must Fail*, authored by the philosopher Bertrand Russell and the second, *Trade Unions – True or False*, was written by Vic Feather the Assistant General Secretary of the British Trade Union Congress (TUC). The Background Books series ran until the end of 1971 and nearly 100 titles and was edited by IRD contractor and former wartime MI5 man Stephen Watts.

One of the titles, an edited collection, pulled big names from the political world. *Why I Oppose Communism* included contributions from the poet Stephen Spender, Bertrand Russell and historian Hugh Trevor-Roper. This edited edition was compiled by another of Sheridan's wartime friends, Colin Wintle, a journalist and literary agent who, as may be recalled, had been the SOE–PWE liaison officer during the war. It was published in 1956 by Phoenix House. Another Background Book was *Africa between East and West*, written by John Dumoga, one of the first indigenous Ghanaian journalists, who later worked for IRD front news agency Africa Features Services. His work also played on the nationalism equals communism trope.

Regime Change and a Massacre

IRD documents released in the National Archives reveal little of the Department's more covert operations. The files released in 2019 under the Foreign and Commonwealth Office (FCO) 168 series were mostly from the early 1960s. Some of these documents confirm my long held suspicion that IRD used forgeries and what we would now call fake news as tools in its anti-communist crusade.[1] For the Lashmar and Oliver (1998b) book, with so few documents released into the National Archives at the time, we made a point of interviewing former participants wherever possible. Perhaps the most revealing was Norman Reddaway, who was interviewed by James Oliver about his involvement in a number of covert operations, where he had secretly intervened in trouble spots across the world. In *Britain's Secret Propaganda War* we were able to reveal

Britain's covert involvement in the overthrow of President Sukarno of Indonesia.

In autumn 1965, Reddaway, a physically rangy and vocally articulate troubleshooter for the Foreign Office, was tasked with a special mission. The British Ambassador to Indonesia, Sir Andrew Gilchrist, had just visited London for discussions with the head of the Foreign Office, Joe Garner (later Baron Garner). Covert operations to undermine Sukarno, the troublesome and independently minded President of Indonesia, were not going well. Garner was persuaded to send Reddaway, the Foreign Office's propaganda expert, to the region to lead the anti-Sukarno propaganda operations run by the Foreign Office and SIS. Reddaway boasted that Garner gave him access to £100,000 in cash 'to do anything I could do to get rid of Sukarno'.[2]

In 2000, Denis Healey, Labour's defence secretary at the time, admitted to James Oliver and I that the intelligence war had spun out of control in Indonesia. He had even had to stop the British service chiefs from taking military action. He said, 'I would not let the RAF drop a single bomb although they were very anxious to get involved' (Lashmar and Oliver 2000: 10). More recently, Aldrich and Cormac have made the point that so many of the British military were secretly engaged against Indonesia (50,000 troops and a third of the Royal Navy) that the government was in no position to act against UDI in Rhodesia militarily (2016: 266).

Reflecting his low opinion of journalists, Reddaway said that 'newsmen would take anything from here, and pestered us for copy'. He suggested that *The Observer* newspaper had been persuaded to take the Foreign Office 'angle' on the Indonesian takeover by reporting a 'kid glove coup without butchery'.[3] Healey admitted to the Foreign Office misinformation campaign:

> Norman Reddaway had an office in Singapore. They began to put out false information and I think that, to my horror on one occasion, they put forged documents on the bodies of Indonesian soldiers we had taken. I confronted Reddaway over this. (Lashmar and Oliver 1998b: 8)

Lord Healey denied any personal knowledge of the wider SIS campaign to arm opponents of Sukarno. However, he added, 'I would certainly have supported it' (Lashmar and Oliver 2000: 10). On 10 March 1966, a defeated Sukarno was forced to sign over his powers to General Suharto, little aware of scale of the US and UK forces that had operated against him. It was not long before Suharto quietly ended the inactive policy of *Konfrontasi*, resulting in a swift improvement in Anglo-Indonesian relations. According to Reddaway, the overthrow of Sukarno was one of the Foreign Office's 'most successful' coups, which he had kept secret until the interview (Lashmar and Oliver 1998a: 10). Suharto, who had proved to be a kleptocratic dictator, was deposed in 1998 after a thirty-one-year reign.

Who Pays the Piper

Many IRD authors established reputations as independent experts in their field after they published books and articles based on information quietly handed to them to them by IRD and often then published by IRD fronts. The doyen of Cold War warriors in Britain, Brian Crozier, explained how the process worked. He had written a report on Sino-Soviet subversion in the third world for IRD, based on material from both GCHQ and SIS. 'After the document had been "sanitised" by the excision of secret material, I was allowed to take the scissored typescript home. The report formed the core of . . . The Struggle for the Third World [1966].' His next book, *The Future of Communist Power*, was written at the IRD offices 'on the basis of a vast supply of classified documents' (Crozier 1994: 57). Earlier, R. N. Carew Hunt, an SIS officer working for MI5, had established a major academic reputation for *The Theory and Practice of Communism*, which had been written by him at the request of Minister Christopher Mayhew. When Stella Rimington joined MI5 as a young woman, Carew Hunt's book was one of the handful of texts that recruits were recommended to read. IRD also issued secret briefings on the Left in Britain, based on the premise that the Communist Party had taken over the trade unions and Labour Party.

Pretty Flamingo

The SIS documents are still held back at the National Archives for many decades so we do not know what they will tell us about British

Intelligence in the post-war years that is new. However, stories of the SIS in those years pop up from time to time, often in unlikely sources. In 2019 yet another story about SIS covert operations made news about events of some sixty years ago. It again showed that despite IRD's wide remit, the SIS liked to keep its own hand in 'front' publishing and using journalists. The story came from the wife and son of a deceased SIS officer called Peter Hornsby.

Hornsby, whose early SIS handler was George Blake, the Soviet double agent, had been recruited as an SIS asset after being elected national treasurer of the National Union of Students (NUS). In 1956, he took up a post with the Coordinating Secretariat of the National Unions of Students (Cosec), an international anti-communist organisation which was also funded by the SIS and housed in the Dutch city of Leiden. In 1960 another one of Hornsby's handlers, Margaret Bray,[4] discussed with Hornsby the idea of setting up one of the first magazines aimed at Afro-Caribbean readers, as a means of monitoring national movements and discreetly recruiting agents.

An SIS front company called Chalton Publishing was set up to produce the magazine and also published *Feline*, a soft porn magazine aimed at the Afro-Caribbean community. Journalists and editorial staff were hired. The exotically titled *Flamingo* was considered an innovative magazine, even in the cultural whirlwind of the 1960s, mixing glamour, sex, culture and international politics. Hornsby's wife and then son told the intelligence writer Stephen Dorril about his work for the SIS. 'In Peter's mind, a magazine focusing on immigrants would make them feel welcome and ease their integration into British society', says Jennifer Hornsby (Doward 2019). The story rang true with Dorril:

> There were people inside MI6 who saw which way Africa was going in terms of politics and nationalism, and were willing to support black students, writers and aspiring politicians who were on the left but who could be persuaded to oppose communism. (Doward 2019)

The SIS used the magazine to push an anti-communist agenda among black and West Indian communities, probably using IRD material.

In the mid-1960s, the Soviets leaked an internal SIS document that stated it was 'of paramount importance to maintain as far as possible the illusion of Cosec's complete independence'. The document continued:

> It seems to us that, if once we attempted to sharpen Cosec as a cold war instrument, we might find it had ceased to have any point at all. Certainly it would be difficult to retain the alliance of member organisations in the uncommitted countries of Asia and Africa, if they suspect that Cosec was being 'run' by the Americans and ourselves. (Doward 2019)

Flamingo ran from September 1961 until May 1965 and at its peak sold up to 20,000 copies in the UK and 15,000 in the USA each month (Doward 2019). It was also distributed in the Caribbean and West Africa, and published dedicated editions in Nigeria, Ghana and Liberia. The reasons for *Flamingo*'s closure are unknown.

The Troubles

Wherever British Intelligence and the security services have operated in the world there has been controversy over selective leaking and disinformation. Northern Ireland was particularly contentious, being part of the UK, and psychological warfare was widely used by the military and security services (as documented by Bloch and Fitzgerald 1983; Curtis 1984; Miller 1993). After close reading of the archives, Cormac concluded that propaganda, conducted by the IRD and military psychological operations, or 'psyops', formed a key part of British covert activity in Northern Ireland.

> Back in 1969, at the outbreak of The Troubles, the Army, which initially took the lead in this area, defined psyops as 'the planned use of propaganda, or other means, in support of our military action, or presence, designed to influence to our advantage the opinions, emotions, attitudes and behaviour of enemy, neutral and friendly groups'. (Cormac 2018: 198)

Cormac observes that such activity covered 'black', 'white' and 'grey' propaganda, and that it was important to remember that the vast majority of information work was overt public relations activity.

'Covert propaganda formed a smaller-scale and complementary activity, used when attribution would undermine credibility' (Cormac 2018: 198).

Cormac discovered that psyops operations had sent army personnel onto the streets to distribute leaflets while disguised in Beatles wigs. IRD staff were particularly keen to find a role in the conflict, given that the receding communist threat had placed their jobs under threat. Whitehall managers slashed the IRD's budget by more than half in 1971, leaving those who survived the axe anxious to safeguard their careers (Cormac 2018: 198). Colonel Maurice Tugwell of the Information Policy Unit (IPU), a former long serving paratrooper, produced an influential yet ludicrously paranoiac appraisal of IRA propaganda predicated on the notion that any organisation criticising British policy in Ireland must be an IRA front. He included not only human rights activists like Father Faul, but also the Irish state broadcaster RTE, and the SDLP, then the main constitutional nationalist party in Northern Ireland (Tugwell 1971). It is little wonder that with the failure of senior officers like Tugwell to understand the realities of The Troubles, British policy in those years was such a disaster.

British military intelligence agents in Northern Ireland used fears about demonic possessions, black masses and witchcraft as part of a psychological war against emerging armed groups in The Troubles in the 1970s. The propagandists were closely linked to IRD though convened in a special regional unit. As The Troubles intensified, Prime Minister Edward Heath also called for unattributable propaganda and Norman Reddaway, back from a Foreign Office posting in Khartoum, and now in charge of all cultural and information work at the Foreign Office, was involved in operations 'overtly and covertly to blacken the IRA' by placing propaganda into the British press (Cormac 2018: 199). The approach was to 'internationalise' the IRA and pose it as tool of foreigners from the Soviet Union to Colonel Qaddafi, rather than an Irish nationalist-based response to overwhelming domestic civil rights abuse over a long period.

Another key figure in Northern Ireland psyops was Hugh Mooney who described himself as a journalist by profession and had worked as subeditor on the *Irish Times*. As a Reuter's correspondent in the Middle East he spent six months in Aden in 1966 and in 1967 reported the Arab/Israeli war. In 1969, he left the BBC External Service to join IRD as a 'Specialist Writer'. He was seconded to Headquarters Northern Ireland (HQNI) circa July 1971. He was there under 'deep cover' as the Information Advisor to the General Officer Commanding (GOC). In a letter, Mooney described his involvement in dirty tricks operations against the Provisionals:

> I hold frequent discussions with senior MOD PR officers on how to react to events so as to present the army in the best possible light and damage the IRA. For example, recently the IRA have started to use heavier weapons, including bazookas. We played down the significance of the weapons, stressing that it was obsolete. We were helped by the fact that the bazooka shells did not explode, because the safety cap was not removed. This latter fact was concealed. Instead, a dummy army order was prepared which said such shells should be tested electrically. This would have the effect of exploding the shell in the tester's hands. Clearance is being sought for this scheme.[5]

When two young terrorists were killed while making a bomb, Mooney said the story was put around that gelignite reacts to changes in temperature.

> We pointed out that the explosion took place on the coldest night of year. Subsequently, there were some very large explosions against soft targets, which led army experts to believe that the terrorists were getting rid of suspect stocks of gelignite. It was at one such meeting that I discussed with the army how to handle the timing of the announcement that the IRA was using hunting ammunition and dum dum bullets.[6]

Tugwell and Mooney also played a part in the post-Bloody Sunday cover-up after British paratroopers opened fire on unarmed civil rights marchers in January 1972 shooting twenty-eight, of whom fourteen died.

Dr Quink

Verifying stories from the world of spies is often difficult. Sources swear hand on heart to extraordinary events but, try as you might, you cannot get corroboration. Sometimes it takes years to crack these stories, even waiting until the once secret files are released into the public archives. However, there are exceptions and in one story, I was able to get compelling proof.

I met Dr Julius Grant in his office in an anonymous Victorian building in the City of London just before Easter 1987. Grant was a leading forensic scientist specialising in the analysis of paper and other writing methods. I was there because we at *The Observer* were sceptical about Colin Wallace, a former British army information officer in Belfast, and a former colleague of Maurice Tugwell and Hugh Mooney. He had offered a detailed account of the tangled web of deceit that the British state had deployed in Northern Ireland in the 1970s. These linked into allegations of an MI5 plot against the Labour Prime Minister Harold Wilson to the Kincora boy school paedophilia allegations. Wallace said he was one of the members of the intelligence agency-led 'Clockwork Orange' project, an alleged attempt to smear various targets including a number of senior British politicians. One was the Prime Minister Harold Wilson.

In 1986, Wallace had recently finished serving six years of a ten-year sentence for the manslaughter of his friend Jonathan Lewis. I had visited Wallace and his wife Eileen in Arundel, in Sussex. Wallace claimed to have been set up for the manslaughter because of his knowledge of dirty tricks in Northern Ireland. I spent a good deal of time corresponding and talking with Wallace. Along with a complex and detailed set of allegations, he said he had paperwork dating from 1974 and earlier that purported to show that a campaign of black propaganda was being discussed, long before these documents became public and controversial in the 1980s. Besides, being a self-confessed propagandist and a convicted criminal Wallace was very slick and always had an answer to every question, and we wondered whether it was a set-up.

We were very suspicious and decided to put Wallace's documents to the test. So with *The Observer* editor's agreement I took the documents along to Dr Julius Grant who had exposed the forged 'Hitler Diaries', which *The Sunday Times* had paid a fortune for and had published the contents as authentic.[7] It took Dr Grant three months to examine the Wallace documents. He told us at *The Observer*, 'I consider that the balance of probabilities favours the authentic origin of the writings attributed to 1974.' The Wallace files contained the first independent corroboration of some of the allegations in Peter Wright's book *Spycatcher* that was the subject of court case, with the British government trying to prevent publication.[8] In our story from July 1987 revealing the results of Grant's tests, we were able to say: 'As a result we can now demonstrate the extraordinary tide of smears, leaks and fabrications that were fed into the British press between 1972 and 1976, many aimed at the incoming government of Harold Wilson' (Leigh and Lashmar 1987a). These included:

- A banner story in the *News of the World* revealing a fictitious 'Russian plot' that Wallace had invented.
- A bizarre speech by the Tory spokesman, the late Airey Neave, about links between the IRA and left-wing MPs, the contents of which were also invented by Wallace.
- The leak by Wallace of a plan to introduce 'community policemen' in Ulster, which deliberately thwarted the then Labour Northern Ireland Secretary, Merlyn Rees.
- Untrue rumours from MI5 files that Wilson was under communist control.

A balding, softly spoken Northern Irish civilian, Wallace was serving as an army public relations officer when The Troubles broke out in 1968. He became a powerful psyops warrior, married into the SIS, leaked against his own government and was eventually sacked by the Defence Ministry. He first used his power to leak stories in the media to persuade the public of non-existent Communist links with the Provisional IRA. In December 1972, the *News of the World* (NoW) printed a front-page splash: 'Russia in IRA plot sensation'. The story claimed that a British RAF reconnaissance aircraft had spotted a Russian submarine off the coast of Donegal. The paper asserted that KGB-trained subversives had been dropped off by boat.[9] The *NoW* story went on to disclose that the British government had dossiers of east European involvement with the IRA. The only problem was that it was not true. The story was part of a disinformation campaign claiming that the IRA was run by Moscow. It was a fabrication by a special IRD offshoot, set up in Belfast shortly after The Troubles had begun. The six-person 'Special Editorial Unit' was operating to place anti-IRA stories into the press.

Now revealed to be almost certainly authentic, Wallace's notes were remarkable. They contained material known only to MI5 at the time – about the suspicions that Labour Leader Hugh Gaitskell had been killed by the KGB; about Wilson's links (via his friend Lord Kagan) with a KGB man called Vaygauskas; about West German links (via businessman Rudy

Sternberg) to Wilson's office. We realised that if Wallace had forged these it would have had to have been after 1980, when the stories had become public. This, for instance, is when the one KGB name, Vaygauskas, finally became public. Dr Grant was able to demonstrate that Wallace's paper and ink were manufactured before 1976. By examining the wood pulp, the starch and the additives used, he found the paper characteristic of a 1970–4 manufacture. However, Dr Grant was not entirely satisfied: 'this does not entirely exclude the possibility that some mill somewhere was making this paper after 1974' (Leigh and Lashmar 1987a). His break-through came through using 'thin layer chromatography' of a pinhead-sized speck of the ink. He proved it had exactly the same components – a mixture of three different blue hues – as a washable Quink ink made by Parker Pens in the early 1970s. By the mid-1970s the formula had been changed.

Colin Wallace had been sacked in 1975 for giving a journalist – Robert Fisk then of *The Times* – an official document. We cautiously note, 'His strange history makes him a difficult witness to believe. But some, at least, of what he says, we have now proved to be true' (Leigh and Lashmar 1987a).[10]

In 1980 Colin Wallace was arrested and subsequently found guilty of the manslaughter of the husband of one of his female workmates. It was alleged that Wallace had beaten antiques dealer Jonathan Lewis to death and the dumped Lewis's body in the River Arun. He served six years in gaol, from 1981 to 1987. Wallace's conviction was eventually overturned and his account of dirty tricks in Northern Ireland in the early 1970s stands. In 1973, Britain removed IRD staff altogether, although they continued to take a keen interest from London. Shortly afterwards, the Army's Information Policy Unit was closed. That is not to say that unattributable – even black – propaganda ended; it continued, often run by MI5.

Reds under the Bed

IRD had another target outside its anti-communist official remit. The Department had been involved in the covert manipulation of the public in favour of the UK's entry into the European Union in 1973, as James Oliver and I were to reveal (Lashmar and Oliver

1998b: 145–51). The official Whitehall line was that IRD was never involved with domestic politics or smears but it did cross that red line on a serious scale, especially against left-wing trade unionists. Cormac's archive trawl revealed that as early as December 1951, the SIS had suggested using satire to ridicule communism, with Norman Brook, the Cabinet Secretary, discussing whether Noel Coward was a suitably reliable comedian to be the figurehead of such a campaign.

> In the same year, the IRD created a small home desk, or English section, which focused on subversion and industry and remained in place into the 1970s. As part of the so-called cultural Cold War, the IRD bolstered purportedly independent domestic writers and presses through moderate trade unions, the BBC, several daily newspapers and the non-communist Left. (Cormac 2018: 199)

James Oliver and I also revealed how MI5 and IRD had worked with the *Daily Telegraph* and *Daily Mail* in the same year as Suez to smear the two leaders of the Fire Brigades Union, General Secretary John Horner and Assistant General Secretary Jack Grahl (Lashmar and Oliver 1998b: 105–8). Both were communists.

More about an IRD anti-trade union smear operation has been revealed more recently, when these government officials, paid for by the taxpayer, covertly smeared representatives of working people. One of the most sinister was IRD's involvement in the building strike in 1972 and concerns Ricky Tomlinson, the now famous actor best known for his part in the 'Royle Family' TV series. Back in the early 1970s he was a plasterer who helped to organise the first national building workers' strike. The strike was marked by great tension and violence between the strikers and the police. Tomlinson was jailed in 1973, along with his 'Shrewsbury Two' partner Des Warren, after being found guilty of conspiracy to intimidate, unlawful assembly and affray, following altercations at a construction site in Shrewsbury. The actor believes to this day that the jury's decision to convict him was prejudiced by an ITV documentary that was aired on the day they retired to deliver their verdict. This was an ITV programme called *A Red under the Bed* and fronted by Woodrow Wyatt. It was a full on attack on 'extremist' trade unionists and claimed that they were involved in intimidation and violence. The day after it was broadcast the accused pickets' lawyers applied for Anglia TV and Woodrow Wyatt to be held in contempt of court but Judge Mais refused and the trial continued. In more recent years there has been a campaign to clear those convicted. In total twenty-four people were jailed over the Shrewsbury strikes. The campaign's researcher, Eileen Turnbull, tracked down the television programme and then applied to have the government files on the programme.

What the researcher found was shocking. Both the government and IRD had been covertly involved with helping the reporter with material for the programme. The decision by the ITV company to broadcast such a closely related 'exposé' the night before the trial seems to have been a clear contempt of court. Yet the judge had rejected the defendants' protestations that the broadcast had prejudiced their trial.[11] Turnbull eventually got the official Whitehall file from the National Archives in 2013 and it revealed the support of the then Prime Minister Ted Heath for the film. Most of the file consists of a transcript of *The Red under the Bed*, obtained shortly after its broadcast on 13 November 1973. A memo from Heath's Private Secretary Robert Armstrong to Cabinet Secretary Sir John Hunt records how: 'The Prime Minister has seen the transcript of Woodrow Wyatt's programme "Red under the Bed". He has commented that we want as much as possible of this sort of thing.' An internal document from IRD elaborated, explaining they had a discreet but considerable hand in this programme:

In February Mr Wyatt approached us direct for help. We consulted the Department of Employment and the Security Service through Mr. Conrad Heron's group, which has been meeting approximately fortnightly for the past year. With their agreement, Mr. Wyatt was given a large dossier of our own background material. It is clear from internal evidence in the programme that he drew extensively on this; there is no doubt, for instance, that he drew on our paper on 'Violent Picketing' to good effect.[12]

Wyatt wrote a regular column for the *News of the World* and was a controversialist – the Richard Littlejohn of his day. He had a long association with IRD and had been shareholder of one of the IRD front news agencies, The Near and Far East News Agency (N&FEN) from 1952. Wyatt had at least two anti-left books published by IRD fronts. Norman Reddaway told us Woodrow Wyatt was a good friend and he supplied a lot of IRD material for Wyatt's column.[13] Wyatt was a Labour MP who moved rightwards as he got older and was a good friend of Margaret Thatcher when she was prime minister. The notion that there were 'Reds under the Bed' abounded in certain circles.

By 1976 there was Labour government and the maverick activities of IRD were causing concern in Whitehall. The Foreign Office had merged to become the Foreign and Commonwealth Office in 1968. Sir Colin Crowe, former High Commissioner in Canada, was brought out of retirement to investigate. Almost £1 million a year was being spent by the Foreign Office on 'unattributable' propaganda (Leigh 1978: 13). Labour Foreign Secretary David Owen was informed of IRD's history and covert operations when he took office and realising the potential for embarrassment from IRD's media manipulation, he authorised the Department's disbandment in May 1977. He was one of several sources who confirmed to James Oliver and me, IRD's role in covert operations with the SIS. On closure, the remaining thirty IRD staff were retired, made redundant or transferred to other departments.

Government propaganda did not stop and a new department, the Overseas Information Department, was set up inside the FCO proper. It was much smaller and had a much wider brief. IRD itself died as it lived for thirty years, a secret kept from the British public. I once heard my editor at The Observer say dismissively that 'Everyone knew about IRD', that was of course except for the people who were paying for it, the public. In the early 1980s Margaret Thatcher wanted to reinstate IRD but was advised not to.

When researching the history of IRD we were always puzzled by the mundanity of the files in the National Archives: they never referred to IRD's involvement with the SIS and CIA. We have assumed that the files were classified as SIS documents in order to prevent their appearance in the archives before seventy-five years had elapsed. However, in 2013 the reporter Ian Cobain may have provided part of the answer by revealing that IRD files were part of a secret and massive cache of documents held in Hanslope Park by the Foreign & Commonwealth Office (Cobain 2013) – a true scandal. The scale of the hidden archive is revealed by an inventory that the Foreign Office (FO) then published, which appears to show that one of the listed items may itself contain 2.9 million documents understood to occupy around fifteen miles of shelving. Since then the FO have been slowly transferring documents to the National Archives.

Certain journalists, selected by the agencies or their officers on a personal, political and informal basis, were uniquely able to access career enhancing information, while all others were excluded. IRD's work was sanctioned at the highest levels in Whitehall and a key part of its role was to create a *cordon sanitaire* so that government inspired information was placed in the public sphere but without attribution. These methods all raised significant ethical issues that were unaddressed at the time. IRD had a grip over journalists as it could provide sanitised intelligence information and assist those journalists to look good to their editors. Whether they were journalists, academics, politicians or trade union figures, IRD – through publishing its chosen people's books, and articles and papers, helping them attend prestigious events often abroad and giving them special treatment and access – hugely promoted their people's careers over less compliant colleagues. Of course, parts of Fleet Street and its lazy journalists played their part. That material could be used without declaration of its real source was an ethical failure.

I believe IRD intervened and skewed the political, media and academic environments by keeping those with left-wing or non-partisan or non-aligned views isolated. It was a corrupting influence. It did this not just in the UK but also across the globe, countering nationalist and anti-colonialist movements and intellectuals. Its legacy remains in RICU, and the controversial Prevent campaign.[14]

Notes

1. https://discovery.nationalarchives.gov.uk/details/r/C16861692 (FO168/267).
2. For a full account of Britain's part in the Indonesian coup, see Lashmar and Oliver 1998b: 1–10.
3. Interview with the late Norman Reddaway by James Oliver, 25 April 1996.
4. Margaret Bray had been Kim Philby's secretary at MI6.
5. Letter from Hugh Mooney to Mr Welser, Bloody Sunday Inquiry, 2 April 1971,

KM6.118/KM6.119, pp. 124–5, <https://assets.publishing.service.gov.uk/government/uploads/system/uploads/attachment_data/file/279155/0029_ix.pdf> (last accessed 29 July 2019).

6. Letter from Hugh Mooney to Mr Welser, Bloody Sunday Inquiry, 2 April 1971, KM6.118/KM6.119, pp. 124–5.

7. The Hitler Diaries were a collection sixty volumes of journals purportedly written by Adolf Hitler, but actually forged by Konrad Kujau between 1981 and 1983. The diaries were purchased in 1983 for nearly 10 million Deutsche Marks by the German news magazine Stern, which sold serialisation rights to several news organisations. One of the publications involved was *The Sunday Times*.

8. *Attorney-General for the United Kingdom v Heinemann Publishers Australia Pty Ltd* (1987) 10 NSWLR 86, 166. Heinemann Publishers Australia was the Defendant, and then the Respondent to the action taken by the United Kingdom Government. It was agreed throughout that Heinemann Publishers would be restrained from publishing *Spycatcher* if the United Kingdom's claim against Wright was successful.

9. In 1990, reporter David Leigh, then at *This Week*, revealed that the story, including 'official documents', had been passed by Wallace and the IRD unit's boss, Hugh Mooney, to the *News of the World* during a secret meeting.

10. For a detailed account of the Wallace story see Foot 1990.

11. <https://www.shrewsbury24campaign.org.uk/the-trial/red-under-the-bed/> (last accessed 19 September 2019).

12. PREM 15/2011 – Woodrow Wyatt's TV programme, *Red under the Bed.*

13. For more on Wyatt see Lashmar and Oliver 1998b: 80, 106, 119.

14. The campaigns around the 2016 UK referendum to decide whether to leave or remain in the European Union (EU) have come to be seen as a nadir in political communication. The 'Remain' lobby unsuccessfully used a campaign of fear. In addition, it is possible that Russian troll factories sought to influence the vote with an aim to break up the EU.

EIGHT

1968 and All That

Decades of war, censorship, propaganda and government control allowed the incompetence, internecine interdepartmental warfare and corruption of the intelligence community to be hidden from the public view. Fifteen years after the end of the Second World War, a new spirit arose, not least in a news media that was more questioning of the secret parts of government. In his examination of the Anglo-American intelligence axis in the Cold War, Richard Aldrich argues that it was in the early 1960s that the 'era of exposure began' citing coverage of the U2 spy plane incident in 1960, the disastrous Bay of Pigs invasion in 1961, the Vassall spy case in 1962 and the Profumo Affair in 1963 (2001: 626–7).

More recently, intelligence historian Christopher Moran has proposed that the earlier 'Buster' Crabb Affair scandal in 1956 was the moment where UK journalists, led by the *Sunday Express*, first widely ignored establishment pleas not to publish a critical intelligence story (Moran 2011). 'The story of one bungling by the SIS' (Moran 2011: 697). Former Navy wartime scuba diver, Lionel 'Buster' Crabb, had disappeared while spying on a Russian warship *Ordzhonikidze*, in Portsmouth harbour. The ship had brought Soviet leaders Nikita Khrushchev and Nikolai Bulganin on a visit to the UK. Recruited by the SIS, the unfit, chain-smoker Crabb had been surreptitiously inspecting the hull as part of an SIS operation to spot signs of state-of-the-art equipment on board the ship. Something went wrong and Crabb did not return.

The press discovered that the operation had been badly planned and organised; indeed, it was a tragic farce. A year after he vanished, a headless, handless body washed up on a beach near Chichester further along the South Coast. Secretary to the Treasury Sir Edward Bridges' withering report into the incident concluded it was a 'thoroughly bad and unplanned' operation. 'No serious steps seemed to have been taken to conceal the movements of the participants or to plan any cover story', it said (Bridges 1956). Bernard Smith, the SIS agent handling Crabb, had used both of their full names and addresses in the registration book of a Portsmouth hotel before the mission. Moran concluded that,

> Increasing press interest in intelligence was arguably indicative of a broader cultural shift in attitudes towards the secret state. Although intelligence had been subject by custom and practice, about which questions were never asked, by the mid-1950s it was fast becoming an area of major public interest. (Moran 2011: 699)

A Crack Down

At that time, except for the selected few with connections to intelligence, the working journalist had no avenue for direct contact with the agencies. As the existence of the intelligence agencies was not officially acknowledged by government, questions about intelligence were directed to designated Home Office or Foreign Office press officers who usually were, at best, as I can vouch, evasive.[1] Despite the Crabb Affair, the government was still keen to crack down on any unauthorised leaks about intelligence operations even as the public's appetite for spy stories grew. It would be another thirty years after Crabb before these services allowed a glasnost.

In 1958, the Oxford University magazine *Isis* found itself in trouble over breaching the Official Secrets Act. Two undergraduate contributors, who were both ex-national service, wrote about British Intelligence operations on the borders of the Soviet Union including fast boats that had been used by the SIS for operations in the Baltic. The two men were prosecuted, under Section 2 of the Official Secrets Act 1911, and sentenced to three months imprisonment (Moran 2013: 189). But from the 1960s there was a demand for intelligence-related news stories as the public became fascinated by glimpses inside a world that has been popularised by Ian Fleming, Leslie Charteris and John le Carré with their fictional characters James Bond, Simon 'The Saint' Templar and, later, George Smiley (see Dover and Goodman 2009: 201–19).

In 1961 when George Blake was apprehended on charges of being a KGB spy, the government used the D-Notice system to ask all Fleet Street editors not to mention in coverage of his forthcoming trial that he had been a long-standing SIS officer. The reason given was that 'that lives of MI6 employees are still in danger'. It was a classic example of national security being cited when the real issue was embarrassment to government and the SIS. D-Notice archives showed that 'every editor played ball' (Wilkinson 2009: 253). However, a German newspaper, which was not part of the UK's D-Notice system, reported that Blake was an SIS officer. It revealed that yet another British spy had betrayed his country and attempts to keep the lid on such intelligence scandals were failing.

A Honeytrap

The Profumo Affair in 1961 was probably the great British political scandal of the twentieth century, and featured some intelligence aspects. John Profumo, the Secretary of State for War in Harold Macmillan's Conservative government, had a sexual relationship with the nineteen-year-old model Christine Keeler that he then denied in Parliament. When it was clear he had lied, he resigned. She was also having a relationship with Captain Ivanov, a Soviet naval attaché at the Russian Embassy, and that raised questions of security. The scandal shook the country, and the press coverage reflected a serious shift away from respect for the establishment and towards a more questioning approach.

If the reporting of the Crabb and other scandals suggested a shift in the UK news media's approach to national security reporting, it was over in the USA that something much bigger was starting that would eventually have a huge impact back in Britain. The seismic shift in the way Western media reported intelligence agencies began in 1964. It went virtually unnoticed at the time in the USA, where it occurred, and is little known in the UK even today. In August of 1964, a leak from a US Congressional investigation into the tax-exempt status of some private American foundations revealed that eight foundations were acting as conduits to launder money from the CIA's secret Cold War funds into international cultural organisations, the media and for events that had an anti-communist agenda. Cord Meyer, a senior CIA officer involved in these operations later noted: 'The story was carried on the back page of the *New York Times* and caused little stir at the time; although within the Agency it caused us anxiously to review and attempt to improve the security of [our] funding mechanisms' (Meyer 1982: 105).

The Underground

The British and American covert narrative is woven tight, not least because of close cooperation between IRD and the CIA in so many projects. In the early 1960s radical journalists working for *Ramparts* stumbled over the first evidence of enormous covert cultural and propaganda operations by the CIA (Richardson 2009: 49). Although the rest of media paid little attention, less than a month later an editorial appeared in *The Nation*, a left-wing political magazine based in New York. *The Nation* had been attentive, and asked two fundamental questions. The first was: 'Should the CIA be permitted to channel funds to magazines in London – and New York – which pose as "magazines of opinion" and are in competition with independent journalism of opinion?' (de Vries 2012: 1078). The second was: 'Is it the "legitimate" function of the CIA to finance, indirectly variously congresses, conventions, assemblies and conferences devoted to "cultural freedom" and kindred topics?' *The Nation* summarised in two sentences a quandary of where the national security remit ends and freedom of speech begins. Should intelligence agencies engineer the political and cultural direction of their own or other nations?

As revealing as the leak from the congressional hearing was, and despite how pertinent *The Nation*'s questions were, even today they are little recognised for their real significance as a landmark moment in the process of changing public attitudes from one of unquestioning patriotic support of intelligence work to a much more critical stance. To that point in time there had been little in the way of challenge to the US intelligence complex. As Loch K. Johnson has dubbed it, 1945–74 was 'the era of trust' for the intelligence agencies characterised by 'benign disinterest' by politicians, the media and the establishment (Johnson 2018b: 90).

In the wake of the Second World War it was viewed as unpatriotic for the media or anyone to challenge the workings of the CIA, and while it was one thing to challenge the FBI and its director J. Edgar Hoover about crime policing, it was not okay to challenge them on national security. Hoover went about his work illegally, blacklisting and harassing anyone who he perceived to be a communist, whether they were part of the Civil Rights movement like Martin Luther King Jr or Paul Robeson or, as Hoover would have seen it, a left-wing and limp-wristed member of the Hollywood elite.

The growing confidence of critics to challenge the national security establishment was to be a slow and virtually undetectable process as the tectonic plates of opinion moved almost imperceptibly but constantly through the 1960s and the pressure gradually built and fractures opened. As former senior CIA officer Cord Meyer noted, *The New York Times* article may have been hardly noticed by the public, but it was most certainly seen as a wake-up call within the CIA. The agency's Cold War warriors realised that it was only a matter of time before some of their covert operations would become public (Meyer 1982: 105). In the web of CIA front organisations including magazines like *Encounter* and its German and French sister journals, writers and editors, who had turned a Nelsonian blind eye to the massive covert funding of these expensive opinion formers, began, queasily, to realise the jig might be up and their reputations as free thinkers open to challenge.

In contrast there was the Californian-based monthly publication *Ramparts*, one of the first of a new wave of 'underground' magazines that sprung up across the USA and the West in the 1960s that challenged authority wherever Cold War orthodoxy could be found. *Ramparts* had started out in 1962 as a Roman Catholic literary journal with 5,000 subscribers. Based in Menlo Park near San Francisco, *Ramparts* was engaged with the Frisco's counterculture zeitgeist under its flamboyant editor, Warren Hinckle. By 1966, it had begun to focus on radical politics and to take an interest in the expanding CIA. Stanley K. Sheinbaum, a former Michigan State University

(MSU) scientist, tipped off the *Ramparts* team about a covert CIA operation. In the 1950s, he had coordinated a development project for South Vietnam called the Michigan State University Vietnam Advisory Group (MSUG).

This project had been secretly financed, and used as a cover by the CIA, so they could train the Saigon police force without revealing US government involvement. The Group also had a hand in writing the South Vietnamese constitution. Sheinbaum had resigned in 1959 after discovering the secret source of the project's funding, which he found incompatible with academic freedom. Six years later, he took his story to Hinckle (de Vries 2012: 1081). Published in April the investigation caused enough ripples for *Ramparts* to win a George Polk Award for Magazine Reporting.

A Shudder

On 14 February 1967 the earth shuddered again, this time more noticeably after *The New York Times* (*NYT*) ran a front page story headlined, 'A student group concedes it took funds from the CIA'. The exposé was by-lined Neil Sheehan, one of the paper's first investigative reporters. It was a tie-in with *Ramparts* where the magazine editorial team had bought a full-page advert in the *NYT* that day to publicise their March issue and Sheehan would develop the story. The advert declared that *Ramparts* would reveal how, for many years, the CIA had sponsored the National Student Association, an umbrella grouping for around 400 student clubs. 'It has used students to spy, it has used students to pressure international student organisations into taking Cold War positions, and it has interfered, in a most shocking manner in the international workings of the nation's largest and oldest student organisations.'

Neil Sheehan investigated further and then confronted the student association chairman Eugene Groves who confirmed the allegations were true. Groves admitted that from the 1950s until 1966 the National Student Association had received around $200,000 a year in CIA subsidies laundered via private foundations as indicated in the 1964 Congressional hearings. The funds were mainly used to send Association delegations to international student meetings where they were expected to counter radical tendencies in other groups. On return, they were debriefed by CIA officials who wanted to know about the student representatives from other countries. The story had come from a whistle-blower called Michael Wood who had been employed by the Association which he noted said it stood for 'a free university in a free society' while in fact being a CIA anti-communist front (Richardson 2009: 47). Uncovering the extent of secret CIA funding escalated through the next couple of months with both the *NYT* and *Ramparts* publishing more stories and other media joining in.

The CIA had discovered that *Ramparts* was delving into National Student Association front organisations long before publication. Richard Helms, the Deputy Director for Plans at the CIA, instigated a series of measures designed to spy, neutralise and discredit journalists at *Ramparts*. As Francis Stonor Saunders who documented the CIA's massive cultural Cold War operations observed, for more than a year the CIA did everything it could to sink *Ramparts* (1999: 481). Deputy Inspector General Edgar Applewhite later admitted:

> The people running *Ramparts* were vulnerable to blackmail. We had awful things in mind some of which we carried off . . . We were not the least inhibited by the fact that the CIA had no internal security role in the United States. (Thomas 1996: 330)

Stonor Saunders noted, 'Amazingly, given the awfulness of the CIA's intentions, *Ramparts* survived to tell the tale' (1999: 382). The CIA's anti-*Ramparts* operations breached the 1947 National Security Act, which specifically prohibited the CIA from acting domestically against American citizens. The *Ramparts* team, like of many of the underground groups coalescing at the time, had little idea of how out of control the national security state in the USA was at the time nor did they yet realise how they were firmly in the CIA sights. That would take half a decade longer to be revealed.[2] That Sheehan's National Student Association story in 1967 had been given front page status and that he was allowed to follow up for many weeks, represented a major change of attitude in *The New York Times* – an opinion setter for the mainstream media. Back in the spring of 1961 *The New York Times*' editors in chief had deliberately made no mention of the CIA's involvement in the disastrous Bay of Pigs invasion in Cuba, which had been designed to effect regime change against Fidel Castro, but the times were a changing.

The close acquaintance between *The New York Times* publisher Arthur H. Sulzberger and CIA director Allen W. Dulles was likely a major consideration. After 1961, within *The New York Times*, an ontological debate then raged about whether their watchdog role extended to national security. The positive outcome was manifest in Neil Sheehan's reporting. De Vries noted the funding of the National Student Association turned out to be the just tip of an iceberg.

> During the weeks that following the *New York Times* articles there were new revelations in the media almost daily about independent American organisations and institution that had received money from the CIA for years via charitable foundations, unbeknownst to the government and Congress. (2012: 1075)

A Tremor

The clashes between national security state and the press increased. The backdrop was the disillusionment of younger Americans with their government over the escalation of the Vietnam War. It was also a failure of the Cold War warriors like Hoover and Helms to understand that these were not communists but a new counterculture that either rejected ideology or were part of the New Left.[3] The proponents of the new politics had little time for the bipartisan politics of the Cold War. It was the next major story that was to cause a cultural earthquake.

Again Neil Sheehan was at the forefront and *The New York Times* published extracts from tens of thousands of pages of secret government documents copied by Rand employee and high-flying administration intellectual Dan Ellsberg. These were to become known as the Pentagon Papers and they unequivocally revealed that the American people had been repeatedly lied to about the conduct of the war, the involvement of the CIA and much more. This was all immortalised in the 2017 film *The Post* where the *Washington Post*'s part in publishing the documents was dramatised and eulogised. It is an excellent film, and deeply moving to investigative reporters of the next generation, but it is easy to forget that the storyline is about the *Washington Post* playing catch-up with Neil Sheehan over at the *NYT*. Sheehan had been given key Pentagon Papers and published them first. Rivalry between the news organisations was a healthy motivator.

This time the story attracted not only the liberal media but also worldwide interest. America's controversially increased involvement in Vietnam did not find favour even with some allies. The UK's Prime Minister Harold Wilson, while sounding supportive to the USA, avoided tying Britain's military up in the Vietnam War. Only South Korea, Thailand, Australia and New Zealand committed troops in small numbers.[4] Nixon's government did everything in its power to suppress the Pentagon Papers. It saw a battle between the news media to publish top-secret documents on the ground of public interest and the administration unsuccessfully going to the Supreme Court in an effort to stop it. *The Post* captures the *Washington Post* owner's conflict, as she has to decide whether publishing the papers is more important than her friendship with Robert McNamara, who as Secretary of Defense had initiated the review of policy that became known as the Pentagon Papers (but by the time of their release was President of the World Bank). The Pentagon Papers were a catalogue of lies, deceits and policy failures in Vietnam foisted on the American public by several administrations. They were never meant to be seen by the public. At the end of *The Post*, there is a droll vignette where Katherine Graham, who is wistfully reviewing the difficult decisions of the past few months, says she hopes she never has to go through something like that again. The film then cuts to a sequence where a security guard in the Watergate complex in downtown Washington, DC, has interrupted burglars at the Democratic National Convention office.

An Earthquake

The story of Watergate has been told many times, not least in the movie *All the President's Men* (1974). It was a profound historical moment in the West; a period that saw not only the established radical press but all mainstream media – led again by the *Washington Post* and *The New York Times* – challenging a corrupted government.

The downfall came from a relatively minor act of criminality, which, upon investigation opened up a culture of malfeasance that thought it was above the law. Nixon's White House team had set up a special investigation unit ostensibly to counter leaks (thus their nickname the Plumbers) and who used illegal methods to achieve their ends. An early covert task for the Plumbers was the burglary of the office of Daniel Ellsberg's Los Angeles psychiatrist, Lewis J. Fielding, in an effort to uncover material to discredit Ellsberg who was facing trial at the time over releasing the Pentagon Papers (he was not jailed).[5] The burglary of the Watergate office took place in 1972 and the CIA was in collusion with the participants: one of the five burglars was a former CIA officer and the unit had a CIA liaison officer, John Paisley.

Over many months of investigation by Bob Woodward and Carl Bernstein and with the help of 'Deep Throat', their confidential source, the result was that the *Washington Post* was able to demonstrate that President Nixon had condoned the burglary of the Democratic Party National as part of extensive dirty tricks operations against the Democrats in advance of the presidential election. On 9 August 1974, Nixon resigned from the presidency as he faced almost certain impeachment and removal from office. He was later issued with a pardon by his successor, Gerald Ford. The scandal resulted in the indictment of some sixty-nine people, with trials or pleas resulting in forty-eight being found guilty, many of whom were top Nixon officials. John Mitchell, Attorney-General and Chairman of the Committee to Re-elect the President that went by the wonderfully apt acronym CREEP, was jailed. Howard Hunt (ex-CIA) and G. Gordon Liddy (ex-FBI) who planned the Watergate break-in were both jailed as was Charles Colson, special counsel to the President. Burglar James McCord (ex-CIA and Security Director of CREEP) was also jailed.

As Watergate was developing, a series of media articles and TV and radio programmes revealed further excesses of the US national security agencies. Unprobed by the previous generation of what Eisenhower had called 'the patriotic press', illegality by the deep state, going back thirty years, was exposed.[6]

Notes

1. It is worth noting that, in comparison to the secretive British agencies, the CIA and FBI have both had Public Affairs offices for decades.
2. For a detailed account of the *Ramparts'* story see Richardson 2009.
3. The failure to understand the New Left also meant that they had no idea how to deal with the dark side of the 1960s 'revolution' with the groups like the Weathermen and the Black Panthers that believed that violence was the only way to make America a fairer place.
4. The war was to cost America 58,220 military killed (<https://www.britannica.com/event/Vietnam-War> last accessed 29 October 2019).
5. I was fortunate enough to meet Dan Ellsberg several times over dinner and to interview him in Washington in the mid-1990s where I was making a BBC *Timewatch* programme about the 'Strangelove' nuclear generals (Lashmar 1996). He was perhaps was one of the sanest, smartest and courageous people it has been my good fortune to encounter as a journalist.
6. For a detailed up-to-date discussion about the nature of the deep state see Lofgren 2016.

NINE

1975: The Year of Intelligence

Watergate and the Pentagon Papers scandals had shocked enough of the American public to spur their representatives in Congress to demand an investigation into the illegal activities of the FBI, CIA, NSA and other agencies. President Richard Nixon had made extensive use of federal resources, including law enforcement agencies, to spy on legitimate political and activist opposition groups including the civil rights movement, Democrats and the New Left. The result of the outcry was the creation of two congressional committees in 1975, one chaired by Frank Church (D-ID) in the Senate and Otis Pike (D-N.Y.) in the House of Representatives.

These proceedings were watched with fascination by British journalists and with horror by the British Foreign Office and intelligence agencies. They had the potential to reveal joint operations between MI6, IRD and the CIA. They revealed CIA operations to penetrate major global press agencies based in London such as Reuters. More importantly, they lent the task of investigative reporting into intelligence and dirty tricks an aura of fourth estate glamour. Bob Woodward and Carl Bernstein turned their story into the best-selling book in 1974, *All the President's Men*, following which it was adapted into a Hollywood film.

Church and Pike

Church and Pike divided the responsibilities of what to investigate, with Church taking illegal activities and Pike analysis failure

(Johnson 2018a). Their hearings exposed secret illegal wiretapping, bugging and harassment of American citizens, including Supreme Court justices, reporters and government officials, who for one reason or another were viewed by intelligence chiefs as a threat to national security. Although initially an American story, this series of inquiries had a global impact upon media reporting, especially in London. British journalists read the *Washington Post* and *The New York Times* daily and asked, what is the British SIS angle on the latest revelation of US intelligence wrongdoing?

The most notorious case, first exposed in the 1960s and fully documented by the Church Committee, was the wiretapping of Martin Luther King Jr by the NSA and FBI under Hoover, who believed King to be part of a Communist conspiracy. In turn, the Johnson administration allowed the CIA to run Operation Chaos, sanctioned by the President, targeting American citizens. The stated mission aim was to uncover possible foreign influence on domestic race, anti-war and other protest movements. However, without any serious evidence of foreign intervention, the mission crept into wholesale harassment and illegality against protestors. Furthermore, revelations detailed how the CIA had been involved in overthrowing regimes in Iran (1953), Guatemala (1954), Congo (1960), Dominican Republic (1961), South Vietnam (1963), Brazil (1964), Chile (1973) and interventions in countless covert operations in other nations. Some of those who had worked for the CIA began to reveal the dirty tricks that the agency had engaged in, most notably Philip Agee who had been a CIA officer based in South America – which the USA viewed as its 'backyard'. He published a highly controversial whistle-blowing book, *Inside the Company: A CIA Diary* in 1975, the same year the USA pulled out of Vietnam defeated.

Such was the tsunami of revelations and investigations so dominating the media in the USA that 1975 remains known as 'the year of intelligence' (Johnson 1988). The CIA became a laughing stock after details of its bizarre schemes to kill Fidel Castro in Cuba, including planting an exploding cigar on the communist leader, became known. The Church Committee said the CIA made at least eight attempts during 1960–5 alone (Church 1975: 71–139). The Cubans say the total is in excess of 600 attempts from 1959 onwards (Cook 2016). Castro died in 2016 of natural causes.

The intelligence agencies and FBI fought tooth and nail against public disclosures. The *Pike Report* was never officially published, but it was, fortunately, leaked to a journalist and while it was a generally limp document, it had moments of interest. In conclusion it notes that, 'all the evidence in hand suggests that the CIA, far from being out of control, has been utterly responsive to the instructions of the President and the Assistant to the President for National Security Affairs' (Pike 1977: 17). The Committee found that at least 29 per cent of the CIA's authorised covert operations were targeted at media and propaganda (Pike 1977: 190). The agency had spent some $265 million on running media operations, as much as the combined budgets of the world's biggest news agencies (Associated Press, Reuters and United Press International) put together. As Nick Davies comments, in practical terms the CIA had the power to fabricate news wherever it wanted, without its hand being seen. 'If there was trouble in Japan, it could feed stories into the *Okinawa Morning Star* (it owned a substantial chunk), or the *Tokyo Evening News* (it owned the whole paper), or the *Japan Times* (it had agents in the paper)' (Davies 2008: 226).

The Church Committee allowed a large amount of CIA material to be withheld from the public record but they did reveal further illegal intelligence activities, often against American citizens. The (1976) report on the intelligence agencies and the media concludes:

> In examining the CIA's past and present use of the U.S. media, the Committee finds two reasons for concern. The first is the potential, inherent in covert media operations, for manipulating or incidentally misleading the American public. The second is the damage to the credibility and independence of a free press, which may be caused by covert relationships with the U.S. journalists and media organizations. (Church 1976: 197–8)

A Triple Whammy

By late 1977, the sheer scale of CIA involvement in the media was revealed in three substantial pieces of journalism. First, Joe Trento and Dave Roman, in *Penthouse* magazine, reported on the relationship of the news agency the Copley Press with the CIA. Trento and Roman showed that the agency owner James S. Copley cooperated with the CIA for over thirty years. Some twenty-three news service employees were also working for the CIA. The second article was by Carl Bernstein. In a 28,000-word article in *Rolling Stone*, he claimed that as many as 400 American journalists had worked for the CIA over the previous twenty-five years. Bernstein detailed the close relationship of many of the American's top journalists of the period with the CIA including Stewart and Joseph Alsop, Richard Salant of *CBS*, Henry Luce, Barry Bingham Sr of the *Louisville Courier-Journal*, Hal Hendrix of the *Miami News*, columnist C. L. Sulzberger, and Philip Graham and John Hayes of the *Washington Post* (Bernstein 1977).

In the third, two months later, *The New York Times* published a series of articles that confirmed much that Bernstein has said, and added a great deal of detail. *The New York Times* disclosed that in the preceding twenty years, the CIA had owned or subsidised more than fifty newspapers, news services, radio stations, periodicals and other communications facilities, most of them overseas. These were used for propaganda efforts, and/or cover for operations. Journalists who were paid CIA agents infiltrated another dozen foreign news organisations (Crewdson 1977: 1). Twenty-two or more American news organisations employed American journalists who also worked for the CIA. At its peak, the CIA's network 'embraced more than 800 news and public information organizations and individuals'. Bernstein alleged that the CIA had paid 400 journalists (Bernstein 1977).

The CIA also used British journalists, as many as fifty, although to this day we do not know who they were, as the CIA has protected their assets (Brandt 1997). The first examples of serious public accountability being brought into the State's intelligence community began in the USA after the continuous stream of revelations of impropriety. The news media were the catalysts for the first major inquiries that were launched in 1975 (see Johnson 1988). The US political scientist Harry H. Ransom notes that in the mid-twentieth century, accountability in this hidden structure of government had been 'sporadic, spotty and essentially uncritical' (1975: 38). A more democratic form of oversight was installed including standing intelligence committees on Capitol Hill: the Senate Select Committee on Intelligence (SSCI) created in 1976 and the House Permanent Select Committee on Intelligence (HPSCI) in 1977.

Senator Ted Kennedy introduced the Foreign Intelligence Surveillance Act (FISA) in May 1977. The Act provides judicial and congressional oversight of the government's covert surveillance activities of foreign entities and individuals in the USA, while, it was proposed, maintaining the essential secrecy needed to protect the United States' national security. This legislation reduced the President's ability to order unilaterally electronic monitoring, in favour of a system requiring parties to demonstrate probable cause to federal judges appointed to the new Foreign Intelligence Surveillance Court (FISC).

It is hard to over-emphasise the impact all these revelations made. The intelligence agencies deservedly took serious reputational damage, the media gained in confidence and the baby-boomer generation felt they were changing the world for the better. Aldrich noted that during the Cold War, journalists were broadly seen as occupying three positions on the landscape of secrecy, namely outrider, renegade or overseer. 'Initially, many American writers and journalists effectively served as outriders, willingly cooperating with the intelligence services both in reporting information and also in the expanding realm of cultural warfare' (Aldrich 2015: 190). Aldrich suggests that finally, from the mid-1970s, a more nuanced relationship developed that embraced the growing panoply of intelligence committees on Capitol Hill. 'Journalists increasingly took a middle path, viewing themselves as an informal part of the new accountability processes that provided the intelligence community with oversight' (2015: 190).

Fleet Street

In the UK, journalists were beginning to probe the most sensitive parts of the state. The most important breakthrough over coverage on Intelligence was *The Sunday Times* reporting of the Philby Affair. The government had done everything it could to play down that one of the most damaging spies, the one who had headed the Soviet section of the SIS, had been for decades a Soviet spy himself. Significantly, late 1967 brought revelations about Philby, which were the result of an eight-month investigation by *The Sunday Times* Insight team (Evans 1983: 4). Aldrich records that this was crowned by the sensational publication of Philby's memoirs in the following year, which dealt in detail with the SIS.

> Whitehall's attempts to control the Philby story had failed. The *Sunday Times* had ignored a D-Notice placed on the story. It also resisted efforts by Dennis Greenhill of the Foreign Office to persuade the editors to print unflattering material about the KGB alongside the Philby material. It is hard to recapture the sense of shock and outrage felt by some members of the establishment at the public parading of these secrets. (Aldrich 2004: 945)

The Sunday Times team featured the sage-like presence of Phillip Knightley, who was to become the doyen of critical intelligence journalists, one of the first to show complete independence from the British establishment.[1]

A landmark investigation known as the D-Notice Affair also occurred in 1967. The reporter concerned was the ubiquitous Chapman Pincher who revealed in the *Daily Express* that British Intelligence was tapping overseas phone calls and opening mail (Moran 2013: 136–76). The paper ignored a D-Notice on publishing intelligence information and as result Prime Minister Harold Wilson was furious with Pincher and the *Daily Express*. The ensuing row lasted several months and had momentous consequences. One of the significant factors in the affair was alcohol, with Foreign Secretary George Brown and the D-Notice Secretary Sammy Lohan[2] acting erratically because of their drinking. Brown was noted for often being drunk and Lohan was known to be 'sometimes fuzzy with drink' in the afternoon (2013: 141). In the modern world alcohol might still be a factor in corners of Westminster late into the evening, but much less so in the past. For journalists – once renowned for their copious drinking – as in the *Private Eye's* satirical character 'Lunchtime O'Booze' it now rarely plays a part in journalists' working lives. In earlier decades, much journalism research was conducted in the pub or over long lunches which loosened tongues and lead to indiscretions.

Popping in and out of the pub through the day was routine in Fleet Street. There were newspapers that held their morning editorial conferences in the pub where everyone drank whisky though it was not even midday. When reading histories of the period it is worth remembering that at key moments many of the participants were probably slightly, or even considerably, drunk. Working with people who were under the influence of drink was just how it was. However, Pincher, a noted fine diner whose favourite eating place was Britain's best French Restaurant *L'Ecu de France*, halfway between Fleet Street and Whitehall, was unusual in his generation as a light drinker and that gave him the edge and an advantage of accurate recall of careless comments. Although Pincher had revealed that British Intelligence eavesdropped on communications, the *Express* did not identify the intelligence agency that organised this work. Within a few years, controversial eavesdropping activities of the GCHQ were to be revealed, by the journalists Duncan Campbell and Mark Hosenball (Campbell and Hosenball 1976).

Pincher was a partial exception to the patriotic press and his relationship with his sources was complex. Sometimes he agreed to withhold stories or even published fake ones if he felt it was in the national interest (Pincher 2009: 155). I spent a good deal of time as a young reporter in the watering holes of Fleet Street with some of this venerable generation of reporters, and while they were often fine journalists, most were imbued with a residue of wartime spirit and not a small measure of Bell's spirit. They bought the establishment's argument that defectors and the incompetent were 'rotten apples' and not a systemic failure.

Ben Bagdikian, who wrote a cover story for *The Atlantic* in March 1977 on the 'Woodstein' phenomenon,[3] summed it up: Bob Woodward and Carl Bernstein

> were young, inexperienced, and not particularly promising in the eyes of their superiors. Working in a city and on a paper where the country's most celebrated journalists were in top command, the two beginners beat them all and became national heroes . . . If they could do it, why couldn't every high school student? (Bagdikian 1977)

The waves caused by Watergate crossed the Atlantic and inspired a new generation of journalists much more willing to take on the establishment. Over in the UK I, like others, felt inspired. We could see the wrongs in society and wanted to do something to counter the hypocrisy, corruption and incompetence.

The Radical Press

Often the new wave of journalists wrote for radical magazines like *The Leveller* collective and *Time Out*.[4] The longer established magazines *Peace News* and *New Statesman* also proved to be prepared to take on the secret state. Reinforced by the exposés in the USA of intelligence excesses these young long-haired journalists with their flared trousers had no reservations penetrating the cloak of secrecy and challenging British Intelligence. They were sick of living with the constant threat of nuclear war, they had caught the spirit of the campus revolutions (many having taken part) that had continued long after 1968, and they were all too well aware of the repressive nature of the British security forces in Northern Ireland's 'Troubles'. The mainstream media could still be timid.

In the UK the mainstream news media were still very cautious about reporting intelligence. If *The Sunday Times* is seen as the home of the first great wave of UK investigative journalism, it did not always publish the national security stories it uncovered. Richard Fletcher, a former Cambridge scientist and Labour Party activist worked with *The Sunday Times* to investigate how the CIA had subverted the British Labour Party, funding many well-known Labour politicians and trade unionists, in an effort to keep left-wingers from any kind of power.

The saturnine Fletcher combined the best skills of the scholar and investigative journalist, drawing on a personal philosophy based in traditional English dissent. He investigated the UK aspects of all the material coming out of the USA about CIA cultural warfare. One of the CIA's prized covert publications, *Encounter*, was largely run out of London by Britons. A little later Fletcher was to become my mentor and entry in investigative journalism. He had some useful methods. Although he had been involved in the Committee of 100 and fought against centrist Gaitskell's leadership bid in the Labour Party in 1960, he looked every inch like a young Cambridge don. If he wanted to interview someone who was involved with the CIA or SIS operations he would write to them on the headed notepaper of his Cambridge college. Usually they agreed to meet and talked very freely on the assumption that the very well-spoken Fletcher was 'one of us'. I still have some of Richard's notes of these conversations.

In such a way he was able to give the first detailed account of the CIA's covert interventions into the British Labour movement (Fletcher 1972). The only problem was, although the story went as far as being typeset for *The Sunday Times* Magazine, *The Sunday Times* editor Harry Evans decided he did not want to print it. Fletcher, never one to be stopped, took the text to a friendly printer and had a samizdat version of *The Sunday Times* Magazine printed with the story told, which he then distributed around left-wing bookstores and organisations. I still have a copy. What this reflected was the caution that still existed in the mainstream press about revealing intelligence operations. I asked Sir Harry why he had not published Fletcher's article and he indicated that, with at such a distance in time, he could not recall the events. However, he noted that *The Sunday Times* editors who dealt with article 'are journalists of the highest integrity, and it's entirely plausible I would have supported their judgment in what seems to be a very faint echo of some of the hotter days of the Cold War'. He adds, 'My considered view of events at that time are set out in *The American Century*, and rightly or wrongly, that remains my view' (Evans 2019).

The Eavesdroppers at GCHQ

An insight into the expansion of intelligence agencies in the UK came in 1976 when the Scot and Cambridge graduate, Duncan Campbell then twenty-four years old and the twenty-six-year-old British-based American journalist Mark Hosenball had pieced enough information together to write a story, 'The Eavesdroppers'. As Ian Cobain has since noted: 'It was seminal piece of post-war British journalism' (2016: 229). This ground-breaking text gave a detailed account of the spying operations, and for the first time named the agency, the Government Communications Headquarters, and revealed it was based in the quiet West of England, very upper middle class town of Cheltenham.[5] The Campbell and Hosenball piece was published in *Time Out* because the radical perspective of the editorial team was immune from the pressures that the intelligence chiefs were usually able to bring to bear on editors of mainstream news media.[6] The Labour government was keen to stop this bleeding of intelligence information into the public domain. The Home Secretary Merlyn Rees signed deportation notices against Hosenball and Philip Agee, who had moved to Britain after whistle-blowing at the CIA.[7] Hosenball was working with Campbell on further revelations about the UK–USA eavesdropping pact.[8] People from what was known as the New Left formed the Agee-Hosenball Campaign to try to stop the deportations. I can recall giving Agee a lift across London in my ancient Bedford van where he chatted about CIA operations against leftist governments in Latin and Central America.

A while after the publication of 'The Eavesdroppers', Duncan Campbell, working with *Time Out* journalist Crispin Aubrey, had gone to meet a potential source, John Berry. The former corporal in the Royal Signals Regiment had engaged in eavesdropping for GCHQ from the British military base in Cyprus. After the meeting in London, the three were arrested by Special Branch and later charged under the Official Secrets Act. This in turn spawned another campaign. At times, the state's effort to tackle these radicals developed a sense of farce. The prosecution in the ABC trial at the Old Bailey produced a senior Royal Signals Regiment officer identified only as Colonel B who was to describe the harm done to national security if the information the three had was released. In its next edition, the radical magazine *The Leveller* printed Colonel B's full name – Hugh Johnstone – and military record, incurring the magazine collective with the real risk of being prosecuted for contempt of court. There was serious side certainly: the defendants in the ABC trial faced long sentences if found guilty. What Campbell was able to show in their defence was that all the information they had gathered was in the public domain, if you knew where to look, and Campbell did. Supposed top-secret government establishments were shown to be listed in the telephone directory.

The revelation of the true nature of the GCHQ marked the exposure of Britain's biggest Cold War secret, and the subsequent ABC trial marked the final collapse of the Cold War consensus around intelligence. Referring to the early days of the Cold War, Aldrich has proposed that initially many writers and journalists willingly cooperated with the intelligence services in the expanding role of cultural warfare. 'Thereafter, during the last two decades of the Cold War, other journalists developed a counter-culture of revelation, focusing the spotlight of investigative journalism upon what they considered to be governmental miscreants' (2009: 13–14).

Open Source Intelligence

In autumn 1975, I had started a three-year course at North East London Polytechnic, given a place by an enlightened admission process. I was a rarity, a working class student in what was effectively an Arts school, even if it was located in the then run-down East End. My year group were exotic and interesting, with quite a few international and mature students. Many of my lecturers had taught at the Hornsey School of Art and supported the famous 1968 student sit-in. For their temerity they were pointed towards the door. One of these lecturers was Richard Fletcher whose muckraking activities caught the interest of this twenty-one year old. I started helping Fletcher with his investigations into the CIA and intelligence excesses. As a natural extension of my interest I began attending the Agee-Hosenball Campaign, then the ABC campaign and started to make very tentative steps as a journalist by involving myself in *The Leveller*. I made a thirty-minute video documentary about the campaign as part of my coursework. I also helped Fletcher to produce pamphlets for the campaigns, typically A4 or A5 twenty-page documents with, say, some of the more interesting sections of the Church Committee report quoted in detail. Picking up the 'open source' approach, it was surprising what you could find in the public domain if you were looking imaginatively.

On one occasion, Fletcher thought it would be a good visualisation for one of our publications to show where the CIA operations to subvert the British Labour Movement were run from. 'What I need is a floorplan of the American Embassy.' Well, I asked, 'where the hell were we likely to get that from – a floorplan of the American Embassy. It must be classified, by definition.' Fletcher patiently explained to me that the Embassy was considered to be an architectural masterpiece by Finnish American modernist architect Eero Saarinen when it was built in Grosvenor Square in

1960. He pointed me to the Polytechnic library some miles away with instructions to look through the architectural magazines of the period. After some hours of sceptical browsing, sure enough, I found the floorplans of the American Embassy as published in 1962. The appropriate floor plan was printed in the next pamphlet suitably adorned with X marks the spot. It was my first lesson in open source research.

We also spent time researching the 1953 Iranian coup, which had appeared a largely popular domestic regime change until new evidence began to emerge. In early 1951 Mohammed Mossadeq, who appeared to be a progressive leftist reformer, was elected Prime Minister of Iran. His government nationalised the Anglo-Iranian Oil Company including its new refinery in Abadan. The then Labour Party Foreign Secretary Herbert Morrison decided not to pursue a legal remedy but decided that a coup was necessary, and set the SIS to depose Mossadeq. They were to work in conjunction with the five-year-old CIA.

The US and UK had no moral justification for the coup, just naked national self-interest. It is an interesting 'what if' question as to what would have happened if Mossadeq had been left in power. Since the violent overthrow of the Western placeman, the Shah, in 1979, Iran has been a hard line anti-Western nation under various Shi'ite fundamentalist governments for which the current version is key to the massive Sunni–Shi'ite power split in the Middle East. As would prove to be the case time after time, covert action looked like a good hairy-chested solution to neutralise truculent states and may well have proved to be in the short term useful to Western interests, but in the long term those interventions may well have backfired badly.

Turbulent Times

As the 1970s passed, the British state was trying to clamp down on all this investigative journalism with arrests and injunctions, but it only encouraged further revelations. Week on week more information became known. Sources – those who had been involved – felt the sense of new era, where repressing nationalist movements in the colonies was no longer seen as a god given right of the British

Empire, and were now prepared to speak out. British Intelligence had been involved in many coups, from Iran to Indonesia, often with unintended and unfortunate consequences. The new generation of journalists remained fully in the public sphere but outside the pre-existing institutional intelligence–media relationships, with their only intelligence sources tending to be dissident officers. The consequence of the new wave was to put pressure on the entrenched cosy London club-based relationships of the old guard that now neither protected the services nor produced front-page stories.

The British security services faced real testing issues in the late 1960s into the 1970s. As consequences of the 1968 student movements across many parts of the world, some participants took up extreme ideological positions. Britain never had a full-blown equivalent to the left-wing revolutionary movements like the Red Brigades or the Red Army Faction. However, it did have the Angry Brigade, a rather less substantial grouping than its German and Italian equivalents, who nonetheless, between 1970 and 1972, launched a bombing campaign with targets including banks, embassies, the 1970 Miss World event and the homes of Conservative Cabinet ministers like Robert Carr. MI5 attributed twenty-five bombings to the Angry Brigade, that mostly caused property damage; one person was slightly injured. But it was a real threat. After a police raid on a house in Hackney, a number of the Angry Brigade were arrested and eventually sent to prison. *The Observer*'s Martin Bright notes that the tabloids had a field day over the trial of long-haired dropouts in communes with stories about orgies. 'The people they arrested that August day on Amhurst Road fitted perfectly the Establishment's picture of dissolute middle-class revolutionaries plotting to undermine civilised values' (Bright 2002a). The rise and fall of the Angry Brigade was another indication that the pacifist ideals of the 1960s were fading quickly, faced with harsh economic reality.

If the country felt tense in the 1970s when Edward Heath and Jim Callaghan were prime ministers, the next election and decade would see the country in strife. In 1979 in a gender and political breakthrough, Margaret Thatcher was elected bringing with her a new style of right-wing politics and now seen as the beginning of the neoliberal turn in Britain. The 1980s were to be marked by further conflict over intelligence and secret propaganda.

Notes

1. Considered one of the best journalists of his generation Knightley died in 2016 at the age of eighty-seven.
2. Lohan was a former section chief at SOE.
3. The new wave of investigative journalism was encapsulated by the work of Woodward and Bernstein and a condensed version of both their names, 'Woodstein', became a signifier of the phenomenon.
4. London's *Time Out* was not then the flimsy giveaway magazine it is now but a substantial, paid for radical magazine with a considerable events listings section.
5. In February 1946 GC&CS begin a reorganisation and five months later was renamed the Government Communications Headquarters (GCHQ) within the jurisdiction of the Foreign Office. In 1952 GCHQ moved its centre of operations and then other sections, including the Joint Technical Language Service and Communications Security, to Cheltenham.
6. Odd as it may now seem, *Time Out's* readers included the 1970s London's radical demi-monde, who were informed in Marxist and Foucaultian analysis, and were genuinely interested in deconstructions of the real nature of the state and power.
7. Agee was accused of having approached the Soviets, who suspicious of him rejected his advances. But then it was claimed he was successfully recruited by Cuban intelligence.
8. Mark Hosenball was and remains a highly respected veteran journalist in the USA.

TEN

The Thatcher Years

I had joined *The Observer* as a researcher in June 1978 – working my way to reporter status. In 1982, I was assigned by *The Observer* news editor to cover the regular Ministry of Defence (MoD) briefings in Whitehall on the progress of the Falklands campaign. Shortly before, on 2 April, an Argentinian naval task force had invaded the Atlantic Islands of South Georgia and the Falklands and proclaimed sovereignty over these distant remnants of the British Empire. It was especially tense for *The Observer* as two of our journalists, writer Ian Mather and photographer Tony Prime, had been arrested along with a *Sunday Times* reporter near the port of Ushuaia in the south of Argentina and charged with espionage. They were not spies – I knew *The Observer* team well – just excellent journalists going about their work.

The Argentinian invasion of South Georgia and the Falklands Islands was a serious intelligence failure for the British, not least because Argentinian intentions had been identifiable for some time. The embarrassing debacle cost the Foreign Secretary Lord Carrington his job. The prime minister's response was to order a British military task force to assemble that was deemed capable of recapturing the Islands even though they are some 8,000 miles away from the British Isles. The task force sailed on 25 April with another *Observer* reporter, Pat Bishop, on board, arriving at the Falklands after a month-long voyage. This counter-invasion had looked fraught, with the Argentine Air Force successfully launching air-to-sea missile attacks on HMS *Sheffield* and HMS *Sir Galahad*.

This demonstrated British military vulnerability in fighting a war many thousands of miles from any base. It stretched the intelligence services, and success was probably made possible by President Reagan's support in providing non-military resources and approving intelligence collaboration. The National Security Agency's intercept of Argentinian communications was particularly useful.

After seventy-four tense days, recapturing the Falkland Islands was hailed as a great success for Prime Minister Thatcher and the British military. Some 900 people, mostly military, from both sides had been killed. After the war, Thatcher appointed a committee of Privy Counsellors, under the chairmanship of Lord Franks, with the following terms of reference.

> To review the way in which the responsibilities of Government in relation to the Falkland Islands and their Dependencies were discharged in the period leading up to the Argentine invasion of the Falkland Islands on 2 April 1982, taking account of all such factors in previous years as are relevant; and to report. (Franks 1983: para. 1)

The Franks Report largely exonerated the government.

The intelligence failure did lead to a major restructuring in the way Britain's spies functioned. It was noted that indications of the invasion were clear from newspapers in Buenos Aires during late 1981 and early 1982. Franks saw all the intelligence available during the conflict and stated that 'the changes in the Argentinian position, were, we believe more evident on the diplomatic front and in the associated press campaign than in the intelligence reports' (Franks 1983: para. 316). Sometimes open source research and reading the news is better than focusing on covert intelligence gathering. After the Franks Report the Foreign Office ceased control over foreign intelligence briefing and the Joint Intelligence Committee (JIC) became a Cabinet Office organisation with direct access to the prime minister. After the success of the Falklands campaign the Conservatives returned to the top of the opinion polls by a wide margin and went on to win the following year's general election. Of the 900 people killed, more than 320 were from the sinking of the Argentinian warship the *General Belgrano*. On the War Cabinet's orders it had been sunk by a torpedo from the submarine HMS *Conqueror* on Sunday 2 May.

The Observer team spent a great deal of time investigating the Belgrano Affair. Controversy arose as to whether the *Belgrano*, which was outside the maritime exclusion zone,[1] was heading for the task force or turning away when it was torpedoed and sunk, and there were allegations that the government had lied that the cruiser was heading towards the task force. I had been working in a partnership with former *Guardian* journalist David Leigh since September 1981 in an attempt to compete with the numerous and heavily resourced *Sunday Times* Insight team. The then news editor, Robin Lustig,[2] proposed the partnership and it worked, and over the 1980s would be deemed a journalistic success.

While the public at large were pleased with the result of the Falklands conflict, which had boosted Britain's flagging status in the world, there was a backlash at the suggestion that it was necessary to kill 320, mostly young, Argentinians if they were moving out of the combat area. David Leigh went to the Caribbean to track down a crewmember from HMS *Conqueror* who was thought to know where the ship's log of the *Conqueror* had disappeared. Finding it might have indicated whether the *Belgrano* was moving further into or out of the exclusion zone. It has never been recovered.

Your Disobedient Servant

Pursuing the *Belgrano* story also brought us into contact with Clive Ponting, a senior civil servant at the MoD. Ponting had discreetly sent two documents, subsequently nicknamed 'the Crown Jewels',[3] to Labour MP Tam Dalyell in July 1984 concerning the sinking of the Argentinian submarine. The documents were internal memoranda concerning the change in the rules of engagement for the British Task Force in the South Atlantic, and a letter drafted by the Defence Secretary, Michael Heseltine, which was never sent. The internal memo recommended how sensitive information about the circumstances surrounding the decision to sink the *Belgrano* be withheld from the Commons Select Committee on Foreign Affairs (Leigh 1984). The government sought to find the source of the leak and after Ponting admitted revealing the information, the Ministry of Defence suspended him without pay. On 17 August 1985, he was charged under Section 2 of the Official Secrets Act of 1911.

David Leigh had dropped a contact note round at Clive Ponting's Islington home address and we met and became closely involved in the case. An intense, slightly built and thoughtful man, Clive Ponting later wrote that he leaked documents because a series of lies led to a two-year-long systematic cover-up designed to stop Parliament and the public from finding out the truth. When he explained what had really happened to an MP, he was prosecuted in a trial which the government ensured was held partly in camera and in which key documents had gone missing or not been revealed.

> The logbook of HMS *Conqueror*, the submarine that sank the *Belgrano*, had been lost in circumstances that have never been explained and even a month long enquiry by Scotland Yard has found no clues. The crucial diplomatic telegrams over the weekend of the sinking have been concealed. Even when I wrote the Top Secret intelligence report now known as the 'Crown Jewels' I was not allowed to see these telegrams. . . . No wonder that Michael Heseltine thought there might be a 'Watergate' in here somewhere. (Ponting 1985: i)

Ponting was later acquitted by a jury that decided, against the direction of the presiding judge, that it was in the public interest for the documents to be released. In the years following Ponting's acquittal, the *Belgrano* question has never completely gone away.

A Country at War with Itself

Britain's spies were the subject of many of *The Observer* stories we wrote in the 1980s. With the Second World War four decades in the past, insiders present at great events were more prepared to talk and a great deal of historical evidence about intelligence operations emerged. It often takes thirty years or more to get any indication of what MI5 or SIS really do.

In 1984 we investigated the case of Michael Bettaney, an MI5 officer who had worked in Belfast and who was jailed in April that year in an Old Bailey court hearing largely held in camera. He had passed secret information on to the Soviets and was sentenced to twenty-three years in prison. It was clear from our research that Bettaney was a very unsuitable recruit and, what was more, he was politicised by the reactionary attitudes he found with Britain's Security Service. MI5's management of Bettaney was a disaster as they failed to notice all the signs of his disillusionment including his heavy drinking. He was assigned to Northern Ireland and was appalled by the British policy there. We noted in our coverage of Bettaney's recruitment that MI5's chief in the 1970s, Sir Michael Hanley, ran a largely unaccountable elite of about 200 predominately public school men. 'They sought out the Oxford research academic Bettaney as a working class intellectual' (Observer Reporters 1984).

Hanley had finally retired in 1978 but little changed. After a brief interim period, Margaret Thatcher promoted Hanley's old deputy, Sir John Jones, to the director's job and we reported some colleagues thought him politically malleable and dim. 'The exposure of the Blunt scandal weakened his position, and Mrs Thatcher ordered an expansion of surveillance, particularly upon CND, miners and sources of journalistic "leaks"' (Observer Reporters 1984). As it says on the MI5 website, the agency's reputation 'had been damaged by the public recriminations provoked by the Bettaney Affair, whose impact had been heightened by the uncommunicative management style of Sir John Jones'.[4] The subsequent Security Commission inquiry into Bettaney's betrayal was critical of the Service's personnel management, and Sir Antony Duff, a senior diplomat, was appointed director general to institute major reforms in the Security Service.

Deception Operations

Over several years in the 1980s, we investigated the plight of British nuclear test veterans of the post-war period who claimed they had been exposed to excessive radiation and were having serious health problems. It took years to prove, but they were right and some died early or suffered illnesses as a result of their military service at the nuclear weapon tests. It was while undertaking this research that I caught a first hint of revival of the genre of intelligence deception campaigns from the Second World War, adapted for the Cold War. Operation Hurricane was the British atom bomb tests that took place in the Monte Bello Islands off the Australian coast in October 1952. A senior official told me of a cunning plan to deceive the Soviets. The military planners did not want the Soviets to know the date of the tests, as they believed that the communists might either sabotage it or undertake air sampling of the fallout, which would reveal a great deal about the design of the bomb. One of the key components of the plot was to plant a story in the *Sunday Express*, designed to mislead the Soviets, along with their usual readers.

Operation Tigress, a deception ruse, was conceived and used Whitehall intelligence contacts with Fleet Street. A features writer of the *Sunday Express*, John Garbutt, and the long-time editor, Harold Keeble, were approached to help with the fake story. Both newspapermen were apparently very keen to help. The *Sunday Express* ran the story with the required deliberately incorrect information.[5] The only person who was apparently upset was Prime Minister Winston Churchill. He had been informed twice of the deception operation, but the briefings slipped his memory. When the *Sunday Express* story was published, Churchill then expressed his ambivalence over the use of deception in peacetime. Lord Alexander, the Minister of Defence, noted that while Churchill accepted the deception had worked, the Prime Minister had then observed, 'but it is a nice question how far this weapon should actually be used in times of peace ...' (Dylan 2015: 4).[6]

On the Edge

In 1984 we were approached by an unemployed former student called Peter Edge, then twenty-eight, who had realised he had been caught between the Stasi and MI5 and wanted to go public. For the previous three years, Edge, a fluent German speaker, had been supplying information on military studies to the East Germans, under instruction from MI5. He had been paid by both sides for his services and until the week before we published he was still in direct contact with both his East German and British 'controls'.

Fearing for his safety, he told his story to *The Observer* and we verified his claims by watching him meet his contacts and checking out his handler's phone numbers. As part of the verification process, on one occasion we watched Edge meet his MI5 contact 'Bill Hackforth' at Temple Meads Station in Bristol. His description of a double agent's uncertain life shed more light on the reality of how the intelligence world operated than did most speculative accounts of the secret service (Leigh and Lashmar 1984b). He had been recruited while living frugally in an anarchist squat in West Berlin in 1981.

Revelation after revelation over intelligence failures were published in 1985. Around this time, I used often to walk pass the MI5 building at 140 Gower Street, which towered over Euston Square tube station, a six-storey building that was anonymous but at the same time ugly and forbidding. MI5 had moved in in 1976. Looking at the windows, which had bomb blast resistant net curtains and security cameras, I would ponder what else was going on in that subdued interior. The allegations of disillusioned former Security Service officers like Cathy Massiter and Miranda Ingram were disturbing. The profound worries expressed by Massiter, a substantial witness, focused on F Branch (counter-subversion) being tasked to provide intelligence in support of the Ministry of Defence which, under Michael Heseltine, had set up an anti-Campaign for Nuclear Disarmament (CND) body called Defence Secretariat 19 (DS19).

Massiter's concern was that MI5 was failing to observe the provisions of the Maxwell-Fyfe directive forbidding it from acting on behalf of a political party or group. Massiter had been responsible for the surveillance of CND from 1981 to 1983, and then turned whistle-blower to a Channel 4 programme *MI5's Official Secrets*. She said that her tasking was determined more by the political significance of CND than by any security threat posed by subversive elements within it, and argued that MI5 was contravening the rules governing its practices. While still at the Security Service in 1983, she analysed telephone intercepts on John Cox, the vice president of CND, and that gave her access to conversations with Joan Ruddock and Bruce Kent. Massiter claimed that the decision was taken to tap John Cox's phone although, 'MI5 had absolutely no evidence, as required by the guidelines, that . . . he was engaged in any major subversive or espionage activity' (Leigh 1986: 1).

Nevertheless, Leon Britain, then Home Secretary, signed the warrant and Cox's phone was tapped. MI5 also placed a spy, Harry Newton, in the CND office who claimed that the campaign group was controlled by extreme left-wing activists and that Bruce Kent might be a crypto-communist. Massiter found no evidence to support either opinion (Andrew 2009: 675).

When we at *The Observer* sought to publish the details of the Security Service lawbreaking supplied by Cathy Massiter, the Treasury solicitor tried to ban us from doing so. Our lawyer Stephen Nathan told the judge in chambers that the application was 'the most iniquitous, outrageous and dangerous I have ever heard in all my career at the Bar' (Leigh 1986: 1). Treasury counsel withdrew halfway through the hearing. It seemed to us there was extensive evidence that the intelligence and security services were not being held to account from within government and were far exceeding their powers. Either that or they were encouraged by the government of the time.

MI5 Vetting of the BBC

In 1985 David Leigh, Mark Hollingsworth and I obtained concrete evidence for the first time of the way the Security Service, MI5, secretly controlled the hiring and firing of BBC staff. The story was splashed across the front page of *The Observer* with the headline; 'Revealed: how MI5 vets BBC staff' and then continued in the main body of the paper (Leigh and Lashmar 1985b: 1, 9).[7] Senior executives at the BBC had revealed to us a series of cases in which the careers of journalists, directors and broadcasters were blighted by MI5 blacklisting. The BBC had always officially denied any interference by MI5 and the most disturbing aspect of the vetting system, aside from that it happened at all, was that often the blacklisting was quite misguided or based on simple errors of fact.

There is no tally but most likely hundreds of people had their careers disrupted by MI5's vetting. To bring home the full inequity of the system we provided a series of case studies. Those blacklisted for periods of their careers include two television directors, Stephen Peet (who later went on to make the 'Yesterday's Witness' series for BBC) and John Goldschmidt; journalist Isabel Hilton;[8] and numerous young film editors, reporters and producers accused of having left-wing sympathies.

In 1984, the BBC had a staff of almost 30,000 and we discovered that all current affairs appointees, together with many of those involved in the actual making of programmes including directors and film editors were vetted. We also established who ran the system. It operated, unknown to almost all BBC staff, from Room 105 in an out-of-the way corridor on the first floor of Broadcasting House – a part of that labyrinth on which George Orwell modelled his Ministry of Truth in *Nineteen Eighty-Four*. We got through the tight security of the BBC reception with help from friends within the BBC who were appalled at the vetting system. We found Room 105 and the legend on the door – 'Special Duties-Management' – gave little away. Behind that door sat Brigadier Ronnie Stonham, 'Sp.A. to D.Pers.' As special assistant to the BBC's director of personnel, his job, with a team of three assistants, was to liaise with MI5, which was then headed by the diplomat Sir Antony Duff. Brigadier Stonham, a signals officer with an intelligence background who left the Army in 1982, had the job of passing the names of successful candidates to MI5 to be vetted. They called what they were doing 'college' or 'the formalities' (Leigh and Lashmar 1985b: 9).

For internal BBC staff who applied for promotion, MI5 kept continuous political surveillance on those it considered 'media subversives' – a category which could include directors, film editors, even actors. Their files were pegged with a symbol that looked like a Christmas tree. That meant that a second, secret file was held in Room 105. Some of these merely contained intimate personal details. If a staff member in this category was shortlisted, the second file, a buff folder with a round red sticker and the legend 'secret', was given to the department head, who had to sign for it. This process was concealed from the individual concerned, who had no idea what was being used against them.

The names of outside applicants were submitted to F Branch 'domestic' subversion desks at MI5. They were fed into a computer containing the details of 500,000 'subversives'. The vetting operation was run by C Branch, who also obtained access to other private information from major private companies. Cathy Massiter, who was a junior officer at MI5 in the mid-1970s, described to us how lists of BBC candidates would pass across her desk for approval. Often the word from MI5 that it regarded a person as a 'security risk' was enough to have him or her permanently blacklisted. Ordinary interviewing board members were not encouraged to ask questions. A particularly bizarre aspect of the system was that BBC boards, when interviewing candidates, were expressly forbidden to ask them openly about their political views.

The blacklisting system had been in place for four decades. 'As early as 1933 a BBC executive, Col Alan Dawnay, had begun holding meetings to exchange information with the head of MI5, Sir Vernon Kell, at Dawnay's flat in Eaton Terrace, Chelsea' (Reynolds 2018). In 1985 we found that senior BBC executives were fearful of speaking out about vetting because of the Official Secrets Act and victims of blacklisting were generally too frightened to admit it. However, two former BBC director generals described the system to us, and executives holding past and current senior BBC posts described what happened in eight specific cases. When MI5's claims were challenged they often dissolved into instances of, at best, over-zealousness and, at worst, false information against the applicant.

Only a year after he had graduated from his art college in London, John Goldschmidt, a bright, young film director, was asked to make a film for the BBC 'Omnibus' series. Goldschmidt could not believe his luck. The year was 1969 and the film was to be about the occupation by students of the Hornsey Art College. During filming, he discovered that police had been checking the details of a car he had hired and had been watching his house. Soon after, without warning, the BBC cancelled Goldschmidt's film on Hornsey without explanation.

Two years later the BBC once again asked him to make a film – this time a *Play for Today* about school-leavers based on an existing script. He was installed in an office in Television Centre and prepared to set about a production. Once again he was stopped from working and an embarrassed executive told him: 'You're not supposed to be allowed to work here.' A major row erupted in the BBC drama department about Goldschmidt's treatment and the truth of his double sacking was revealed. He had been blacklisted and Goldschmidt's 'offence' was to have taken part in an exchange of students between his art college and a Czech film school, spending a few weeks in Czechoslovakia. He was not, nor ever had been, a communist. After an outraged deputation went to see Huw Wheldon, at that time Managing Director, Television, the banning was eventually lifted. But Goldschmidt was by no means the only victim of the BBC's secret blacklisting system.

At about the same time that Goldschmidt had been cleared, one of the BBC's brightest graduate trainees, Michael Rosen, known as an Oxford student activist, was blacklisted by MI5. Rosen had caused ripples during his BBC training by making a radio documentary about the French Marxist, Regis Debray, and the US Embassy in Grosvenor Square had complained about another Rosen project, which used film clips of US soldiers being tested with the drug LSD.

In 1972, Rosen was sacked. He was told that no department was prepared to offer him a job. This was quite untrue. John Laird, then in charge of graduate recruitment, said: 'I was called by the chairman of one board, who said "You'll be glad to know we've appointed Rosen." Then he called again, embarrassed, and said it had been "blocked."' Rosen had made no secret of his political attitudes when he was originally appointed, telling the board he had Marxist views. He has subsequently become something of a national treasure. He served as Children's Laureate from June 2007 to June 2009, and he has been a TV presenter and a political columnist.

The following year, 1973, MI5 attempted to blacklist Isabel Hilton from a job as a TV reporter in Scotland, based on secret allegations that were, as it turned out, completely false. By chance, the then controller of BBC Scotland, Alastair Hetherington, former editor of *The Guardian*, knew her personally. When we put Ms Hilton's name to him, he confirmed the case:

I refused to accept it. It was inconceivable. There was obviously some mistake. As a result of my protests, eventually a personnel man came up from London and said she was an organiser of a pro-Chinese group-SACU, the Society for Anglo-Chinese Understanding. It was a clerical error. She was a Chinese linguist and had agreed to act as secretary to a completely different academic body based in the Chinese Department at Edinburgh University: SCA, the Scottish China Association. (Leigh and Lashmar 1985b: 9)

Hilton, having despaired of delays lasting weeks, described by the BBC as 'administrative referral to London', decided to leave Scotland and accepted a job elsewhere. She is now one of the UK's most respected journalists. She was shocked when we told her why she had been denied the Scottish job: 'I suppose what those people did change my life without me ever knowing' (Leigh and Lashmar 1985b: 9). She was lucky, had Hetherington not discovered the mistake and followed it up, she would have been permanently blacklisted, and kept in the dark.

In 1981, a board met to consider whom to appoint as editor of the *Listener*, the BBC's own magazine for its radio audience. After a brilliant presentation from Richard Gott, later *The Guardian*'s features editor, he was chosen. However, MI5 had other ideas. 'His file went off for "colleging" said one senior executive, and it was blocked. They said he was an ultra-leftist. The phrase was: "He digs with the wrong foot"' (Leigh and Lashmar 1985b: 9). After an unexplained delay, another applicant, Russell Twisk, was appointed editor. Some years previously Gott stood as a by-election candidate for the Radical Alliance against the Vietnam War. He also spent three years in Latin America where he openly supported Che Guevara and the Bolivian guerrillas. The Bolivian regime arrested him alleging he was engaged in communism. He had also caused tension when broadcasting on the Foreign Office-funded BBC World Service and supporting trade unionists in the then British colony of Aden.

Later Gott's own actions were to cause him embarrassment. Gott became literary editor of *The Guardian*, but resigned from the latter post in December 1994 after it was alleged in the *Spectator* and *Sunday Times* that he had been an 'agent of influence' for the KGB. These were claims he rejected, arguing that 'Like many other journalists, diplomats and politicians, I lunched with Russians during the Cold War.'[9] He asserted that his resignation was 'a debt of honour to my paper, not an admission of guilt', because of his failure to inform his editor of three trips abroad to meet with KGB officials at their expense.[10] He is probably an example where MI5 might reasonably say that history has shown that they were right. The six victims of blacklisting were prepared to be publicly identified but others were not. I can recall spending a very long session in the pub with a man who became a well-known BBC broadcaster who had been blacklisted and his career put on hold. However, he ultimately decided that it was not a smart move to go public about a 1970s fling with Maoism.

In 1952, General Sir Ian Jacob was appointed Director General by Churchill. He remembered during his induction at the BBC: 'I was shown lists of communists in the BBC. It was handled by the Controller of Administration. A relative of mine was actually on the list: he had a Communist wife' (Leigh and Lashmar 1985b: 9). Throughout the 1960s, Hugh Carleton Greene, as Director General, headed a new liberalisation of the stuffy BBC. However, behind the scenes vetting continued at that time under the head of administration, John Arkell. By the time Ian Trethowan, a man of known ultra-conservative views, became Director General in 1975, the vetting system was elaborate and extensive. Trethowan thought the BBC's political balance was too left-wing.

> One BBC old hand John Laird recalled a conversation when he asked me why I had hired so many reds as general trainees. 'I said they weren't Communists but Trotskyists, Maoists, all sorts of groups. All the brightest young people were left wing in those days. Trethowan said, "They're all the same to me. They're all Commies."' (Leigh and Lashmar 1985b: 9)

When publishing we made the point that even if the system was cleaned up and acknowledged: 'The real "moles" – if they exist – are buried too deep to be discerned by such an inaccurate and incompetent vetting procedure' (Leigh and Lashmar 1985b: 9).[11]

As a consequence of our 1985 articles the BBC staff and the National Union of Journalists eventually had the vetting system overturned, although it did not cease entirely until the 1990s. The story of MI5 vetting (or, more accurately, blacklisting) at the BBC has resurfaced from time to time as more information has been uncovered. In late 1987, we had found another case study. MI5 had tried to have broadcaster Anna Ford secretly sacked from the BBC on the grounds that a former boyfriend, Trevor Hyett, had once been a communist (Leigh and Lashmar 1987b). A senior executive fought for her to remain on the *Man Alive* programme. Later Ford became ITN's first female newsreader.

Vetting popped up again in the news when, in 2006, the *Sunday Telegraph* obtained confidential papers that revealed that the BBC had allowed MI5 to investigate the backgrounds and political affiliations of thousands of its employees, including newsreaders, reporters and continuity announcers. It reported: 'The files, which shed light on the BBC's hitherto secret links with the Security Service, show that at one stage it was responsible for vetting 6,300 different BBC posts – almost a third of the total workforce' (Hastings 2006).

Thirty years later, I am more convinced than ever that secretly vetting and blacklisting people without giving them a chance to challenge the veracity of the information on which their blacklisting was based is an insidious breach of their human rights (Lashmar 2015d: 598). In these acts we also find MI5 denying the rights of others to enter the public sphere. What David Leigh and I did not know until 2018 was that, at the same time, Margaret Thatcher's government drew up a secret blacklist of its own civil servants thought to be 'subversives' in order to keep them under observation and block their promotion. Whitehall departments worked with MI5 to identify 1,420 civil servants to be closely watched and, where possible, kept away from computers and revenue collection roles (Cobain 2018b). The majority, 733 people, were identified as Trotskyists, and another 607 as communists. Forty-five were said to be fascists, and thirty-five Welsh or Scottish nationalists, 'black or Asian racial extremists' or anarchists. According to documents released into the National Archives, MI5 also compiled lists of suspect local councillors and active trade unionists deemed to be of similar concern.

Robert Armstrong (who was later to give evidence in Australia against the publication of *Spycatcher*) and other senior civil servants then decided to revive a 1970s Whitehall body known as the Inter-departmental Group on Subversion in Public Life (SPL) with representatives from MI5, Scotland Yard's Special Branch and each of the major government departments. It had four staff members – including two senior MI5 officers, Royd Barker and Stella Rimington – and produced annual reports. One SPL chair, John Chilcot – who later conducted the inquiry into the Iraq War – wrote in June 1988: 'It is right on balance to continue with this exercise, despite its acute sensitivity and the high risk of embarrassment in the event of any leak' (Cobain 2018b). Three decades after the end of BBC vetting, it has not become, despite the warnings of these establishment figures, a Marxist cabal.

Sources

Working as an investigative team, the Leigh and Lashmar stories came from a variety of sources. Sometimes we just dug deep into the current running big story. Other times proven sources gave us a tip. We were getting a strong roster of inside sources in Whitehall, intelligence, the law and in law enforcement. In other cases, freelance journalists brought stories to us knowing we were the most likely paper to further research, pay the freelance for their time and get their story in print. We also started to cooperate with TV journalists. This had been beyond the pale for print journalists in the past but we took the view at *The Observer* that it increased our research resources and, ultimately, TV and print were not in direct competition. Then there were people who approached us for the first time and we had to verify who they were and what they claimed. Some stories were discarded quickly; others made the newspaper and sometimes the front page. One story came from a freelance journalist's tip off and proved to be a very peculiar tale.

Notes

1. On 2 April 1982 Britain declared a maritime exclusion zone (MEZ) of 200 nautical miles around the Falkland Islands within which any Argentine warship entering the MEZ might be attacked by British submarines. On 30 April it was upgraded to a total exclusion zone.
2. After a period as a distinguished foreign correspondent, Robin Lustig later became an anchor on BBC Radio 4's *The World Tonight* for many years.
3. <http://belgranoinquiry.com/sound-archive/clive-ponting-the-crown-jewels> (last accessed 29 October 2019).
4. <https://www.mi5.gov.uk/fr/node/310> (last accessed 20 September 2019).
5. DEFE 28/133, Text of Sunday Express article 'Atom Bomb', 15 August 1952.
6. I never did develop the story to the point where it could be published, but more recently the Kings College academic Huw Dylan did research and publish a full account.
7. This story was something of a peak for the Leigh and Lashmar partnership and was a major reason why we were awarded 'Reporters of the Year' in the 1986 UK Press Awards.
8. In 2019 Isabel Hilton was the distinguished chair of The Centre for Investigative Journalism (TCIJ).
9. Richard Gott, letter to the *The Sunday Times*, 24 September 2000.
10. Richard Gott, letter to the *The Sunday Times*, 24 September 2000.
11. The vetting system failed to pick up Guy Burgess who was a Soviet spy who worked for the BBC in two stints after 1936.

ELEVEN

Spycatcher

The most bizarre story we wrote in the 1980s concerned the recording of a purported sinister Reagan–Thatcher telephone conversation. The cassette tape of the transatlantic call, apparently picked up by anonymous eavesdroppers, had been widely circulated. A cover letter with the faked tape said it had come from a source at British Telecom (then the UK national telephone company) and that it had been overheard on a crossed line.[1] The jumpy and clipped conversation leapt from Reagan urging restraint on Mrs Thatcher in the Britain–Argentina Falklands War and criticising her actions, to an incredulous Mrs Thatcher questioning Reagan about nuclear war in Europe. The tape has Reagan saying, 'In conflict, we will launch missiles on allies for effective limitation of the Soviet Union' (Leigh and Lashmar 1984d).

A Crass Hoax

The tape had been taken seriously by some and played on national TV news. *The Sunday Times* published a story about the tape. The front page story was headlined 'How the KGB fools the West's press' (Ellsworth-Jones 1984: 1). The CIA and the State Department had taken the bait and said it was an example of the Soviet KGB intelligence agency's attempts to fool the Western press. The State Department had said:

From the drift of the tape, the evident purpose was to cause problems for Mrs. Thatcher, by blaming her for the sinking of the British destroyer

Sheffield, and also for us by stirring trouble on the INF [Intermediate Nuclear Forces talks in Geneva] issue. (Ellsworth-Jones 1984: 1)

A contact tipped me that the tape was in fact a fake produced by the Crass punk band and anarchist collective. I rang and asked to visit and drove to the farm in Essex where the collective lived. Two members of Crass, Andy Palmer, then twenty-seven, and Pete Right, thirty-four, guitarists and spokespersons for the band, admitted immediately that they had faked the tape as an anarchist statement and showed me how they had made the tape. They had clipped individual words from both Thatcher and Reagan news interviews and strung them together. 'It is a hoax. We intended it to be a hoax, but what we said in the tape we believe is true', Palmer said, laughing. 'All this thing about the KGB press shows that the techniques they (the Americans) use aren't quite as infallible as we think they are.' Right said that making the tape was a three-month process of deciding on a script, making a 'rough cut . . . then an increasingly fine cut . . . making words out of syllables' (Leigh and Lashmar 1984d). It remains remarkable that the intelligence services took this tape in any way to be real.

The 1980s were prove an incomparable period for reporting on intelligence spy stories and they appeared in profusion. It was partly the breakdown of the 'Empire of Secrecy' leaving participants in the intelligence world far more prepared to talk openly. In 1986 David Leigh and I covered for *The Observer* the row over BBC Scotland's intention to broadcast a programme, part of a series called *Secret Society* made by the intelligence specialist, investigative journalist Duncan Campbell, which revealed that the government was intending to build a top spy satellite called Zircon without informing Parliament. As Zircon was deemed top secret, the Special Branch raided BBC Scotland's offices at the end of January 1987. The programme was never broadcast and Zircon was never built.

Leigh and I were also covering the Stalker Affair and working with our *Observer* colleague Jonathan Foster. We obtained evidence that undercover British death military squads had operated in Northern Ireland for a period, though we never discovered whether or not these had been officially sanctioned. These were strong stories that produced many column inches of stories over the months. We were also involved in a swathe of investigations in this period that had nothing to do with intelligence matters.

The Tasmanian Devil

One of the biggest stories in the 1980s was that of former MI5 senior officer Peter Wright. In 1984, *The Observer* ran a 'World Exclusive' about Wright's forthcoming book, a memoir written in retirement in Tasmania (Davies and Leigh 1984). A few weeks later we reported that the intelligence agencies were bringing a lot of pressure on three publishers to stop them bringing out memoirs by former intelligence officers. The story notes that both MI5 and GCHQ 'have threatened the publishers with prosecution under the Official Secrets Act or with expensive civil injunctions' (Leigh and Lashmar 1984c). This was a time when the intelligence agencies enforced an *omertà* on publication by their people except when it suited their own agenda.

The first and really the least appropriate target were the memoirs of Joan Miller, who was by then dead, who had worked for the wartime MI5 some forty years earlier. It was little different from a number of MI5 approved books like *The Man Who Never Was* by Ewen Montague which told tales of derring-do from the 1930s and the Second World War. Miller's book had been sent to the D-Notice Secretary, Admiral Ash, and he declared the text 'completely innocuous' but MI5 then threatened the publisher saying the manuscript 'included confidential material obtained by her in the course of her employment' (Leigh and Lashmar 1984c). The second book was an exposé of poor security and corruption at GCHQ's outstation in Hong Kong by a former radio traffic analyst, Jock Kane. An injunction was sought and obtained by legal officers on behalf of GCHQ. The third, and as was shortly to emerge, the most important, was the autobiography of Peter Wright. Miller's book was eventually published, initially in Ireland, away from the reach of the UK authorities. Kane's book remains banned to this day though most of the allegations had appeared in the *New Statesman* via intelligence journalist Duncan Campbell.

It was the third book that was to trigger a major legal battle with the British government. Peter Wright had written a book called *Spycatcher* about his time at MI5. We had first heard about Wright's book a few months earlier. *The Observer* had been working with Paul Greengrass of

Granada TV's *World in Action* programme.[2] He had filmed Peter Wright talking about betrayal and incompetence at MI5 and in July *The Observer* reported Wright's claims and that he had dossier on problems at MI5. He said he was prepared to defy the Official Secrets Act and told *The Observer*: 'Even now the service has failed to protect itself adequately against future penetration and the Bettaney case has just show how easy it still is' (Davies and Leigh 1984).

Peter Wright claimed in *Spycatcher* he was tasked to identify a Soviet mole in MI5. He claimed that his evidence showed the mole was the former MI5 Director General Roger Hollis. However, Wright's allegation that is now best remembered was of an abortive plot by MI5 officers against the left-of-centre British Prime Minister, Harold Wilson. He detailed numerous historic MI5 operations, many of which had been illegal. Wright recalled having fun in the 1950s: 'For five years we bugged and burgled our way across London at the State's behest, while pompous bowler-hatted civil servants in Whitehall pretended to look the other way' (Leigh and Lashmar 1984c).

According to Wright, in 1955, MI5 had initiated a covert operation called 'Party Piece' to obtain the secret membership list of the Communist Party. They knew the files were secreted in the Highgate house of a family called Berger who included members of the CPGB. An undercover MI5 officer became a tenant of the family. When it was known the family were away for the weekend, MI5 struck. They had assembled a team of burglars, a locksmith and a photographer, all protected by an MI5 team of watchers. 'In less than twelve hours – while the owner was away for the night – all 48,000 files had been stolen, their contents photographed and files replaced' (Wright 1987: 54–5).

A powerful motivating force for Wright to undertake publishing the book was that he had been infuriated by Mrs Thatcher's Commons statement in 1979 saying that there was insufficient evidence to prosecute Anthony Blunt, one of the Cambridge ring of spies who had been recruited to MI5 during the Second World War. An art historian by training, Blunt had gone on to become an establishment figure as the Surveyor of the Queen's Pictures. Wright thought that the Prime Minster had misled the House or had herself been misled by MI5. He then compiled a dossier on Soviet penetration.

In 1980, Wright had, at the prompting of former MI5 officer and member of the banking family, Victor Rothschild, showed his 150-page dossier to

Chapman Pincher, who used it for his book *Their Trade Is Treachery*. Wright had told Chapman Pincher about Party Piece and that the membership files revealed a series of public figures, top trade unionists and thirty-one MPs were covert members of the Communist Party. Wright received £30,000 for this collaboration, but to his profound disappointment, Pincher concluded that there was no need for an inquiry – the thing Wright wanted above all.

Pincher said that he decided not published the story of Party Piece 'because I judged it to be really damaging to national security' (Pincher 1987: 72). Wright told him the names of the some of the secret members, several of whom were still in the Commons or the Lords or were at the top of the trade union movement at the time. It was one of the many omissions in Pincher's book on Wright (1981). In this case, Wright sought to expose those public figures that had been in the Communist Party; he said they were all overtly members of the Labour Party.

These and many other omissions were his prime motivations to write *Spycatcher*. At *World in Action* and *The Observer* we were astonished at the cavalier way MI5 treated the law and also the rampant internal disputes which clearly had seriously hampered the organisation's efficiency. After a good deal of discussion, the editorial team took the view that the skulduggery at MI5 was a matter of public interest and should be published. We felt the public had a right to know. In *Spycatcher* Wright outlined an SIS plot to assassinate President Nasser at the time of the Suez Crisis and MI5's eavesdropping on high-level Commonwealth conferences (Wright 1987). Wright also revealed how the Egyptian codes were broken by GCHQ. Other allegations included:

- All diplomatic conferences at Lancaster House in London throughout the 1950s and 1960s were bugged by MI5, as were the Zimbabwe negotiations of 1979.
- Britain bugged diplomats from France, Germany, Greece and Indonesia, and used microphones hidden behind cipher machines.
- Soviet leader Nikita Krushchev's suite at the up-market hotel Claridge's was bugged during his 1950s visit to Britain.
- The Soviet spy Guy Burgess attempted unsuccessfully to seduce Churchill's daughter on Soviet instructions.
- The central allegation of his book was that Sir Roger Hollis (the head of MI5 from 1956 to 1965) had been a Soviet spy.
- There was also, almost incidentally, a reference to a plot by thirty MI5

officers to destabilise Harold Wilson's government in 1974. Wright
wrote that he was tempted to join the plot but instead decided to name
the conspirators to Sir Michael Hanley, then head of MI5.[3]

Wright detailed how MI5 had engaged with Cecil King, the chairman of
the company that owned the *Mirror* group of newspapers and part of the
Harmsworth publishing dynasty. The plot was to bring down the Wilson
government and replace it with a coalition led by Lord Louis Mountbatten,
a member of the royal family and a war hero. Wright claimed that: 'Cecil
King, who was a long-time agent of ours, made it clear that he would
publish anything MI5 might care to leak in his direction' (Wright 1987:
369). The *Mirror*'s editor Hugh Cudlipp arranged for King to meet Lord
Mountbatten, who had recently retired as Chief of the Defence Staff, and
who had been privately highly critical of the defence cuts made by the
government.

According to Cecil King's account in his memoirs, *Without Fear or
Favour* (1971) when he told Lord Mountbatten of his plans, Mountbatten
replied that there was anxiety about the government at the palace, and
that the Queen had had an unprecedented number of letters protesting
about Wilson. More evidence of a planned coup was to emerge later.
Dorril and Ramsay, the authors of *Smear! Wilson and the Secret State*
(1992), state King then delivered a version of his preoccupations at the
time – approaching economic collapse and ineffective government, with a
prime minister no longer able to control events. Public order was about to
break down leading to social chaos. There was a likelihood of bloodshed
in the streets. Within forty-eight hours, King had an op-ed published in the
Mirror, 'Enough is enough', under his by-line. In this confrontational piece of
rhetoric, he proclaimed:

> Mr Wilson and his government have lost all credit and we are now
> threatened with the greatest financial crisis in history. It is not to be resolved
> by lies about our reserves but only by a fresh start under a fresh leader.
> (Donnelly 2012: 144)

Less than month later the board of International Publishing Corporation unanimously dismissed King.

David Leigh and I investigated Wright's claims by talking to as many
former MI5 officers and Whitehall officials as possible. Soon it was clear:

Wright was accurate when he claimed MI5 had been riven by internal disputes and mutual suspicion for many years (it was very much in line with the political thinker Poulantzas' (1975) concept of elite schisms). Pessimistic about its chances against the British government, the publishers might have given up had not Malcolm Turnbull, a young Australian lawyer, taken the challenge offered by the case. Publication was to be in Australia. The British government sought to ban it in the Australian courts. The case was set for trial before Mr Justice Powell in the Equity Division of the New South Wales Supreme Court in 1986 (*Daily Telegraph* 1995).[4] On 22 June 1986, we published a story, 'MI5 memoirs to be revealed in courtroom' outlining what would come up in the court case (Leigh and Lashmar 1986).

That week the government took legal action against *The Observer* and *The Guardian* and during the following week and on 27 June obtained injunctions to ban us from reporting the contents of Wright's book. It was tense in the editorial offices that week — it was taken very seriously that the British government had injuncted us. Such an action had great potential for reputational loss and hefty legal bills for a paper that did not have enormous funds. We decided the best tactic was to point up the farcical nature of the government's attempts to close the stable door long after Wright had bolted. On 13 July we printed the same story as we had on 22 June, but this time with all the redactions we were required to use under the injunction to visually illustrate the extent of the farce.

However, on 26 July 1986 we failed in the Court of Appeal to lift injunctions. Sir John Donaldson, Master of the Rolls, sitting with Lord Justice Mustill and Lord Justice Nourse, said that freedom to publish the information from a former Security Service worker could not possibly be justified on the evidence before them. Sir John added that he regarded it 'in the highest degree unlikely' that publication could be justified on any further evidence that might be available at a full trial. Outside court, David Leigh told other journalists, 'The injunction is worthless because everything in the articles we have already published has now been said on the floor of the House of Commons.'

However, the government was still seeking to stop publication in the Australian courts. In a hearing that lasted five weeks, the British government stuck to its contention that Wright owed a duty of confidentiality, and that *Spycatcher* would damage the security services and help the Soviets and terrorists. Sir Robert Armstrong, the Cabinet Secretary, was the key witness for the British government and his evidence was widely ridiculed by the British press for its ambiguity and seemingly deceptive nature dominated by his one, supposedly light-hearted admission, that he had, on one occasion been 'economical with the truth' (Leigh 1987: 6).

When it came to his turn in the witness box, Wright presented himself as a patriot whose sense of duty gave him no choice but to break silence. The judge was persuaded, dismissing the proceedings and awarding costs to the defendants, rejected the claim that *Spycatcher* would harm British security. He noted that the government had done nothing to stop Pincher's book or programmes about MI5; he also said that much of Wright's information was old.

In mid-1987, a UK High Court judge lifted the ban on English newspaper reportage on the book, but in late July, the Law Lords again barred reporting of Wright's allegations. On 31 July the *Daily Mirror* published upside-down photographs of the three Law Lords, with the caption 'YOU FOOLS'. The UK edition of *The Economist* ran a largely blank page with just a box saying that in all but one country, their readers have on this page a review of *Spycatcher*. 'The exception is Britain, where the book and comment on it, have been banned. For our 420,000 readers there, this page is blank — and the law is an ass.'[5] Meanwhile in the USA where the book had been published trouble free, *Spycatcher* was shooting up the bestseller list to the number one position. I recall it was seen as a status symbol by many members of the public to have their own copy of the American version smuggled in personal baggage back to the UK.

The government's long battle ended in 1988, when the Law Lords unanimously rejected the government's demand for a blanket injunction to prevent the media's use of allegations by former Security Service officers. Later in 1988, the book was cleared for legitimate sale in the UK when the Law Lords acknowledged that overseas publication meant it contained no secrets and any damage to national security has already been done by its publication abroad. However, they agreed Mr Wright's book had indeed constituted a serious breach of confidentiality, the principle at the heart of the government's case against him for the last three years. Wright was barred from receiving royalties from the sale of the book in the UK. For us at *The Observer* it had been nerve-wracking year but it was also a significant one for press freedom.

The newspapers that had been injuncted took the case to the European Court of Human Rights to prevent future prior restraint becoming a government tool to block publication in other cases. In 1991 we partially won our case against the government in the Court, where the judges ruled that the British government had breached the European Convention of Human Rights in gagging its own newspapers. Their judgment has been seen as a keystone in the argument that the media must be able to publish freely as they play a 'vital role of public watchdog' and have a duty to impart information of public interest and the public had a right to receive it.[6] *Spycatcher* was to sell more than two million copies. In 1995, Wright died a millionaire from the proceeds of his book. It may have not been Wright's intention, but perhaps the most damning revelation was of the incompetence and exaggerated, destructive paranoia of his MI5 generation.

Official Contacts

In the 1980s the British government still did it best to prevent the identification of the heads of the British Intelligence agencies. In December 1985, the small para-political magazine *Lobster* published the name of the new head of SIS, Christopher Curwen.[7] A row broke out in Fleet Street about the naming but several mainstream news organisations identified Curwen. It was hardly a surprise that this man was a spy chief, at least for anyone who was familiar with his entry in the Diplomatic List. It was possible to work out who were SIS officers by using the 'open source' annual Diplomatic List that gave thumbnail sketches of the career of all Foreign Office staff and looking at the location and the timings of postings. All it required was a visit to the St Martin's Lane Library in central London, which was noted by researchers for having the most comprehensive collection of Diplomatic and Military Lists. Sir Christopher Curwen's biographical information showed that he had joined the Foreign Office from the Army in 1952 and had been posted to Thailand in 1954 and Vientiane, Laos, in 1956. He returned to London in 1958, had another spell in Bangkok from 1961 and then two years in Kuala Lumpur. Other posts followed. *Lobster* did this in the pre-internet age. The subsequent growth of the World Wide Web as a research tool has facilitated those who wished to identify British spies.

Back then a number of favoured journalists like Chapman

Pincher and Conservative MP and author Nigel West still had direct contact with the intelligence and security services. Yet there was still the political pretence that the agencies did not exist. They did not have a formal press officer, so most reporters were unable to contact them in order to ask questions and check facts. This *omertà* may have enhanced their mythical status but did not always work in the interest of the intelligence agencies. There was a constant flow of news stories published about the doings of Britain's spies. These stories would be attributed to 'sources' within MI5 or SIS or more generally 'intelligence sources'. Many were entirely speculative, even just plain made up, but effectively protected by the government position of neither confirming nor denying anything about intelligence. Therefore, journalists and editors could run any story they liked about spies in the less scrupulous media without fear of official contradiction.

The red-baiting *Daily Express* was the most enthusiastic purveyor of such stories but it was far from being on its own. Early in my career, I sat across the desk in the investigations office from an ambitious freelance who had a series of 'exclusives' he apparently sourced from within MI5. This reporter often made a show of seeming to call the MI5 contact on the phone in front of others and me. Then the reporter would discuss the phone call delivering the 'exclusive' with the editor, nonchalantly seeking support from his desk sharers as witnesses. After observing a couple of these calls I realised there was no one at the other end of the phone and it was all for show. However, as government policy was to 'neither confirm nor deny' intelligence matters no one officially challenged these stories.[8] It took a while for the freelancer's perfidy to be noticed and his work for the paper curtailed.

Editors did have routes to the intelligence agencies and I recall at *The Observer* in the 1970s and 1980s there was a back channel to MI5 via the editor Donald Trelford to the MI5's legal adviser Bernard Sheldon. It was used rarely and only when a story did have serious national security implications. I have no doubt this channel was available to other major national organisations. The channel mostly worked with a concerned Sheldon ringing Trelford after MI5 heard of our latest investigation. David Leigh and I manipulated this system; if we needed confirmation of a story, we would make sure that MI5 became aware that we were publishing something about the Security Service. If the editor then got a back route call from MI5, it gave us additional confirmation of the story. Chapman Pincher did not need to use such ruses as he handled both his relationship with Mandarins and spy chiefs, mostly conducted over expensive lunches around SW1, and his material carefully so as not to upset his key contacts.

Pincher was not alone in having contacts in British Intelligence. When he retired, Sandy Gall, the ITN foreign correspondent who graced TV screens from many a tricky location, talked about his relationship with the SIS. He spoke of meeting the head of SIS and other senior officers in Stone's Chop House in Piccadilly in the 1980s. It was the time of the Afghanistan mujahedeen guerrilla warfare with the Soviet occupiers. As Stewart Purvis noted, hacks talking to spooks has always been a sensitive subject in British journalism.

> The fact is that when British journalists return from places where dip-lomats find it hard to get to the Foreign Office will invite them in for a chat. If they go along it is, in effect, a de-briefing. Some will go along out of patriotic duty, others because they think that in return they will get information which means they will hopefully get to know more about what's going on. (Purvis and Hulbert 2013: 257)

The resourceful Gall infiltrated his team into Afghanistan for ITN:

> Soon after I returned to London', he stated in his memoirs, 'I received an invitation to have lunch with the head of MI6 . . . I was flattered of course, and . . . resolved to be completely frank and as informative as possible, and not try to prise any information put of him in return. (Gall 1994: 116–18, 158)

Apparently, 'C' – the head of SIS – wanted to ask Gall a ques-tion from the then Foreign Secretary: How can the war between the mujahedeen and the Red Army be kept centre stage? Gall told them get TV cameras in there, filming the action. Thereafter the SIS encouraged TV crews to get into Afghanistan. The Chop

House relationship continued with Gall reporting back to the SIS over more English culinary fare. In their book, which examined whether famous journalists crossed the profession's sacred ethical and professional lines, Stewart Purvis and Jeff Hulbert looked at Gall's admission and clearly believe that Sandy Gall stayed just the right side of the line (Purvis and Hulbert 2013: 260). While researching this book a few more journalists who had worked with or for British Intelligence in the past decided to tell their stories. After many years of denial that he had worked for the SIS, the famous British thriller author, Frederick Forsyth, admitted he had worked for the Service for two decades, from the 1950s, unpaid as he had perceived it to be his 'patriotic duty' (Forsyth 2015). He was a correspondent for the BBC and then the Reuters news agency, covering some highly sensitive areas, including postcolonial Nigeria, apartheid South Africa and East Germany during the Cold War. Forsyth was keen to make the distinction: he was not a spy for the SIS, but an asset. 'There was nothing weird about it; it was the Cold War', he claimed pointing out that an awful lot of the strength of British Intelligence came from the number of volunteers.

> A businessman might be going to a trade fair in a difficult to enter city and he'd be approached, quite gently, with a courteous "If you would be so kind to accept an envelope under your hotel door and bring it home ..." so that was what I did. I ran errands. (BBC 2015)

I had similar though less dramatic experiences. In one instance after I returned from a discreet half holiday, half journalistic tour of Equatorial Guinea in 1992, my travel companion and I were invited to the Foreign Office for a chat. I went along as much out of curiosity as anything else. There were no British government representatives in the strange two-site nation (a strip of mainland West Africa and an island once known as Fernando Po) of Equatorial Guinea. While we were there, we popped into the American Embassy and had a chat with the available embassy official, who, we later worked out, was the CIA station chief. For a small nation, Equatorial Guinea was riddled with intrigue, but it was becoming apparent that it had enormous gas and oil reserves. Combined with a corrupt dictator,

Equatorial Guinea had enormous potential for venal capitalists (see Lashmar 1992: 326).

Death on the Rock

The next major intelligence-related story for us at *The Observer* came in 1988, after three unarmed IRA operatives were shot dead in Gibraltar in March of that year by an SAS unit. There were suspicions that these deaths were an extension of an informal 'shoot-to-kill' policy against the IRA in Northern Ireland. An ITV channel, Thames TV, had a long-standing and highly regarded current affairs series at the time called *This Week*. Two journalists from the programme investigated and claimed that the IRA trio had been killed, without any opportunity to surrender. The programme, which went out some weeks after the killings, was widely criticised, really for even daring to question the morality of the killing of the terrorist trio. Under the editorship of Andrew Neil, *The Sunday Times*, in a flourish of patriotic fervour, launched a full-out attack on the *This Week* programme. Approached by a beleaguered *This* Week team of Julian Manyon and Chris Oxley, David Leigh and I at *The Observer* then agreed to undertake a forensic investigation. I was doubtful there was a news story about the actual killings. Some facts about Gibraltar were clear. The IRA was planning a 'spectacular' and the target was a military ceremony, to be attended by members of the public, many of whom would have been killed and injured. The plan had been uncovered by British Intelligence and initiating Operation Flavius, they liaised with their Spanish counterparts to prevent the bombing.

A fierce propaganda battle followed over the actual events. According to British officials immediately afterwards, the trio was said had been in the actual act of planting a bomb and had been shot in a firefight. The BBC reported that the bomb, which had been left in a car on Gibraltar, 'would have done enormous damage. It was something like five hundred pounds of explosives, packed with bits of metal, shrapnel and so on' (BBC *Radio 4 News* 1988). ITN said that 'a fierce gun battle broke out' and that 'army explosives experts used a robot to defuse the bomb' (*ITN News* 1988). These were incorrect reports. As broadcaster Jonathan Dimbleby put it in his introduction to the resultant *This Week* programme: 'The question, which goes to the heart of the issue, is this: did the SAS men have the law on their side when they shot dead Danny McCann, Sean Savage and Mairead Farrell, who were unarmed at the time?' (Bolton 2018). After reading through the huge bundle of witness statements we could see why the *This Week* team were concerned about the SAS operation. There was no evidence the Special Forces team were ordered to shoot to kill. However, their instructions and the operation made it extremely unlikely that the three unarmed IRA operatives were going leave Gibraltar in anything other than a coffin. Certainly, the intelligence they were operating on was right about the big picture – this was an active IRA cell. However, what we do not know to this day is how accurate the detailed intelligence briefing to the SAS actually was about the trio's plan.

So we investigated, and after some weeks work showed that there was substance to *This Week*'s allegations and there were inconsistencies in the government version of events.[9] However, our strongest story, 'Insight into distortion', published in early 1989, asserted that *The Sunday Times* (who were our major rivals) had published a distorted counterattack against *This Week*. We discovered several members of *The Sunday Times* investigation team were profoundly unhappy about the way the story had been handled by senior editorial staff, to the point that they wrote detailed memos of complaint to their bosses, copies of which we were able to obtain (Leigh and Lashmar 1989). *The Sunday Times* attack on *This Week*'s *Death on the Rock* programme remains controversial to this day. We also wrote another six stories in those months about a variety of inconsistencies in the evidence to the inquest into the shootings. *This Week* were courageous for broadcasting such a sober, controversial and anti-jingoistic programme asking the difficult questions, but such was the anger of Prime Minister Margaret Thatcher it possibly cost Thames TV its franchise.[10]

Decades later *Death on the Rock* remains controversial. In 2018, *The Sun* newspaper – stablemate of *The Sunday Times* – rasped in doggerel:

It is 30 years since TV journalists were condemned by the British
government for questioning the killing of an IRA squad

Thames Television can wriggle like a puff adder.

They can posture like Mick Jagger.

They can hold all the inquiries they wish into the truthfulness of
witnesses and the integrity of their journalists.

But they cannot alter basic truths.

Their programme, 'Death on the Rock', was an irresponsible,
mischievous, deeply shaming episode.

It should NEVER have been made.

It should NEVER have been broadcast.

As we entered the 1990s the world was changing both personally and politically. David Leigh and I had both left *The Observer* as the owner 'Tiny' Rowland's personal agendas leached across from the business section, where it had festered for some time, into the main body of the paper. We both went to TV current affairs and our separate ways.

Notes

1. Back in the pre-digital age, it was common for telephone calls to be suddenly interrupted by an unexpected caller, misconnected by the analogue technology. This was known as a crossed line.
2. Paul Greengrass would later go on to be a successful Hollywood director of films like the 'Bourne' series and *United 93*.
3. Wright's actual involvement in the Wilson Plot was later made clear. The Cabinet Secretary Lord Hunt authoritatively confirmed the central allegation. Hunt, who conducted a secret inquiry, said in August 1996: 'There is absolutely no doubt at all that a few, a very few, malcontents in MI5 . . . a lot of them like Peter Wright who were right-wing, malicious and had serious personal grudges – gave vent to these and spread damaging malicious stories about that Labour government. (Leigh 2009).
4. Turnbull would become the Prime Minister of Australia some thirty years later.
5. Editorial in *The Economist*, 25 July 1987. (UK edition)
6. *The Observer and Guardian v. The United Kingdom*, 51/1990/242/313, Council of Europe: European Court of Human Rights, 24 October 1991, <http://www.refworld.org/cases,ECHR,3ae6b7234.html> (last accessed 5 August 2018). See also <https://www.echr.coe.int/LibraryDocs/DG2/HRFILES/DG2-EN-HRFILES-18(2007).pdf> (last accessed 29 October 2019).
7. *Lobster* is published by Robin Ramsay from his home in Hull and is an amazing resource, pulling together information about intelligence from many different sources.
8. In the USA this is known as the Glomar Response.

9. MI5 have stated that the programme contained a number of errors (see Andrew 2009: 743–5).

10. It is often suggested that Margaret Thatcher made it clear that she did not want Thames TV's licence renewed because of *Death on the Rock*. It was not renewed in the next licence round but we do not know if the programme was the reason.

TWELVE

The Wall Comes Down

Britain's intelligence services were as taken as much by surprise by the Berlin Wall coming down in 1991 and the collapse of Communism as the public at large. The communist bloc disintegrated at a remarkable rate and with the sudden disappearance of the prime target of four decades of the Cold War, the intelligence and security services no longer had much of a party to go to. Mrs Thatcher and President Reagan assisted the transformation of the new Russia into an unfettered capitalist state by sending waves of neoliberal advisers to show the new 'democratic' government how to privatise the country's industries and natural resources.[1]

In the early 1990s, there was a new lighter mood in Britain and part of that was a desire for more openness and transparency in government and Whitehall. 'The Iron Lady', Margaret Thatcher, had been forced to resign as prime minister by her ministers in 1990. The first sign was a relaxation of the previously rigid rules that withheld government documents from the public for a minimum of thirty years.[2] This policy was driven by government minister, William Waldegrave, with the full approval of Margaret Thatcher's successor as prime minister, John Major. The 'Waldegrave Initiative for Open Government' was a milestone in open government in Britain. Speaking on the Radio 4 *Analysis* programme on 25 June 1992, Waldegrave said,

> I would like to invite serious historians to write to me . . . those who want
> to write serious historical works will know, probably better than we do, of

blocks of papers that could be of help to them which we could consider
releasing.

Many historians did write detailing documents that they believed
had been withheld past the Thirty Year Rule without justification.
To coincide with the publication, the government released some
intelligence documents for the first time, albeit for the period
1791–1909, a move that attracted a great deal of media attention.

In November 1993, I was involved with the Institute of
Contemporary British History (ICBH) conference to discuss
the progress of the initiative. An indicator of the new mood in
Whitehall was that the heads of the Departmental Record Offices
of several key ministries attended. They said that by the end of
1993 they hoped 6,000 sensitive files previously withheld beyond
the thirty-year period would be released. I wrote a piece for *History
Today* on the Waldegrave Initiative cautiously welcoming the
change (Lashmar 1994). Another consequence of this policy was
that the intelligence agencies MI5 and SIS would start to release
their older files. I recall MI5 chief Sir Stephen Lander speaking at
the Institute of Historical Research – where he had undertaken
post-doctoral research – about this liberalisation of policy. The first
official release of MI5 files to the National Archives took place in
1997. The 'new openness' would also result in a new wave of official histories including Christopher Andrew's *Defence of the Realm*,
a measured history of MI5 approved by the agency that would be
published in 2009, followed Keith Jeffery's *MI6: The History of the
Secret Intelligence Service* published a year later.

Out of the Cold

In the early 1990s, the SIS, supported by Prime Minister Major,
decided the time had come for the agencies to develop more formal
(if still opaque) contacts with some 'responsible' major media
organisations. The institutional relationships conducted in London
panelled-wall clubs, while reposed in leather armchairs over cigars
and port, were in desperate need of resetting. As a trial, the SIS was
prepared to talk to one link reporter in a few selected major UK
media organisations. It was discreetly promoted to participants as a

step towards glasnost but, actually, it worked to improve SIS's reputation and get its version of events into the public sphere. David Rose, then Home Affairs editor of *The Observer*, later detailed how he came to be an 'accredited reporter'. The paper's editor, Donald Trelford, proposed him as the intermediary between the paper and SIS in spring 1992. Over lunch, his new SIS contact (who Rose gave the alias Tom Bourgeois) told Rose that the SIS 'had always had a few, very limited contacts with journalists and editors, it now felt the need to put these arrangements on a broader and more formal basis'. Rose added:

> From time to time, he went on, it might be possible to 'give me a steer', and if things worked out we might progress from meeting for tea to luncheon . . . Nevertheless, there would be things I might find interesting that would not compromise sources or security. Anyway, here was his number. (Rose 2007)

Rose was told that the conversations would be off the record and the relationship with the intelligence services blossomed according to Rose:

> Later, there were boozy dinners at headquarters with C or MI5's director general, flanked by their brightest and best; briefings not just from the deniable PR man but officials involved with operations; and, most useful of all, a mobile phone number in case of urgent need at evenings and weekends. (To my chagrin, I never got as far as one reporter colleague who was plied with champagne and strawberries as a guest of SIS at the centre court for the Wimbledon men's semi-final.) (Rose 2007)

This was a major change in the relationship between the two entities, as it is official, acknowledged by both sides, but not attributable. Rose said he had had stories leaked to him by the SIS. The intelligence services were keen to take the opportunity to be proactive 'primary definers' in the public sphere and on occasion to shape the news agenda.[3]

Accredited Reporters

Deemed a success, the pilot of the accredited reporter scheme was extended. Now based in their new iconic headquarters on the Albert Embankment, the SIS was keen to appear part of the modern world. MI5 and SIS would separately develop a more overt media network. The other major intelligence service, GCHQ, does have a press office but does not often discuss its secret work with journalists and when it does it is usually to a BBC national security reporter. Expanding their range of media contacts, though, meant the 'rules of engagement' were to become tighter and the agencies were not to plant stories (at least not to the new intake of accredited journalists). In exchange for a wider set of institutional links, the agencies were prepared to respond to stories but able to retain some control over their shape.

My own period as an accredited reporter with the intelligence services began, sometime after David Rose, as staffer for the *Independent* newspapers. Intelligence and terrorism were part of my beat and the approach was direct. MI5, at least, demonstrated a sense of humour, as the location for our first meeting, chosen by the MI5 contact person, was in a restaurant called 'KGB' in Central London. Further lunches occurred about every six months to a year. Throughout, given the so-called war on terror was in full swing, there were many phone calls, especially when terrorism was in the news. The terms were much the same as dictated to David Rose. There would be no direct quotes attributable to MI5; instead the sources would be much vaguer, usually 'a Whitehall source'. MI5 were not keen on the phrase 'a security source' as it pointed too closely to them.[4] On one occasion when a news desk subeditor changed the phrase and made the source clear, I had to get the editor to send a letter of apology. The arrangement between the news media and MI5 was later to become fraught.

Turf Wars

As part of the post-Cold War 'bonus', intelligence budgets were cut. Towards the end of the Cold War, the (still) Secret Vote had been £1 billion. By 1998 it was to be down to £693 million (Smith 2003: 22). In 1991 in a clever Whitehall campaign orchestrated by Stella

Rimington, MI5's Director General, the hole in MI5's remit created by the end of the Cold War was filled. Against vehement opposition from the police, MI5 won its hostile takeover bid of Irish counter-terrorism, convincing the then Home Secretary, Kenneth Clarke, that it was uniquely placed to lead the fight against the IRA.

In the early 1990s, I watched as Whitehall turf wars between intelligence and police burst into life, much as it had done in the earlier 1920s. By 1994, MI5 could also see that The Troubles in Northern Ireland were coming to end. David Rose asked in one article, 'whether if peace comes to Northern Ireland, 1,000 Security Service staff could be out of job. So, will the spies turn to cracking crime?' (Rose 1994: 27). The police had always played down the notion of UK organised crime. MI5 grabbed the opportunity, breathed life into the concept and saw that by taking on the mantle of a British FBI they could move into policing. In fact, organised crime, if always a nebulous term, was a problem in the UK long before the services cast around for something to do in the post-Cold War lull.

Several national newspaper reporters got involved in the battle, lobbying for one side or the other for supremacy. According to a well-publicised MI5 brochure (MI5 1993)[5] about their work, by 1996 only a fifth of MI5's resources were devoted to counter-espionage – 'significantly less than in the period prior to the fall of President Gorbachev, when it was 50 per cent'. However, 'although the level of threat is no longer the same, spying still continues. In Russia, the process of democratic reform within the security and intelligence agencies is not so far advanced as among her former allies in the Eastern Bloc.' In other words, the KGB (by then split into the FSB (Federal Security Service) and SVR) and military intelligence GRU were back, and renewed their efforts to post intelligence officers to London.

ECHELON the All Seeing

The king hath note of all that they intend. By interception which they dream not of. (Shakespeare, *Henry V*, II, ii,)

If the end of the Cold War suggested a scaling down of the intelligence agencies, there was one agency where the rapid changes in technology was making their work more, not less important. Eavesdropping technology was much cheaper than running a large number of spies across the globe. GCHQ has played a pivotal role in the British Intelligence community and with the proliferation of commercial and intelligence satellites in space its importance has increased. There is little doubt that GCHQ was important in the Cold War and in conflicts since, including the Gulf War, Kosovo and Afghanistan. Indeed, by the early 2000s it probably produced more than 70 per cent of all the intelligence gathered by the UK. Occupying, in more recent years, its 'Doughnut' (on account of its shape) building near Cheltenham, in the West of England, GCHQ is the largest UK intelligence agency.

As Campbell revealed, GCHQ's principal task is SIGINT: providing 'clients' from intelligence and law enforcement agencies with information derived from intercepting, eavesdropping or spying on the communications of others.

> Every detail of GCHQ's size, mission and methods was unknown to the public, press and most of Parliament for more than half of its 70 years so far. The agency's capabilities – and, importantly, the limitations of these capabilities – are little understood. (Campbell 2010)

Reviewing Richard Aldrich's 2010 book on GCHQ, Campbell wrote:

> Richard Aldrich, an accomplished cold war intelligence historian, has taken a decade to produce the first substantial account of what is known about the agency, and what can be gleaned from recently released official archive material. He charts how, by 1964, GCHQ's demands and hidden financial allocations exceeded the entire cost of the Foreign Office. Its managers lobbied for a string of ambitious and costly projects: a nuclear-powered, aircraft-carrier-sized spy ship (never built); a small force of sky-sweeping Nimrod spy planes (flying from Lincolnshire now); and a spy satellite, Zircon (which never left the ground). (Campbell 2010).

As investigative reporter Duncan Campbell points out, GCHQ was unmasked in the summer of 1976 by a ground-breaking article, entitled 'The Eavesdroppers', that he and Mark Hosenball wrote for *Time Out*, then a London-based magazine. As he points out, 'The agency's unwilling transition into public awareness was consolidated by the subsequent "ABC"

Official Secrets Act trial of 1978, directed at myself and two others' (Aldrich 2010: 8). As an expert of GCHQ, he explains there is an elaborate structure behind and in front of GCHQ: these are the collectors and the recipients. 'The collectors use a wide range of methods and technologies bringing in signal intercepts. The recipients are the select few with clearance to see the "sensitive compartmentalised information" that is produced' (Campbell 2010).

The collection of SIGINT from the Mediterranean region was considered so important that the resident British military presence in Cyprus was there mainly to maintain a convenient base for a large GCHQ outstation.[6] Ambitious joint global projects were launched. The ECHELON programme was created in the late 1960s to monitor the military and diplomatic communications of the Soviet Union and its Eastern Bloc allies during the Cold War, and was formally established in 1971. It would not be until the Snowden leaks that the full importance of ECHELON became clear to the wider public (see Chapter 14).

The first hint had come with the 'D-Notice Affair' of 1967 featuring Chapman Pincher's clash with the Labour government about the wholesale collection of all overseas telegraph messages and their delivery to GCHQ (see Chapter 9). Before the controversy subsided, GCHQ was busy constructing at Morwenstow, six miles north of Bude in Cornwall, receiver dishes that would track and copy all communications passing through Western communication satellites. In 1972, former NSA analyst Perry Fellwock, using the pseudonym Winslow Peck, first blew the whistle on ECHELON to *Ramparts*, where he wrote a commentary revealing a global network of listening posts and his experiences of working there, but not identifying the codename.

The dogged Duncan Campbell exposed the much-expanded Five Eyes' ECHELON programme in 1988. In Britain as in the USA, the means to tap, track, store and assess this data were embedded in secretly spliced optical fibre cable connections that loop around national telecommunications systems, which suck every sort of communication into vast data warehouses. It took a decade for legislators to wake up to the human rights implications of ECHELON and its monitoring of all phone calls, faxes and emails, and it was the subject of an inquiry launched by Euro MPs in 1999. The same Duncan Campbell was chosen as the researcher and author of the European Parliament report on Anglo-American eavesdropping. As I wrote at the time, one British Member of the European Parliament (MEP) observed: 'Our

European counterparts are asking whose side are we on, the European Union or the Americans?' (Lashmar 2000c: 6). America considered the ECHELON system so crucial that the NSA appointed its deputy director Barbara MacNamara to become the London liaison officer between the two countries' eavesdropping agencies (Lashmar 2000c: 6).

I worked with Duncan Campbell from time to time trying to ascertain the extent of GCHQ operations and the civil liberties implications. In 1993, I made inquiries at Lackland Air Force base in Texas, a vast expanse of fenced off land that housed an impressive array of NSA antennae. It was for the Channel 4 *Dispatches* programme, 'The Hill', which detailed the SIGINT network that spread out from the NSA's base at Menwith Hill on the Yorkshire Moors (Campbell 1993). While working on *The Independent* I again collaborated with Campbell. He had identified that another GCHQ project involved the construction of an £18 million tower in Cheshire that tapped British Telecom's network to intercept communications with the Republic of Ireland (Campbell and Lashmar 1999).

We also obtained documents that revealed how ECHELON had been used to spy on British and continental European companies. ECHELON allegedly cost Airbus Industrie GIE a £8 billion contract with Saudi Arabia in 1994, after the US government intercepted phone and fax messages between Riyadh and Airbus headquarters in Toulouse. Although Britain stood accused by its European partners of aiding and abetting American spying, the British do not necessarily know what the Americans use the network for (Campbell and Lashmar 2000). Each participating ECHELON country could choose what it targeted. The French led attacks on ECHELON but British and American officials have accused them of hypocrisy because France runs its own global eavesdropping system, nicknamed 'Frenchelon'. Though the European Parliament mandated extensive action against mass surveillance in 2001, a few days later the Twin Towers were destroyed in the 9/11 terrorist attack. Campbell wistfully observed, 'Any plans for limiting mass surveillance were buried with the victims of 9/11' (Campbell 2014).

The increasing emphasis on signals intelligence in the war on terror saw the NSA and GCHQ work ever more closely together. Just how close was very clearly indicated in 2003 at the time of the Iraq War when Katherine Gun, a GCHQ linguist, leaked a top-secret memo that had been sent from the NSA to GCHQ. This memo asked GCHQ to aid (in what was a secret and illegal operation) the NSA to bug the United Nations (UN) offices of six 'swing' nations whose delegates were to attend the United Nations

Security Council meeting that was going to decide on whether to support the invasion of Iraq. The idea was get a steer on the swing states' positions so they could be countered in the Bush/Blair march to war. The memo was published by reporter Martin Bright in *The Observer*. Gun admitted the leak and was charged with an offence under Section 1 of the Official Secrets Act 1989. When the case came to court in February 2004, the prosecution declined to offer any evidence and case was dropped. Dan Ellsberg, who had supported Gun at the time, recently described Gun's decision to leak this memo as more important than his to leak the Pentagon Papers (Ellsberg 2017).[7]

The secret ECHELON programme's ability to invade citizens' privacy would become a testing issue again in 2013 (see Chapter 14).

Still Meddling

The Information Research Department might have been shut down in 1977, but the SIS retained the capacity to use the media for its own agenda. Stephen Dorril states, in his history of the SIS, that the service had started 'a pattern of disinformation' in the 1990s:

> A former SIS officer has alleged that the 'bread and butter work' of the Services' psychological warfare I/Ops section is in 'massaging public opinion into accepting controversial foreign policy decisions'. In particular, he cited 'the plethora of media stories about Saddam Hussein's chemical and biological weapons capability' – the 'ante was upped so that there would be less of a public outcry when the bombs started to fall'. (2000: 766)

Suspicion arose of MI6's continued meddling after two articles appeared in *The Spectator* in early 1994 under the by-line Kenneth Roberts. Datelined Sarajevo, Roberts was described as employed by the UN in Bosnia as an adviser. At the time, Bosnia and Croatia were the targets of attacks from Bosnia's own Serb minority supported by the Serbian government in Belgrade. Atrocities by Serbian forces were the focus of some passionate reporting by British journalists. The first article on 5 February considered arguments for a UN withdrawal, noting that all sides had committed atrocities. The second piece complained distorted and inaccurate reporting by journalists, including the BBC's Kate Adie.

The editor was the well-connected Dominic Lawson, whose father had been the Conservative Chancellor of the Exchequer and his brother-in-law, Anthony Monckton, a serving SIS officer, who was the Zagreb station chief from 1996. Kenneth Roberts was an alias for an SIS officer called Craig who was undercover as a civilian 'attached' to the British military's Balkan secretariat. Investigating the publication of the articles, David Leigh wondered if Roberts was acting on his own behalf or not.

> It is possible, of course, that Craig was merely overcome with private liter-
> ary urges whilst marooned in the Balkans, and thought it more politic to
> express his own opinions under a *nom de plume*. But one of the traditional
> roles of I/Ops is to plant stories. (Leigh 2000)

There are still occasional glimpses of deliberate intelligence leaks into the public sphere through trusted journalists. In the late 1990s, the *Sunday Telegraph* alleged the son of the then Libyan Leader Colonel Gaddafi was involved in a criminal enterprise with Iranian officials that involved counterfeit notes and money laundering in Europe. This backfired as the *Sunday Telegraph* could not evidence the allegations and the resultant libel action ended up with the paper issuing a retraction. The story was written by Con Coughlin, the paper's then chief foreign correspondent, and it was attributed to a 'British banking official'. It emerged in the trial that, in fact, SIS officials, who had been supplying Coughlin with officially sanctioned leaks, had given the information to him (Leigh 2000). This was an officially sanctioned informal leak. David Leigh claims that intelligence agents routinely approach reporters:

> I think the cause of honest journalism is best served by candour. We all
> ought to come clean about these approaches and devise some ethics to deal
> with them. In our vanity, we imagine that we control these sources. But the
> truth is that they are very deliberately seeking to control us. (Leigh 2000)

Leigh gave an account of his own experience when, in August 1997, the then foreign editor of *The Observer*, Leonard Doyle, was in contact with the SIS who supplied him with intelligence information about an Iranian exile. While running a pizza business in

Glasgow, the exile was also attempting to lay hands on a sophisticated mass spectrometer, which could be used for measuring
uranium enrichment – a key stage in acquiring components for a
nuclear bomb. According to Leigh, they were supplied with a mass
of apparently high-quality intelligence from the SIS, including
surveillance details of a meeting in an Istanbul hotel between the
pizza merchant and a representative involved in Iranian nuclear
procurement. Leigh emphasised that they did not publish merely
on the say-so of the SIS.

> We travelled to Glasgow, confronted the pizza merchant, and only when
> he admitted that he had been dealing with representatives of the nuclear
> industry in Iran did we publish an article. In that story we made it plain
> that our target had been watched by Western intelligence. (Leigh 2000)

The experience was not a happy one for Leigh although they had
confirmed the story:

> Nevertheless, I felt uneasy, and vowed never to take part in such an exer-
> cise again. Although all parties, from the foreign editor down, behaved
> scrupulously, we had been obliged to conceal from our readers the full
> facts and had ended up, in effect, acting as government agents. (Leigh
> 2000)

In 2002 Martin Bright, the Home Affairs editor of *The Observer* and
accredited with MI5, wrote the first critical article on the accredited
reporter system between the media and the agencies. 'Most journalists agree that this is less compromising than the old system, but it
is far from ideal' (Bright 2002b). He suggests that most journalists
feel that, on balance, it is better to report what the intelligence services are saying, but whenever the readers see the words 'Whitehall
sources' they should have no illusions about where the information
comes from. 'In the period immediately following the events of
September 11 and up to the new internment legislation, these journalistic briefings were used to prepare journalists for what was to
come' (Bright 2002b).

Renegades

It was not just the liberal media that raised concerns about the activities of MI5 and SIS; these agencies also produced several notable dissidents in the 1990s. Questionable practices by the intelligence services did not end with the Cold War, and two disaffected young officers in MI5 and SIS, David Shayler and Richard Tomlinson, spoke out about dubious operations, including domestic political surveillance and an alleged SIS plot to assassinate Libyan leader Colonel Muammar Gaddafi. Academic Mark Phythian notes that, 'This stream of revelations has resulted in a pronounced ambivalence in attitudes toward the intelligence services – attraction to the James Bond myth coexisting alongside a degree of scepticism and mistrust' (2005: 656–7).

Shayler's partner of the time, Annie Machon, herself an MI5 officer, also resigned and expressed serious concern over the politics of senior staff within MI5. She was not indiscreet about specific operations, confining her criticisms to more general policies and was not prosecuted. However, she has been a measured critic of MI5 ever since. I was to meet all three. Richard Tomlinson was not what you would expect of a renegade SIS officer. When I first interviewed him, in May 1999, he was living in exile in a private hotel in Geneva. He was tall, handsome and lean – more James Bond than Kim Philby – his appearance suggesting a man of action rather than a skulking double dealer. There was nothing furtive or obsessive about his manner. On the one hand, he clearly retained a great affection for the SIS and was proud to have worked for it. On the other hand, he was also very bitter at his treatment by the SIS, and was prepared to detail SIS practices he thought unacceptable in a democracy. He said he wanted to do a deal with the SIS to allow him to return to England, but then he was continuing to leak secret material that made his return less and less likely. The SIS and MI5 each had renegade officers loose who could compromise the innermost secrets of both agencies. An attempt in late 1998 to extradite MI5 agent David Shayler from France to face Official Secrets Act charges failed. Shayler continued to talk about MI5 operations and in May 1999, for example, he had given a detailed account of MI5 operations to an Arab satellite TV station.

In the case of Tomlinson, it was clear that some of the fault lay with an old-fashioned, macho management style at the SIS. Tomlinson had been working for Booz Allen Hamilton when he was recruited by the SIS. The rookie spy had worked undercover during the Bosnian War and says he witnessed some horrific scenes. On one occasion in Sarajevo, he said he had seen a young woman walking ahead of him in the street killed by an exploding shell. On a personal level when he returned to London, his girlfriend died slowly of cancer. Tomlinson confided to his personnel officer at SIS's headquarters on the South Bank of the Thames that he had become suicidally depressed.

By then most organisations, including the military and the media, had established counselling procedures for personnel suffering with personal problems, or with imminent or recent experience of war zones, so such individuals are not stigmatised. This was not the case in the SIS, where the rule of the stiff upper lip continued. Tomlinson explained to me that he was firmly told to pull his socks up – he was in the SIS. Then in 1995, Tomlinson who was still struggling, was informed that his career as a spy was finished. He says that the SIS threw out a few hints about finding him a job in the City, and then cut him loose.

When Tomlinson had joined the SIS in 1991, he seemed destined for great things. Unusually, he told me, he was sent straight out to work in the field, rather than to the conventional backwater posting. He claimed that in 1992 he successfully carried out a tricky, six-month undercover operation in Moscow and then infiltrated an Iranian organisation, which the SIS believed was trying to buy chemical warfare equipment in Britain. Next came the Bosnian experience. Whether he was as suited to the spy trade as he says he was, I do not know. However, to dispense with him without a cushion seems to have been a major error of judgment.

Dumped, Tomlinson's singular personality came into play. He went to John Wadham, of the civil liberties organisation Liberty, who took on the role of Tomlinson's solicitor in his efforts to get redress. Tomlinson tried to take the SIS to an industrial tribunal, but the SIS is protected from such public accountability. Tomlinson began to write a book about his SIS experiences. Offered a pay-off, as long as he dropped his claim for unfair dismissal and handed over the book manuscript, he agreed. However, the SIS discovered that he had gone to talk to a publisher in Sydney about the project. Worried about unauthorised disclosures, the British authorities charged him under the Official Secrets Act. In a trial that was largely held in camera, he was found guilty and jailed for six months. Released from Belmarsh Prison in April 1998, he left Britain. In France, after being briefly arrested at the behest of the British authorities and having his computer seized, he moved to Switzerland, which was indifferent to English law. There he decided it was time to cut a deal with the SIS that would allow him to return to England without fear of arrest.

In Geneva in September 1998 came the next security breach. Tomlinson resorted to a local internet cafe to communicate securely with John Wadham. However, he left the file on the computer, where it was found by Swiss journalists. They published on their website two letters written by Tomlinson to Wadham that outlined his concerns about SIS operations. The first letter detailed how the SIS had recruited a high-level mole inside German's central bank, paying him large sums of money to betray his country's most sensitive economic secrets. The mole, codenamed Orcada, was said to have betrayed Germany's negotiating position during talks on the Maastricht Treaty. The second letter was possibly more damaging. It revealed a 1992 plan by a member of the SIS to assassinate President Slobodan Milosevic of Serbia. This in turn revealed the names and positions of eight senior SIS officers. The British press did not publish the names, but they were published elsewhere. Tomlinson's less than compelling defence to this security breach was that it is the British authorities' fault for having his personal computer seized and forcing him to use a public computer.

Next, a list purporting to identify over 100 SIS recent or serving officers was posted anonymously online in 1999 at the time of the Richard Tomlinson Affair. Tomlinson was accused of posting the list, which he denied. No UK mainstream media published the names. To compound matters, the *Sunday Business* newspaper revealed that Tomlinson was claiming that the editor of a national newspaper was an SIS agent. Why the British authorities chose to dump Tomlinson remains a puzzle. To make Tomlinson feel more and more isolated as he ran out of money in Geneva seemed pointless and dangerous.

When Tomlinson's book *The Big Breach* was published, it revealed a great deal about SIS methods and operation. Tomlinson alleged that, in 1991, the SIS had tried to discredit Dr Boutros Boutros-Ghali, the then soon to be elected United Nations Secretary-General, by planting stories in the British press saying he was mentally unbalanced because he believed in unidentified flying objects (UFOs) and extra-terrestrial beings. Tomlinson claimed that the CIA (prevented under United States law from manipulating the media itself) had asked the SIS to spread the smear against Boutros Boutros-Ghali because it suspected him of being pro-French (Cockburn and Lashmar 2001). There were more allegations unproven to this day. Eventually, sometime after his book was published, Tomlinson came to an arrangement with the SIS. Last interviewed in Antibes in 2006, he talked about moving to Australia. He then faded from public view.

Prison versus Identifying Sources

The Shayler Affair also threw up a case that again exposed the fundamental tension between freedom of the press and the national security state: that a journalist might have to go to prison rather than reveal any information that could endanger their source. *The Observer* reporter Martin Bright had visited Shayler in Paris where he was in self-imposed exile. Bright had returned with a story saying Shayler had released the names of two SIS officers whom Shayler implicated in an attempt to assassinate Colonel Gaddafi. After publication, the Special Branch contacted *The Observer* and demanded Bright's notebooks, along with any documents and emails, stating they were investigating an offence under the Official Secrets Act. He and his paper refused.

Bright was ordered by an Old Bailey judge in March 2000 to hand over documents relating to the renegade MI5 officer. The prospect of jail or a fine was hanging over the head of several journalists at the time who had been told to hand over confidential material to the courts. 'The prospect of jail really is my worst nightmare', Bright told me at the time.

Let's face it, I'm a middle-class journalist and have no idea what it is like to be in prison. I would be lying if I said I wasn't worried about doing time, no matter how remote the possibility. Who knows how a journalist might get treated once inside. It doesn't bear thinking about. (Lashmar 2000b)

Working on intelligence and security are beats more likely to bring journalists into conflict with the authorities than most. Ed Moloney, Northern Ireland correspondent of *The Sunday Tribune* newspaper, who has been through the courts over source material, agreed with Bright that defying a court order is stressful. He told me in 2000:

I don't think I realised how serious the personal effect had been until the end, when we won the case. I was very emotional. There were a lot of tears all over the place, I can tell you. I don't think I realised until then how much of a strain, even torment, the case had been on me. (Lashmar 2000b)

An old Belfast hand, Moloney was approached in 1999 by the RUC detectives reinvestigating the death of human rights lawyer Pat Finucane nearly a decade earlier. Moloney had interviewed a loyalist witness, who had claimed to be an RUC informant and nine years later had become the prime suspect. The RUC wanted Moloney's notes, although the interview had been on a confidential basis. Ed Moloney refused, and the RUC went and got a court order. The decision to withhold the information was not a hard one to make. Moloney knew that he had a great deal to lose if he complied with the court order because of the kind of journalism he was involved with in Northern Ireland, which sometimes required dealing with people to whom discretion was a matter of life and death. If he handed over information to the RUC, he said,

It would ruin me as a journalist. Indeed, I saw it as part of the motivation by the people behind the court order that they knew this was a threat hanging over me and they knew I'd have comply with it or fight it off at great personal and financial risk. (Lashmar 2000b)

In the end, Moloney won his case, when Ulster's Lord Chief Justice, Sir Robert Carswell, dismissed the court order. Moloney said his editor and paper were very supportive.

> Once they saw what was happening, they got right in there behind me. We were lucky we won in the end, and the majority of our costs are borne by the taxpayer. If we hadn't, for a small paper like the one I work for, a bill of £200,000–£250,000 and could have cost jobs. (Lashmar 2000b)

Moloney was left with a lingering suspicion over the motives of the RUC:

> I got the distinct impression that part of the exercise was punishment. The state acts in these circumstances to send a warning to all journalists that if you delve into these areas, if you take an interest in matters we consider no business at all of the public, then there will be a price to pay. At the very least, we will make your life uncomfortable for several months. (Lashmar 2000b)

It has been nearly six decades since a British journalist was last given a prison sentence for refusing to disclose sources. In 1963, Reg Foster of the *Daily Sketch*, and Brendan Mulholland, of the *Daily Mail*, refused to disclose their sources for stories about the Vassall spy case. Each was sentenced to six months in prison and they became Fleet Street legends for their prison time. Mulholland had a bar named in praise of him in the *Mail*'s then Fleet Street drinking den, The Harrow pub. The case set a legal precedent that journalists, like priests, doctors and bankers, had no immunity from legal obligations to disclose information to a court. There are parallels with the Martin Bright case.

The UK's journalistic community saw Bright's case as a ludicrous attempt to frighten them away from the Shayler story. 'Journalists are notoriously competitive, but when something like this happens, they do tend to be supportive. I have had a lot of calls', said Bright. 'But the support of the editor and colleagues at the paper has been great. Without them, my stance would be impossible' (Lashmar 2000b). In July 2000 the appeal court dismissed attempts by the police and state prosecutors to order *The Guardian* and *The Observer* to hand over any material they had relating to the former MI5 officer, David Shayler. In a stout defence of press freedom and the newspapers' right to publish allegations by whistle-blowers, as *The Guardian* reported, Lord Justice Judge told the court: 'Inconvenient or embarrassing revelations, whether for the security services or for public authorities, should not be suppressed.' Otherwise, he said 'legitimate inquiry and discussion' and the 'safety valve of effective investigative journalism' would be 'discouraged, perhaps stifled' (Norton-Taylor 2000).

At this point in the book, some themes and patterns have begun to emerge: how spies have used the media as part of their operation; the politicisation of intelligence; where journalists are co-opted by intelligence as propagandists; and where spies have used journalistic cover and the risks that entailed. We can also see changes over nearly a century. How a new breed of journalists began to bring an ad hoc form of accountability to intelligence agencies and how the intelligence agencies had become increasingly sophisticated in their handling of the media. As the millennium passed, events were to unfurl that highlighted all these issues and many more.

Notes

1. Later, this would be seen as a serious policy mistake, with Russia developing as a major long-term national security threat. However, at the time the Reagan and Thatcher administrations believed a more cooperative, less threatening Russia would emerge.

2. Each New Year all the withheld documents from thirty years earlier were released in one go at the National Archives in Kew in West London. Journalists were given a preview opportunity and each year TV news cameras would film the journalists running to see the new documents and get the best scoops for the year. I did this job for *The Observer* for many years.

3. Stuart Hall and his co-authors suggested in their widely influential book, *Policing the Crisis*, that there were a group of sources who had privileged access to the media and called them *primary definers*. These are credible individuals and institutions granted media access which enables their initial framing of events that are assumed to be within their area of competence: for example, experts, official sources, courts, leading politicians and senior religious figures (1978: 58).

4. The only formal comment about this system came from the Director General of MI5, Jonathan Evans, who said, in an address to the media in 2007: 'I am, on the whole, impressed with the media's sense of responsibility and its understanding of our concerns. In addition, as the demand for news increases, we cannot

afford to let this understanding fall away, because there is no contract between the security and intelligence agencies and the media. There is no memorandum of understanding between us. It is a matter of trust' (PA Mediapoint 2007).

5. Authorised for public distribution by the soon to be retired Stella Rimington and meant to signal the new 'openness'.

6. In February 2019, a United Nations court declared that the British deportation of the islanders had been illegal.

7. In 2019 a Hollywood film, *Official Secrets*, was released starring Kiera Knightley portraying Katherine Gun.

THIRTEEN

The 'War on Terror'

Sir Harold Evans, the former *Sunday Times* editor, pointed to failures by the American news media in the months prior to 11 September 2001 (9/11). And in light of 9/11 how to report terrorism would raise major questions about the practices of journalism. Evans was scathing about the fact that 'not a single major newspaper' had taken seriously the February 2001 report by Senators Rudman and Hart[1] that gave warnings about the likelihood of such a terrorist attack (Evans 2006). He admitted that following 9/11 a wave of patriotism in the USA made criticism and dissent much harder. He said: 'I felt rage myself. I was in New York.' However, he states, it required the press to stand back and take stock rather than be caught up in the emotion (Evans 2006). After the terror attacks of 9/11, the world, not least for the media and the intelligence community, was a very different place.

As Evans notes, prior to 9/11 there had been an escalation of terror attacks against Western targets, emanating from fundamentalist terror groups coalescing around the leadership of Saudi citizen Osama bin Laden under the collective title al-Qaeda. These had included the attacks on US embassies in East Africa and the sea-borne attack on the USS *Cole* off Yemen in the late 1990s. There had been some reporting and some investigative journalism but the Western media evaluated it not to be significant news. The idea of an anti-Western global terror network lead by a dissident Saudi did not fit with the prevailing news narratives of the period. Following up the story, I reported for *The Independent* in the immediate aftermath of the Embassy bombings how the trail was leading to Osama bin Laden:

> Behind the scenes a breakthrough was taking place. On the day of the bombing the Pakistan police had arrested a man arriving from Kenya on a Yemeni passport but immigration authorities noticed the photograph did not match the carrier.
>
> Under interrogation he began to crack, admitting he was really a Palestinian engineer called Mohammed Saddiq Odeh. Gradually he boasted he had been the mastermind behind the Nairobi bombing. He was part of Osama bin Laden's terrorist organisation.
>
> It was arranged for Odeh to be shipped back to Nairobi. When he arrived, he explained to the FBI and Kenyan CID [Criminal Investigation Department] that he had booked into The Hilltop hotel in Nairobi four days before the bombing with three accomplices. The bomb had been completed the day before the attack. (Lashmar 1998)

I had been working with moderate Saudi dissidents in the mid-1990s who provided me with compelling detail of the corruption of the al-Saud family. They told me stories of massive external political donations to the West that to this day I have never been able to confirm. The dissidents went on to secretly film beheadings and official beatings in Riyadh. Osama bin Laden was a mujahedeen who had been important in the guerrilla war against the Soviet occupiers in Afghanistan and whom the West had covertly supplied and supported. Then to turn against his allies seemed ungrateful to the West and much of its news media. Having been once part of the Saudi establishment the austere fundamentalist well knew the pragmatic, if morally hypocritical, policies of the West and particularly of Britain, France and the USA in supporting the autocratic and kleptocratic Saudi royal family.

With the hijacked airliners caught on multiple camera phones as they crashed into the World Trade Center, the drama and impact of the attacks and 2,995 deaths on 11 September 2001 (CNN 2019) really do justify using the term 'paradigm shift'. Seen from a Western perspective the world was suddenly a very different political environment. Global attention had fixed on a few acres of smouldering blackened rubble in the centre of Manhattan. For other parts of the world, such devastation was not entirely new, but for the USA, nothing after Pearl Harbor compared. The search, by government and media alike, for the behind the scenes instigators of this unparalleled act of terror began instantly. In retrospect, we can see the tone of reporting after 9/11 was set in reaction to the horror of the event, which muted objective critical reporting. There was considerable critical reporting on whether the USA should have been better prepared and whether the US authorities had ignored early warning of the attacks.

There have been few events in history that have attracted as much media coverage. After 9/11 every journalist instinctively wanted to engage in what was likely to be the most important story of a generation. 9/11 changed many lives. James Gordon Meek was a reporter covering politics and campaigns in Washington, DC. He was reporting from the scene of the attack on the Pentagon within an hour. 'It changed the course of my life', he said, years later. He became a national security investigative journalist for ABC News covering the post 9/11 wars, terrorism and the trial of Khaled Sheik Mohammed – the organiser of 9/11 (Meek 2018). 9/11 also changed the direction of the author's life. At a point where I was looking to move more into making television history programmes, I was drawn back into Fleet Street and was able to be on hand to witness history as it was made.

The War on Terror Launched

In the USA, media attention focused on the antecedents of the terrorists and the possibility of covert Saudi Arabian involvement in the attack. Meanwhile further terrorist attacks were attempted. Richard Reid, a British national who had converted to Islam in prison, was arrested in December 2001 on a transatlantic flight having attempted to set off a bomb in his shoe. With the emergence of a British-born Islamist terrorist the focus for the UK media began to shift to the threat within the UK.[2] In the atmosphere of shock and revenge, the media were often outright supportive of the American led invasion of Afghanistan in the same month and the removal of al-Qaeda's hosts, the Taliban, from government. All knew that America would respond with force.

In his address to Congress a few weeks later, US President George W. Bush defined what he saw as the new global order. 'Our war on terror begins with al Qaeda, but it does not end there. It will not end until every terrorist group of global reach has been found, stopped and defeated.'[3] Ever since Bush uttered it, the term 'war on terror' has been contested and has come to encapsulate diverse counter-terrorist interventions and invasions. Academics Reese and Lewis note: 'The cultural construction and political rationale supporting this slogan represents a powerful organizing principle that has become a widely accepted framing; laying the groundwork for the invasion of Iraq' (2009: 777). Melley proposes that:

> The declaration of the War on Terror was thus marked by a paradoxical epistemology. It was to be a mighty struggle whose two shadowy protagonists – 'the global terror' network and the state's vast security apparatus – would remain largely invisible to the democratic public on whose behalf the war would be waged. (Melley 2012: 2)

Others believe the phrase disguised the neo-conservative, neo-empire ambitions of the USA. Pilger commented: 'It is not a war on terror but a war of terror' (Pilger quoted in de Burgh 2008: 191).

9/11 was a historical moment that brought terror to the centre of the global stage and the media. Since, the study of terrorism has expanded rapidly from an established canon (e.g. Sobel 1975; Laqueur 1977, 1978; Wilkinson 1986) as have the related fields of surveillance studies and intelligence studies (e.g. Dover and Goodman 2009; Bakir 2015). The counter-terrorism theorist Paul Wilkinson defined the problems facing the liberal democratic state in confronting terrorism, observing that the primary objective of counter-terrorist strategy must be the protection and maintenance of liberal democracy and the rule of law.

> It cannot be sufficiently stressed that this aim overrides in importance even the objective of eliminating terrorism and political violence as such. Any bloody tyrant can 'solve' the problem of political violence if he is prepared to sacrifice all considerations of humanity, and to trample down all constitutional and judicial rights. (1986: 125)

Weapons of Mass Destruction

I had left *The Independent* for a planned sabbatical from journalism in May 2001. Three days after 9/11, I was phoned at home in Dorset by Michael Williams, the deputy editor of the *Independent on Sunday* (*IoS*), who asked me to rush up to London to lend a helping hand with their coverage. He said they urgently needed someone on the team who had experience of reporting on intelligence and terrorism. My relationship with the *Independent on Sunday* was to last over six years.

Journalists are well aware that the main objective of terrorism is publicity, and reporting of terror has to be sober and responsible. At the *Independent on Sunday* we covered the aftermath of 9/11 and the American led response to the 'war on terror' including the invasion of Afghanistan. Later, stories investigated the European connections of 9/11 terrorists, their relationship with radical preachers and al-Qaeda networks. We were to learn the threats posed by 'lone wolf' and 'home grown' terrorists.

After the invasion and regime change in Afghanistan, the US and UK governments turned their attention back to the repressive dictatorship of Saddam Hussein and put it under intense scrutiny and criticism. There was a feeling that the West had failed to tackle Saddam Hussein effectively at the end of the First Gulf War in 1992 when they had driven Hussein's invading army out of Kuwait, causing enormous casualties to the Iraqi military. Claims were made that there were links between Saddam and bin Laden and that would come to justify another invasion. The *IoS* team reported on US and UK government claims that Saddam Hussein was evading the UN weapons security conditions and developing weapons of mass destruction (henceforth WMD). When did the 'war against terror' become a campaign against Saddam Hussein rather than Osama bin Laden? Less than a month after the September 2001 attacks on the World Trade Center and the Pentagon, some hawkish members of the US administration were stressing a connection with Iraq, but the shift did not become clear until George Bush's State of the Union address in January 2002, when the 'axis of evil' was unveiled. Suddenly Baghdad was in the frame, and al-Qaeda took a temporary back seat.

For some months, the name of Osama bin Laden was hardly referred to by President Bush. He had name-checked al-Qaeda in the 2003 State of the Union speech but its leader was not mentioned. Instead, Washington has acted as though the link between Iraq and terrorism were self-evident. The intelligence that supports government policy is rarely revealed publicly but when it came to Iraq the Western governments were so keen to manipulate public opinion they placed some intelligence in the public domain. The US Chief of Staff Colin Powell's detailed presentation at the UN showing images, documents and wiretaps to 'conclusively' give evidence of WMD in Iraq is probably the most notorious moment. Some of his supporting material proved to be bad forgeries.

As the war on terror progressed, serious questions arose about the veracity of intelligence-based information released by the UK government. Former senior intelligence official John Morrison later claimed that the Tony Blair/Alistair Campbell school of media manipulation had infected the agencies: 'There was a culture of news management which came in after 1997 which I had not seen before, and intelligence got swept up in that' (Norton-Taylor and White 2004). For the journalist to get access to high-level sources is a great resource but it can be hard to resist the danger of 'going native'. By the early 2000s, in the run-up to the actual invasion, the intelligence community and especially the SIS was successfully manipulating parts of the news media using what we know is called strategic political communication techniques (Bakir 2013). Only later was the full extent realised.

At the *Independent on Sunday*, we picked up that there was a discontent within the SIS about the way senior officers and the government were using intelligence. After consulting my sources we wrote a piece headlined, 'On the brink of war: The spies' revolt MI6 and CIA: The new enemy within', where we revealed Tony Blair and George Bush were encountering an unexpected obstacle in their campaign for war against Iraq – their own intelligence agencies. We reported that Britain and America's spies believed that they were being politicised, that the intelligence they provided was being selectively applied to lead to the opposite conclusion from the one they had drawn, and that Iraq was much less of a threat than their political masters claimed (Lashmar and Whitaker 2003). The politicians were even 'tweaking' the material to ensure a better fit. At the time, I was also dealing with non-official, long-standing contacts within the intelligence agencies. Talking to these unsanctioned contacts became particularly difficult around the time of the David Kelly Affair. The government expert on WMD was revealed as BBC journalist Andrew Gilligan's source. He had made the claim that the Blair inner circle had 'sexed up' their dossier – used to justify the invasion of Iraq – by claiming that Iraqi could deploy missiles with weapons of mass destruction within 45 minutes, and that they could hit British bases in Cyprus. Comments by inside confidential sources were embarrassing the government. Home Secretary John Reid lambasted these unofficial sources as a 'rogue element' on the BBC's *Today* programme, specifically referring to my sources:

> I said a rogue element because I thought there was one that was briefing Andrew Gilligan or indeed I said indeed [sic] elements because there may be the same source, there may be the same person, who is briefing the *Independent on Sunday* and various others, I don't know. But they are very much in the minority. (*Today* 2003)

Behind the scenes, Whitehall spent a lot of time trying to identify and close down these sources. The picture the insiders – my sources – had given was different in key ways from the official line and helped to produce much more nuanced journalism. As they were widely recognised as having entered the public sphere, the intelligence agencies were now caught in the political crossfire. A lot of journalists bought the misinformation. David Rose later wrote an apology article in the *New Statesman* admitting he had got too close to his intelligence contacts:

> To my everlasting regret, I strongly supported the Iraq invasion, in person and in print. I had become a recipient of what we now know to have been sheer disinformation about Saddam Hussein's weapons of mass destruction and his purported 'links' with al-Qaeda – claims put out by Ahmad Chalabi and his Iraqi National Congress. (Rose 2007)

I too received the same UK intelligence briefings as David Rose and I was also consistently told with great certitude that there were WMD in Iraq until about seven weeks after the invasion was completed (Lashmar 2013). Infamously, in September 2002 Downing Street produced a dossier on Iraq's WMD. The JIC signed off on a document that clearly exaggerated the threat posed by Iraq, to a point where it could barely, if at all, be supported by the available intelligence. Tony Blair's team used this material to persuade journalists to support their decision to invade. In contrast to its most obvious rival *The Observer* and many other papers that were still in a hawkish patriotic phase suppressing stories that indicated invading Iraq was a mistake or that Saddam's 'hidden' WMD did not exist (see Davies 2008: 329, 356), the *Independent on Sunday* was sceptical and critical of the Blair government's intent to invade Iraq.[4] This policy grew organically within the news team and was ratified at senior editor level. The arrest of the 'shoe bomber' Richard Reid in January focused us upon the domestic side of terrorism and the growing radicalisation of some Muslims in the UK. Indeed, the reporting provided a developing narrative on radicalisation that shaped the *IoS* commentaries on 7/7 for some years.

The Counter-Narrative

Quality information on the fast-changing events of the war on terror was limited. The *IoS*, as with other news outlets, relied to a considerable extent on politicians' public interviews, the then much rarer public statements from intelligence chiefs, the comments of retired security officials, and academics with expertise on terrorism. At this time, contacts with security services were either informal (confidential sources) or formal (if non-attributable). In a September 2004 *IoS*, I reported on the MI5 assessment of the number of plots. It would be an example that showed how the accredited reporter system did produce MI5 assessments and actual figures:

> Since 9/11, MI5 has monitored those it suspects of close links with al-Qaida, most of North African birth and believed to number around 30. In addition, there is a concentric ring of between 300 and 600 supporters and active sympathisers. A worry for MI5, reflected by a spate of arrests, is

a small but growing number of British-born Muslims becoming al-Qaida supporters. (Lashmar 2004)

Nonetheless, our determination to evaluate claims where possible led to questioning in our reporting, for example this story in November 2004, whether there really had been a terror plot to attack Canary Wharf.

> It was a terrifying image – a flashback of the horror of 11 September – hijacked planes coming out of the sky to smash into Britain's tallest office blocks at Canary Wharf in London. And the timing could not have been better. The front page of the *Daily Mail*, and the ITV News bulletins quoted authoritative but anonymous 'senior sources' as saying that the latest grim al-Qa'ida conspiracy had only recently been foiled.
>
> The reports came on Tuesday, the morning of the Queen's Speech, when Tony Blair was due to announce that security was the key component of this year's legislative programme, including another Terrorism and Crime Bill, and the highly contentious Identity Cards Bill, which will be published tomorrow. (McSmith et al. 2004)

As we noted, the timing was so neat in fact, that it aroused suspicions of a government spin machine at work, creating a climate of fear that would serve as an appropriate background to a Queen's Speech dominated by security matters.

For journalists, it is often difficult to evaluate the claims about plots that emanate from security sources. On the one hand, these people are in a position to have this privileged information and there are good reasons why they cannot detail the specifics. In practice, we journalists at *IoS* would take official information on the basis that we could search for corroboration where possible and would return to such claims in future editions. In July 2003 an article I filed was somewhat buried in the paper on page 10 and was just 343 words I thought it explained what most people had missed about WMD. I was disappointed with a major word reduction and lack of prominence at the time but such is life as a journalist. The short report provided a compelling explanation for why evidence of weapons of mass destruction had not been discovered in Iraq. The interview was with an intelligence expert who believed that Iraq dismantled its weapons in the mid-1990s.

> Professor Richard Shultz, one of the United States' top intelligence experts, contends that at some point before 2000 the Iraqis changed their strategy. 'I think US intelligence misunderstood the WMD issue. But then so did everyone else,' he said. Prof Shultz, of the Fletcher School of Law and Diplomacy at Tufts University in Boston, says that American intelligence was convinced that Saddam Hussein had 'hidden actual weaponised WMD'.
>
> 'It is almost certain that Saddam ordered the weapons dismantled or destroyed sometime in the 1990s. Sanctions had seriously impeded the Iraqi efforts to obtain materials and equipment for their WMD programmes'.
>
> 'The Iraqi strategy was to get sanctions lifted and they mounted a deception . . . But then Osama bin Laden got in the way. After September 11 the Bush administration turned its attention firmly to Iraq,' says Prof Shultz, who believes that the World Trade Centre attacks disrupted the Iraqi strategy. (Lashmar 2003)

7/7 and 21/7

At peak commuter travelling time on 7 July 2005, four 'home grown' Islamic terrorists separately detonated three bombs in quick succession aboard London Underground trains across the city and, later, a fourth on a double-decker bus in Tavistock Square. Fifty-two people, all UK residents, but of eighteen different nationalities, were killed and more than 700 were injured. Two weeks later on 21/7 a second set of terrorist tried to repeat the attacks on the London public transport system. The bombs were poorly assembled and failed to go off. The *IoS* described the problems of trying to tackle al-Qaeda – never an organisation with a clear hierarchical structure:

> It has always been as much an ideology as a tangible group. 'Trying to hit al-Qa'ida is like trying to hit jelly,' said one intelligence source. 'One minute you think you know who is running it, and next minute you feel you have no idea'. (Whitaker and Lashmar 2005)

'Home grown' radicalisation became the main theme in intelligence briefings. David Rose's fury at being fed deliberate lies is very apparent in his mea culpa. In the same article, after attacking his US sources for misleading journalists, he moves on to the UK Security Service stating that more recent media briefings seem equally questionable. He recalled that after the 7 July 2005 London bombings, MI5 told its stable of reporters that the bombers had all been 'clean skins' who had been completely unknown to them. Only two years later, thanks to evidence given in criminal trials, did it become clear that MI5's claims were false.

> In fact, the two leaders of the 7/7 gang, Mohammad Siddique Khan and Shazad Tanweer, had been observed by MI5 surveillance officers at least four times, and were known to be connected to another, now convicted, terrorist cell. But MI5 had decided to leave them alone while both men had apparently trained in Pakistan, at the same time as the 21/7 group. (Rose 2007)

I reviewed the evidence for the Khan case as I too had had these briefings. The evidence suggested MI5's record is better than MI6's record and the Security Service briefers did not deliberately lie over Khan. True, early briefings did not accurately portray how frequently leader of the 7/7 bombers had come up on MI5's 'radar'. However, perhaps they were suffering from the 'fog of war'; working on the best information available, while still analysing and collating evidence. While the political bias of MI5 is a concern throughout this book there is no evidence MI5 was politicised by the Blair government to support policy (Lashmar 2013).

Politicisation

Did the British Intelligence community become politicised by Tony Blair's government pressures? My own non-official and proven inside sources of the time deny that MI5 became captive, like the SIS, to Downing Street's political agendas. There is compelling evidence that the SIS was politicised at a senior level after 9/11 and did proffer information as credible that in fact was poorly evidenced.

The whole issue over the source known as 'Curveball' was a nadir for the Western intelligence community (Drogin 2007). Even the sceptic could be swayed by the certainty that emanated from the SIS about the existence of WMD and of Saddam Hussein's imminent aggression. If the UK media were too willing to publish the government's claims of WMD, in the build up to the Iraq invasion, eventually the journalists settled back into a more fourth estate role.

The formal relationship between intelligence and news media remains difficult. In a couple of decades we have moved from a situation where the intelligence services used to say nothing or would only leak to their advantage, to a situation where they try to respond to journalists in a fast changing situations. It is a very different environment. If the news media want fast moving operational information that later is proved not to be accurate, journalists need to think carefully before accusing agencies of lying. As Rose suggested, the SIS may have even been convinced themselves but, in that case, their misjudgment was enormous. It would be a long time before journalists were able to trust the SIS, and even now there is reserve.

Terror plots continued and in July 2006 we covered Operation Overt which was to thwart attacks on airliners:

> The biggest surveillance operation in British history is under way this week as the authorities seek to track what the Home Secretary, John Reid, has called 'dozens' of terror plots. While every police force in the country is now involved in investigating the alleged plot to bring down transatlantic airliners, MI5, the main counter-terror agency, is being strained to the limit as it seeks to head off the next threat.
>
> The one thing we can be sure of is that there will be a 'next one', said a Whitehall source. 'The big question, indeed, is "Where next"'. (Whitaker et al. 2006)

The expansion of the intelligence services was in full swing. They were operating across the world and the gloves were off. New methods, technologies and weapons were to be used, all supported by the Five Eyes agencies. It would prove controversial. The role of the New Labour government, notably Tony Blair and his then

Foreign Secretary Jack Straw, on a particularly unsavoury episode of SIS operations, in conjunction with the CIA, has not been fully disclosed a decade and half after events.

Torture and Rendition

In the early 2000s, Abu Omar, an Iman, was granted asylum in Italy. On 17 February 2003 Abu Omar was walking along a street in Milan on his way to noon prayers at the local mosque. As he strolled along the Via Guerzoni, he was kidnapped by a CIA snatch team and bundled into a car. Abu Omar was rushed to the air base at Aviano. Later that day he was flown in a US Air Force jet to Ramstein airbase in Germany and there put on a CIA hired aircraft and flown on to Egypt. Abu Omar was suspected by the USA of plotting terrorist acts. The CIA plane landed at Cairo and Abu Omar was put into the hands of Egyptian intelligence (the Mukhabarat). The Egyptians believed he belonged to al-Gama'a al-Islamiyya, an organisation they had designated as illegal as its aims were said to include the overthrow of the democratically elected Egyptian government. Al-Gama'a al-Islamiyya was considered a terrorist organisation by the USA and European Union. Rendered to Cairo, Abu Omar claimed he was tortured both by the CIA and by State Security, Egypt's feared secret police. He was kept locked up for many months and, he said, torture ranged from hanging him upside down and applying electric shocks to his genitals to putting him in a room where loud noise was played, damaging his hearing. He was interrogated as to whether he was an al-Qaeda militant. Then after thirteen months he was suddenly released and told to keep his mouth shut. An Egyptian court had ruled his imprisonment was 'unfounded' (Nasrawi 2007).

Italian prosecutors began an inquiry and that would reveal that a group of Italian secret service officials colluded with the CIA in the kidnap of Abu Omar. As a result, European arrest warrants were issued in December 2005 and Italian security service (SISM) officers were among those arrested. Investigative journalist Stephen Grey points out that Abu Omar's is only one of many cases of rendition, the details of which have been revealed as a result of painstaking forensic work by journalists and aircraft enthusiasts (Grey 2006: 170–90). It is estimated that at least 100 'suspects' were rendered (Grey 2006: 170–90). As Grey notes the outlines of the CIA's rendition programme have emerged not from any single piece of reporting by a journalist or any single disclosure by a public official. Instead, details have come to light piecemeal fashion. Grey went to great lengths to find and contact eyewitnesses, sources, participants, victims and experts and made use of thousands of flight records that revealed the exact movements of CIA planes. He also made sophisticated use of the relatively new art of data journalism, crunching data to separate rendition flights from routine civil aviation flights.

The work of this loose cooperative (see below) are detailed in Grey's 2006 book, *Ghost Plane*. They had painstakingly identified over 1,000 CIA 'ghost flights' criss-crossing the globe after 2001. Many of these flights were for 'extraordinary renditions' where, simply, terror suspects were secretly taken by force from one country to another. As Bob Baer, a former CIA operative in the Middle East, commented: 'If you want a serious interrogation you send a prisoner to Jordan. If you want them to be tortured you send them to Syria. If you want someone to disappear . . . you send them to Egypt' (Grey 2004). Rendition flights were not used to move suspects from war zones like Afghanistan or Iraq to the USA where these alleged terrorists could be charged and tried. The receiving nation was always a third country where the security services were sympathetic to the USA and cooperative with the CIA. These third-party states include Egypt, Jordan, Syria, Morocco, Thailand, Uzbekistan and possibly Poland. Suspects could then be incarcerated, interrogated and in many cases tortured to extract their alleged knowledge of al-Qaeda. Some of the suspects died in custody.[5]

Reporters like Grey who have followed this story worked cooperatively – not in concert but by picking up pieces of the jigsaw puzzle disclosed by others – and then added new pieces to the picture (Grey 2006: vii). Bakir cites a number of examples of international cooperation (2013). It was indicative of new developments to monitor the covert operations of the burgeoning Western intelligence complex. Bakir also pointed out that a strength of investigative journalism is that a reporter can write a series of agenda-building articles.[6]

> Investigative journalism gives leakers a place to leak and allows in-depth examination of leakers' claims. A further strength is that investigative journalism can now exploit the data-dumps of secret information that websites like WikiLeaks (that has experimented with journalistic collaboration) enable – such as the Cablegate dump and the Guantánamo Database. (Bakir 2013)

While investigative journalism in the media often lacks resources and is hampered by commercial imperatives, the mode of investigation is moving into philanthropically funded bureaus and civil society (NGOs, unions, campaigns and civil rights organisations) and becoming a much more powerful anti-corruption tool.

Domain Expansion

After the Second World War, the British Customs and Excise organisation had been the only organisation that had proved consistently capable of tackling international forms of organised crime like drug smuggling and value added tax (VAT) fraud. However, their investigative capability was degraded when Tony Blair decided it would be a good political 'big idea' to set up 'a British FBI' in the form of the Serious and Organised Crime Agency (SOCA). In was launched in 2006 under the chairmanship of the former head of MI5, Sir Stephen Lander, and the director was a police officer, Bill Hughes. It was disastrous venture at every level. It was meant to absorb the best investigators from Customs and Excise, the police and other agencies to produce a super detective agency. The canny senior Customs officers I knew, including some of the best crime investigators in the business, wanted nothing to do with what they foresaw would be a hodgepodge (see Lashmar 2007a).

SOCA quickly developed a secretive and worrying neo-intelligence ethos as SIS officers were seconded to the Agency. And unlike any previous policing organisation, it had very limited accountability. I wrote a number of articles about its poor performance and its dubious claims of unprecedented levels of Class A drugs seizures.

Oddly, given the profusion of intelligence officers, it did not adopt the rather effective 'intelligence led' approach to dealing with organised crime used by Customs. Instead it targeted 130 what it called 'core nominals', or in newspaper parlance 'Mr Bigs'. It was a major mistake as the drugs market was fragmenting and on SOCA's watch the amount of drugs in circulation increased and the price of drugs actually fell (Lashmar 2007a; see also Lashmar 2008b). It also engaged in empire building, absorbing the very effective Asset Recovery Agency (ARA), which stripped criminals of their ill-gotten gains. Within SOCA, this agency was emasculated (Lashmar 2007b). My critical stories for *The Independent* sufficiently annoyed Sir Stephen Lander that he called me in to their high security headquarters in Westminster and told me at some length that I was impacting SOCA's morale. For my part, I was using my excellent inside sources to report how ineffective Britain's FBI was turning out to be. It was a bad time to try out a new agency and the experiment failed. Eventually, SOCA became a political embarrassment and was replaced by National Crime Agency in 2013, which has done a much better job.

Drones

On 21 May 2016, Mullah Akhtar Mansour, the leader of the Afghan Taliban, had just returned from Iran and was being driven by a rental car driver across Balochistan, a lawless region of Pakistan which was home to the Afghan Taliban's leadership in exile. At 3.00 pm local time a missile attack from US drones blew up the car killing Mansour and his driver. According to the *Wall Street Journal*, the strike took place on the N-40 National road from the Iranian border to Quetta. The drone attack, one of many against the Afghan Taliban, produced a muted response from the Pakistan government. Many newspapers celebrated the attack. Britain's *Daily Express* summarised it as 'GOT HIM: Taliban leader WIPED OUT by furious firepower of multiple drones' (Wood 2016).

Initially, drones were passive intelligence gathering platforms but technology enabled them to become remotely controlled weapons, in some cases capable of carrying American manufactured Hellfire missiles. As the US approach to intelligence gathering developed a much more aggressive stance, acquiring intelligence became a routine precursor to the assassinations of targets. The USA has been carrying out targeted killings with drones around the world since 2001.[7] As the rate of drone strikes increased so too did criticism from human rights groups and civil liberties advocates.

The UK's Bureau of Investigative Journalism's (BIJ's) 'Drone Wars' project logged Mansour's death; just one of many it recorded. Usually drone attacks are unreported, the Western military are reluctant to speak about them and logging them was difficult work. The BIJ had been tracking and investigating drone strikes for more than eight years, monitoring and recording the date, time and location; and importantly, the number of those killed. Drone strikes tend to occur in locations which are extremely dangerous for journalists to work and most news organisations did not have the resources to monitor the drone war.

The BIJ is part of a developing model of journalism, philanthropically funded and able to undertake important fourth estate investigations that other news organisations would say are expensive, are risky and lack audience impact.[8] Although many journalistic organisations in the USA now work using the philanthropic model, like the news agency ProPublica, it is still rare in the UK. The BIJ is the outstanding example.[9]

The Bureau systematically built up a network to gather reports on drone strikes and then verify the information – it was an extraordinary piece of journalism. It is an example of international cooperation and philanthropic funding of investigative journalism, and the work of the project has become the go-to place for information on the effects of drone warfare. It of course mirrors the difficulties for intelligence agencies in targeting these strikes. They too need to build reliable networks and also to verify the information. The consequences of the two different approaches are very different.

Minimum confirmed STRIKES – 4,809
Total killed – 7,584–10,918
Civilians killed – 751–1,555
Children killed – 252–345[10]

The Bureau noted that there is just one law that underpins the whole basis for the USA being at war with al-Qaeda – the Authorisation for the Use of Military Force Act – drafted by the Bush White House in the week after the 9/11 attacks.[11] At its heart is a sixty-word sentence that gives the US president the power to 'use all necessary and appropriate force against those nations, organisations, or persons' that he or she determines was behind or helped the people who carried out the attacks. On 16 September 2001 it was passed into law by Congress. Drones have been used in military contexts by the USA and UK in Afghanistan, Iraq and Libya – situations of recognised armed conflict under the Geneva Conventions and international humanitarian law. The USA has also flown drone strikes in Pakistan, Yemen and Somalia.

The BIJ started the drone wars project because there had been next to no official transparency about the US drone war. Their concern was focused on the number of 'collateral' civilian deaths. Their work has also revealed some of the political and oversight issues for intelligence agencies engaged in drone wars. The Obama administration did bring in rules to govern the use of armed drones. This included putting the military in charge of the lethal end of drone operations and limiting the CIA to providing intelligence. However, the Trump administration put the CIA back in charge, which has had a dampening impact on transparency.

General Joseph Votel, the man in charge of US Central Command (Centcom), testified before the Senate Armed Services Committee apologising for the killing of between four and twelve civilians in a botched special operations raid and drone attack in Yemen in January 2017. Seven months later, it turned out he got the numbers wrong. An investigation by NBC News revealed internal US estimates showed at least sixteen civilians died (McFadden et al. 2017). Centcom said that Votel spoke 'with the best information he had at the time'. Yet both figures are lower than the twenty-five civilian deaths uncovered by researchers working with the Bureau, who visited the scene of the strike.

An Unfinished Task

Covering the war on terror has been among the most difficult and demanding jobs in journalism in recent history. Domestically, the probing journalist is up against the wilderness of mirrors created by the intelligence agencies, terrorists and politicians. Terrorists are by their very nature secretive, and their hinterlands, whether at home or abroad, are potentially dangerous places to operate. Covering Afghanistan, Iraq and the battlefields of this war has been more dangerous for journalists than previous any war (Lashmar 2008a: 194). A number of the news and current affairs organisations responsible for dogged coverage of intelligence from the 1970s to the 1990s no longer exist or have lost their engagement in public interest stories. For example, the current affairs series: *World in Action*, *This Week* and the *London Programme* are all moribund.

Coverage of intelligence was always ad hoc, but with fewer resources available to interested journalists it is now also inconsistent. Only recently have we begun to understand how much secret surveillance journalists come under once they attract the attention of the UK's 'Secret State'. Reporting on the war on terror in the UK after 9/11, I was fascinated by the difference in the portrayal and reality of the opponents in this counter-terrorism battle. The Regulation of Investigatory Powers Act 2002 allowed police forces to investigate journalists' sources and the Investigatory Powers Act 2016 allows the electronic monitoring of journalists.

US writer Timothy Melley proposes that as a result of the war on terror we have seen the rise of the 'covert sphere' – as opposed to the public sphere. He notes that there is a massive expansion of the intelligence sphere. 'The covert sphere is a cultural imaginary shaped by both institutional secrecy and public fascination with the secret work of the state.' Further, he suggests that:

> Unlike the supposedly 'rational-critical' public sphere, the covert sphere is dominated by narrative fictions, such as novels, films, television series, and electronic games, for fiction is one of the few discourses in which the secret work of the state might be disclosed. The projection of strategic 'fictions,' in fact, is a primary goal of clandestine agencies. (Melley 2012: 5–6)

The portrayal of security forces as superheroes and the terrorist as dastardly villains, all with something akin to superpowers, is a manifestation of the desire to fictionalise facts. Reality is mostly different. Close examination of the evidence of the terror trials after 2001 shows frequent blunders to the point that I was surprised that anyone was arrested and that any of the terrorists actually made a viable bomb. I spent some years as a consultant to Chris Morris for his film *Four Lions* (2012), which being a dark comedy, in the spirit of Stanley Kubrick's *Dr Strangelove*, made this point. The intelligence community and the terrorist organisers now tend to be more professional having experienced seventeen years of the war on terror. Yet the landscape of terrorism is constantly changing. Now, the most effective means of Islamist terror is not so much those who have guns or bombs but those who use everyday items such as kitchen knives, cars and trucks to wreak havoc suddenly on unsuspecting members of the public. In 2017 there were five successful terrorist attacks in the UK, four of which were Islamist inspired, but the head of MI5 Andrew Parker told the Cabinet during a presentation in December that a further nine had been stopped (Asthana 2017).

Notes

1. The Rudman and Hart Commission was also known as the US Commission on National Security/21st Century (USCNS/21) and was tasked 'to analyze the emerging international security environment; to develop a US national security strategy appropriate to that environment; and to assess the various security institutions for their current relevance to the effective and efficient implementation of that strategy, and to recommend adjustments as necessary'. The Commission released its third report in February 2001 (USCNS/21 2001).
2. According to al-Qaeda operative Mohammed Mansour Jabarah (who was captured and interrogated in Oman in 2003), Reid was a member of al-Qaeda and had been sent on the bombing mission by Khaled Shaikh Mohammed.
3. 'President Declares Freedom at War with Fear', <https://georgewbush-whitehouse.archives.gov/news/releases/2001/09/20010920-8.html> (last accessed 30 July 2019).
4. I, like the rest of the team, had no sympathy with Saddam Hussein who had a large number of his own people tortured, raped, murdered and gassed and, in addition, Saddam had caused my former *Observer* colleague, Farzad Bazoft, to be hung on trumped up espionage charges.
5. The Trump nominated head of the CIA Gina Haspel was in charge of the Thai black prison from mid-2002. The Thais insisted on the removal of prisoners by 2004, as embarrassing stories about cooperation with the CIA began to emerge.
6. For example, look at the persistence of certain reporters who investigated torture and extraordinary rendition. They included Dana Priest (2002–5) for the *Washington Post*; Neil Lewis (2003–5) and Douglas Jehl (2004–5) for *The New York Times*; Seymour Hersh (2004–7) and Jane Mayer (2005–7) for the *New Yorker*; Michael Isikoff for *Newsweek* (2004–9); Brian Ross and Tichard Esposito for ABC News (2005–7); and freelancer Stephen Grey (2004–7).
7. <https://www.thebureauinvestigates.com/explainers/history-of-drone-warfare> (last accessed 29 October 2019).
8. Further funding for the drone project came from the Joseph Rowntree Charitable Trust and the Freedom of the Press Foundation, through a crowdfunding initiative.

9. The model is expanding across globe. Another notable example is the Organized Crime and Corruption Reporting Project (OCCRP). It is a non-profit media organisation providing an investigative reporting platform for the OCCRP Network, and 'connects[s] 45 non-profit investigative centers in 34 countries, scores of journalists and several major regional news organizations across Europe, Africa, Asia, the Middle East and Latin America'. They say: 'We work to turn the tables on corruption and build greater accountability through exposing the abuse of power at the expense of the people. We serve all people whose lives are affected by organized crime and corruption' <https://www.occrp.org/en/projects?option=com_content&task=view&id=17&Itemid> (last accessed 23 September 2019).

10. <https://www.thebureauinvestigates.com/projects/drone-war> (last accessed 29 October 2019).

11. <https://www.govtrack.us/congress/bills/107/sjres23/summary> (last accessed 23 September 2019).

FOURTEEN

Citizenfour

On Saturday 20 July 2013, in the basement of *The Guardian*'s Kings Cross offices, a senior editor and a computer expert used an angle grinder to destroy the hard drive containing data leaked by the former NSA contractor Edward Snowden while GCHQ technicians watched on. The highly classified data provided extensive evidence of unsuspected invasive surveillance, even by diligent spy watchers, and hacking by Western intelligence agencies including Britain's own eavesdropping agency, GCHQ.

The decision to destroy the hard drive was taken by *The Guardian*'s then editor Alan Rusbridger after a threat of legal action by the UK government, which would have been meaningless, disruptive and expensive, yet was not over any fundamental point of press freedom. However, this bizarre exercise – given Snowden's data was also stored in the cloud out of reach of *The Guardian* – was a clear demonstration of the very real tensions between intelligence agencies and the media. It was an existential example of their differences and while both maybe devoted to collecting information, the ethos of intelligence is dissemination to a handful of authorised persons only, while the *raison d'être* of the media is to publish as widely as possible if they think it is in the public interest.

The Era of Data Leaks

The 'era of data leaks' began in 2006 when WikiLeaks was set up by its ever controversial founder, the shock haired Australian, Julian

Assange, as an extra-territorial online entity to encourage and disseminate leaked data, most especially from within governments. The ad hoc international group released a series of prominent data dumps. Early releases included documentation of equipment expenditures and holdings in the Afghanistan war and a report containing information on a corruption investigation in Kenya. In April 2010, WikiLeaks released the deeply disturbing *Collateral Murder* footage from the 12 July 2007 Baghdad helicopter gun attack in which Iraqi journalists from the Reuters agency were among those killed.[1] Other WikiLeaks releases that year, working in conjunction with the mainstream news media, included the Afghan War Diary and the Iraq War Logs. The latter allowed the mapping of 109,032 deaths in 'significant' attacks by insurgents in Iraq that had been reported to the Multi-National Force – Iraq, including about 15,000 that had not been previously published. WikiLeaks also released a huge batch of diplomatic cables, classified cables that had been sent by embassy officials across the globe to the US State Department, a leak known as 'Cablegate'. Prior to WikiLeaks, journalists had been experimenting with computer-aided research utilising large data releases for stories.

In the early years of my career, most leaks with supporting evidence involved paper documents that had 'arrived anonymously in brown envelopes', and we would be delighted if we were given anything as substantial as a lever arch file of revealing material. With governments and companies starting to store data online, investigative journalists needed to adapt. Computers gave us the capability to analysis large quantities of information and get stories that way. In 1996 I worked with a computer programmer to structure a large local government data set[2] so that it revealed which UK local authorities were the most efficient (Lashmar and Oliver 1996). This project, which ran for two years, led to me being identified later as Britain's first data journalist (Egawhary 2010).

From 2003 Gavin MacFadyen, the inspired director of the London-based The Centre for Investigative Journalism (TCIJ), annually brought over pioneering US data journalists to train reporters and activists how to use software to enhance their journalism. It required the ability to take 'dirty' data, structure it, verify it and clean it up so that it met ethical and professional standards.

With WikiLeaks, this was not without its problems. Assange and his people worked with *The Guardian* on releasing the Iraq War Logs. Assange, a self-described libertarian activist, wanted to put all the data online but the then head of investigations at the paper, David Leigh, insisted anything that might put a life in danger should be not be published. For instance, a number of alleged informers were identified in the documents who might have been murdered if their names were made public. Assange was angry with *The Guardian* for withholding this kind of data and through mutual antipathy they did not work with each other again. Each subsequent data release has presented journalists with a new set of problems, not least the growing size of the data being managed. In 2013 there was to be a huge data leak revealing startling details of the Five Eyes network.

NSA Contractor

In 1943, in the middle of the Second World War, the British and Americans had signed the BRUSA intelligence agreement to share information and resources; it was an unprecedented and embracing pact that continues, amended and expanded, to this day.[3] With the rise of international terrorism this pact has grown to be the 'Five Eyes' surveillance network that covers the globe.

Edward Snowden (born 1983) is an American computer specialist, a former CIA employee and contractor to the NSA who established unauthorised contact with journalist Glenn Greenwald and filmmaker Laura Poitras from late 2012. He had copied some 60 gigabytes of data from the NSA system without approval.

Snowden had been a computer systems administrator for the CIA. Next, he was hired by the NSA contractor, Booz Allen Hamilton for whom he worked for some months. On 20 May 2013, Snowden flew to Hong Kong after leaving his job at an NSA facility in Hawaii, and in early June, he gave Greenwald and Poitras access to this material, which revealed the Five Eyes global surveillance programmes run with the cooperation of telecommunication companies and other governments. From June 2013, a range of Snowden's leaked documents were published by media outlets worldwide, including *The Guardian* (Britain), *Der Spiegel* (Germany), the *Washington Post* and *The New York Times* (USA), *O Globo* (Brazil), *Le Monde* (France), and news outlets in Sweden, Canada, Italy, Netherlands, Norway, Spain and Australia.

Although only a small percentage of Snowden's estimated 1.7 million documents have been published, these reveal structural details of a global surveillance apparatus jointly run by the Five Eyes in close cooperation with their commercial and international partners.[4] Snowden said he was motivated to leak because: 'I do not want to live in a world where everything I do and say is recorded.' He added, 'My sole motive is to inform the public as to that which is done in their name and that which is done against them' (Snowden quoted in Gellman 2013). Snowden said his 'breaking point' was 'seeing the Director of National Intelligence, James Clapper, directly lie under oath to Congress'. Clapper had given testimony in which he denied to the US Senate Select Committee on Intelligence that the NSA wittingly collects data on Americans. In an interview with the *Washington Post*'s Barton Gellman, Snowden said he wanted to 'embolden others to step forward' by demonstrating that 'they can win' (Snowden quoted in Gellman 2013).

The US investigative journalist Seymour Hersh is certain that the NSA whistle-blower, 'changed the whole nature of the debate' about surveillance and that that while he and other journalists had written about surveillance, Snowden provided hard conclusive evidence:

> Duncan Campbell [the British investigative journalist who broke the Zircon cover-up story], James Bamford [US journalist] and Julian Assange and me and the New Yorker, we've all written about the notion there's constant surveillance, but he [Snowden] produced a document and that changed the whole nature of the debate, it's real now. (O'Carroll 2013)

In an interview, Duncan Campbell told me that the scale of the ECHELON operation alone revealed by Snowden had shocked even him: 'The NSA and its partners had arranged for everything we communicated to be grabbed and potentially analysed', he said. 'ECHELON was at the heart of a massive, billion-dollar expansion of global electronic surveillance for the 21st century' (Campbell 2017).

'Collect it all'

From Snowden's documents we know that metadata from personal communications is being copied into huge data stores that allow the agencies to sift for useful information.[5] Snowden has also revealed that the agencies have secretly negotiated for 'backdoors' in the security of many computer programs, social networking sites, websites and smartphones. Glenn Greenwald, the former *Guardian* journalist who worked with Edward Snowden, notes the Five Eyes mantra of 'Collect It All':

> At the top of the document, it said 'new collection posture'. This is the NSA describing its new collection position, and right underneath is a really ugly, though helpful, circle with six points on it. Each of the six points has a different phrase that elaborates on the 'Collect It All' mandate. So you go clockwise around the circle, and the top it said 'Sniff It All' and then it said 'Know It All', 'Collect It All', 'Process It All', 'Exploit It All', and then the last one is 'Partner it all'. (Greenwald 2017: 45)

He adds that this then is the institutional metadata mandate for the NSA – it is collecting billions and billions of telephone calls and emails every single day from populations and nations all over the world including our own (2017: 45).

The sheer scale of NSA–GCHQ operations surprised many politicians who thought they had been kept informed of the activities of the intelligence agencies. Chris Huhne, a former UK Cabinet minister, said that ministers were in 'utter ignorance' about even the largest GCHQ spying programme, TEMPORA,[6] and its US counterpart, the NSA's PRISM, as well as 'about their extraordinary capability to hoover up and store personal emails, voice contact, social networking activity and even internet searches' (Huhne 2013). An Australian journalist who has also worked in government and politics, Phillip Dorling, noted, 'Edward Snowden's revelations about the mass acquisition of telecommunications data and bulk interception of internet traffic by the US National Security Agency provide a salutary warning of how technological change has developed the architecture for a surveillance state' (Dorling 2013).[7]

Snowden's documents provided official confirmation of the

ECHELON programme, the electronic eavesdropping project. Duncan Campbell had first revealed its existence in 1988 and he notes that the Snowden documents revealed for the first time that ECHELON was part of a larger programme, codenamed FROSTING that was set up in 1966. One part of FROSTING, called TRANSIENT, targeted the Soviet Union's then new Molniya [молния or 'Lightning'] communications satellites. These were used for military and government communications.

> The second part, ECHELON, targeted the west's planned Intelsat satellites. These satellites were to be built and run by a consortium of western countries, the International Telecommunications Satellite Organisation (Intelsat). Intelsat satellites were and are used for TV broadcasts and for private, government and commercial communications.[8]

Snowden's material did not just raise questions over intelligence gathering, but also covert operations. A story run by NBC News described techniques developed by a secret GCHQ unit, called the Joint Threat Research and Intelligence Group (JTRIG), as part of a growing mission to go on the offensive and attack adversaries ranging from Iran to the hacktivists of Anonymous (Greenwald 2014). According to the documents, from internal presentations prepared in 2010 and 2012 for NSA cyberspy conferences, the agency's goal was to 'destroy, deny, degrade [and] disrupt' enemies by 'discrediting' them, planting misinformation and shutting down their communications. The PowerPoint presentations detail 'Effects' campaigns that are divided into two broad categories: cyber-attacks and propaganda operations. The propaganda campaigns use deception, mass e-messaging and 'pushing stories' via Twitter, Flickr, Facebook and YouTube (Cole et al. 2014).

JTRIG also uses 'false flag' operations, in which British agents carry out online actions that are designed to look like they were performed by one of Britain's adversaries (Cole et al. 2014). The leaked documents also revealed that some in GCHQ did not see journalists as the fourth estate but as a threat, as profiteers who were little better than terrorists. A GCHQ document in the Snowden cache warned of 'journalists and reporters representing all types of news media represent a potential threat to security' (Ball 2015).

With a vitriolic turn of phrase it continued: 'Of specific concern are "investigative journalists" who specialise in defence-related exposés either for profit or what they deem to be of the public interest' (Ball 2015). As the documents were gradually released more worrying information emerged. For instance, in October 2014 it was further admitted that GCHQ views material gathered by the NSA without a warrant (Ball 2014). Journalists interpret whatever snippets come into the public domain from intelligence. One, a nugget from the Snowden documents, reveals that GCHQ was prepared to hack the content of journalists' emails as early as 2008. This suggests that the agency has the confidence of political support for an action that would have been considered completely unacceptable in a modern democracy until quite recently, infringing, as it does, the freedom of the press (Ball 2015).

The UK investigative journalist, a specialist writer on electronic intelligence and interviewee Duncan Campbell pointed out that the Five Eyes operational network does now perform the anti-terrorism role well:

> It does work. It is what people want. It's what journalists absolutely do not seek to expose and that is shown in the Snowden case which is dripping with this stuff that I doubt will ever see the light of day because it is about anti-terrorism. (Campbell 2014)

Eternity in Moscow Airport

As the first Snowden-based stories began going public in June 2013, he left Hong Kong and flew to Russia where he has remained ever since. He told reporters he had destroyed his own copies of the secret documents and did not have access to them in Russia so he could not be compromised by the authorities there and branded a traitor. Snowden's revelations reached a global audience, and in terms of considering privacy and surveillance there is a watershed of before and after Snowden. When the Snowden revelations were published by major news media, including *The Guardian*, in a number of Western countries they polarised public opinion. The Snowden Affair was a fractious clash between the national security nexus and the media in developed Western countries. It highlighted the variations within democracies as to what is the right balance between security and civil liberties. Some commentators unreservedly attacked Snowden for his leaks and news organisations for publishing them. Charles Moore, the former editor of the *Daily Telegraph*, said:

> In traditional accounts of Hell, sinners end up with punishments that fit their crimes. Rumourmongers have their tongues cut out; usurers wear chains of burning gold. On this basis, it will be entirely fitting if Edward Snowden spends eternity in a Moscow airport lounge. (Moore 2013)

The UK government and the then Prime Minister David Cameron attacked *The Guardian* for giving succour to the enemy:

> As we stand today, there are people in the world, who want to do us harm, who want to blow up our families, who want to maim our country. That is a fact, it's not a pleasant fact, but it's a true fact. (Hope and Waterfield 2013)

Cameron maintained that the UK's intelligence agencies were fully accountable:

> So we have a choice, do we maintain properly funded, properly governed intelligence and security services, which will gather intelligence on these people, using all of the modern techniques to make sure that we can get ahead of them and stop them, or do we stop doing that? What Snowden is doing and to an extent what the newspapers are doing in helping him is frankly signalling to people who mean to do us harm, how to evade and avoid intelligence and surveillance and other techniques. (Hope and Waterfield 2013)

On the one hand, there was public shock at the surreptitious and massive expansion of surveillance capability On the other hand, in the face of escalating Islamist and far right terror, many members of the public expressed support for the agencies. Britain was noted for the intense level of criticism of Snowden. German commentators are among those most puzzled by the British reaction. Substantial parts of the British news media have a tendency to put aside objectivity in times of stress and replace it with 'patriotic journalism', falling in behind the government. However, in a rapidly globalising media world, patriotic journalism looks increasingly parochial.

The Snowden documents also reveal large-scale specialist hacking operations into target computers especially by the NSA's Tailored Access Operations (TAO) group – a cyber-warfare unit (Walters 2013). There has been one ominous glimpse of the potential of Five Eyes hackers to intercept and use journalists' private communications. According to *Der Spiegel*, the NSA hacked the computers of *Al-Jazeera* journalists in Qatar in search of terrorism contacts. One such document, dated 23 March 2006, revealed that the NSA's Network Analysis Center managed to access and read communication by 'interesting targets' that were specially protected by the news organisation (*Der Spiegel* 2013).

If eavesdroppers are able to identify sources and locations of sources from within the private computers in news organisations, this has serious ramifications. Journalists may well have contacts in terrorist groups as a legitimate part of their work. However, what happens if their contacts are hacked, identified and eliminated? How should journalists react if they now know that a source may be tracked and then, say, killed in a drone attack because eavesdropping agencies were able to break into journalists 'secure' communications?

Duncan Campbell remains frustrated that Snowden coverage had been so focused on bulk collection – all the data that the Five Eyes sucks out of the world's communication networks including phone and email metadata – and no one had asked what GCHQ did with the mass of data it collected. He points out that,

> The fact of the matter is, to understand in its context the harm or good that may be done by signal intelligence agencies, you have to look at the tasking, the collection management, the analysis process and above all the consumer reporting channel. (Campbell 2017)

His point is that GCHQ has customers: other agencies. These are drivers for government to fund GCHQ.

He says we need to know more about what happens to the information collected by GCHQ once it is passed on:

So if the Snowden documents, which they do on some occasions, speak to all of those processes, they clearly have more force and show more of the picture and when they don't, they certainly show collection capability and scale. But what is done with it? (Campbell 2017)

Damage Assessment

While journalists published documentation from Snowden, they sought to act responsibly, and concentrated on material that demonstrated the extent of mass surveillance and any other areas where the legitimacy and oversight is questioned (Lashmar 2017b). *The Guardian* editor told a parliamentary committee that the paper consulted with government officials and intelligence agencies, including the GCHQ, the White House and the Cabinet Office, on more than 100 occasions before publication (Rusbridger 2013). Those who have had access to the Snowden documents have told me there is a considerable amount of material on actual UK anti-terrorist operations. Estimates of the number of documents in the Snowden cache ranged from 150,000 to 1.7 million; only 7000, less than half of one per cent, have been published.[9] None published was from active anti-terrorist operations.[10]

With the exception of the USA, new laws have been passed to enhance the power and scope of the intelligence agencies. In some cases, the laws were scheduled at the time Snowden leaked the documents and in other cases the Snowden Affair was either part or all of the reason for new laws. The Investigatory Powers Act (IPA) passed into law in October 2016. Snowden tweeted: 'The UK has just legalised the most extreme surveillance in the history of western democracy.' The IPA is just one example of national security bodies being given more powers.

It is noteworthy that during the Snowden revelations, in the UK the Conservative partners in the coalition government would not acknowledge why critics of mass surveillance were so concerned, though it was really a continuation of a well-established debate over privacy that has run for several hundred years. The Liberal Democratic partners had understood such concerns, to the point of vetoing the first ill-fated manifestation of the Communications Data Bill, dubbed the 'Snooper's Charter', in 2013. The republican political theorist Quentin Skinner challenged Foreign Secretary William Hague's assertion that that no one has anything to fear so long as they have done nothing wrong. Skinner and Marshall pointed out he was missing an absolutely crucial point about the nature of freedom:

> to be free we not only need to have no fear of interference but no fear that there could be interference. But that latter assurance is precisely what cannot be given if our actions are under surveillance. So long as surveillance is going on, we could always have our freedom of action limited if someone chose to limit it. (Skinner and Marshall 2013)

They noted the situation is much worse once you come to know – as all of us now do – that we are in fact subject to surveillance.

> For now there is a danger that we may start to self-censor in the face of the known fact that we may be being scrutinised by powerful and potentially hostile forces. The problem is not that we know that something will happen to us if we say certain things. It's that we don't know what may happen to us. (Skinner and Marshall 2013)

And they made the point that people must know in advance exactly what activities are subject to surveillance, and why, and what penalties will potentially be incurred. 'And the use of surveillance will have to be undertaken by bodies that have to respond to Parliament, not merely to the Executive, which we often have no good reason to trust' (Skinner and Marshall 2013). Skinner and Marshall were referring to what is called 'the chilling effect' where people alter their behaviour because they think they are being observed. I would suggest this is already happening. As Bakir noted the 'chilling effect' of mass surveillance was formally recognised months after the Snowden leaks, 'as the UN General Assembly adopted a Resolution that ties the right to privacy to the right to freedom of expression: if people are subject to mass surveillance they are no longer able to express themselves freely' (2018: 8).

Notes

1. <https://collateralmurder.wikileaks.org/> (last accessed 23 September 2019).
2. The late lamented Audit Commission's local authorities' performance indicators data set.
3. This was formalised as the UKUSA agreement in 1946.
4. At the time of writing some 7,000 of these documents had entered the public domain.
5. Metadata is defined as data about data and in this case is information that accompanies and individually defines emails, phone calls, texts and other electronic communications but is not the actual content. Both the NSA and GCHQ are building huge warehouses for servers so that huge quantities of metadata can be collected and stored.
6. TEMPORA is the code word for GCHQ's surveillance programme that taps fibre optic cables for data.
7. The Five Eyes agencies argue that bulk collection is not the same as mass surveillance. They argue that you can pinpoint targets retrospectively if you have undertaken bulk collection. That is not the same as watching large numbers of people all the time.
8. <http://www.duncancampbell.org/content/nsa-yes-there-echelon-system> (last accessed 17 June 2019).
9. In May 2019 The Intercept controversially closed down the online archive of Snowden documents saying it was no longer cost-effective. For a critique of this decision see: 'The Snowden files: where are they and where should they end up?', <https://electrospaces.blogspot.com/> (last accessed 31 October 2019).
10. On the issue of acting responsibly, it is worth noting that the name and the home location of the MI6 handler for Sergei Skipral is well known to journalists but the DA-Notice committee has asked that they are not uploaded online, printed or broadcast. All UK mainstream media organisations have at the time writing abided by that request. The handler is identified in many non-UK news stories and has had prolific coverage on social media.

FIFTEEN

Lives at Risk

During the Snowden revelations intelligence chiefs and politicians claimed that publication of the Five Eyes secret documents put the lives of intelligence agents at risk. In four decades of covering intelligence agency activities I have seen many exposés of illegality, incompetence or unethical behaviour by the intelligence community and, often, the intelligence chiefs, their political masters and commentators' response has been to accuse editors and journalists of 'putting lives at risk'. It is true that there was a period post-Watergate when naming serving intelligence officers was considered to be in the public interest because of the extensive anti-democratic actions of the agencies in the early Cold War. That was short-lived and naming a serving intelligence officer without an exceptional public interest defence is now extremely unlikely. Naming serving intelligence officers was made illegal in the USA after Philip Agee's books named many CIA officers.

At the heart of this recurring problem is the balance between national security and the freedom of the press to inform the public over matters of genuine concern. My own research suggests that proven instances of people being killed as a result of media exposés of intelligence are very few, if any, and that the accusation does not have a lot of traction.[1] Arguments that exposure impacts on reputation and intelligence tradecraft are more compelling but require nuance. As with the Snowden documents, journalists and editors have not published specific details of anti-terrorism operations and have shown restraint. Over recent years, I have interviewed twenty or so investigative journalists from the Five Eyes countries. All have untaken national security investigations and indeed, in most cases, have broken major national and international stories in this specialist area. All were deeply sceptical of the 'putting lives at risk' intelligence agency counter-narrative to their stories (Lashmar 2017b, 2018b). They saw this response by agencies that had been caught behaving badly as disingenuous. The fourth estate is a pithy aspiration for the journalist, but before journalists get too pompous, it does represent a flawed concept as it does not encompass the other less high-minded pressures journalists can come under to publish, ranging from economic and market forces to career enhancement (Hampton 2010). And so it has been shown in the UK context with the phone-hacking-related scandals that have had an enormous impact on trust in the media

Putting Lives at Risk

If spies claim that journalistic exposés place them at risk, it is worth looking at the flipside. Take for example American journalist Peter Theo Curtis who was kidnapped in Syria, by the al-Nusra Front in October 2012. His hostage takers believed him to be a CIA agent and tortured him, convinced he was a spy because he was so knowledgeable about the Middle East and Islam and fluent in Arabic, French, German and Russian. Curtis had written about the Middle East for such magazines and online news sites as the *New Republic*, the Huffington Post and the *London Review of Books*. He had entered Syria with the intention of writing an article about journalist Austin Tice, who had been kidnapped two months earlier. Curtis's cellmate was American war photographer Matt Schrier who escaped after seven months of captivity. Peter Curtis was released after two years when his family paid a ransom. The whereabouts of Tice, an American photojournalist, remains a mystery.[2] There is no evidence that any of these men were ever spies.

In another example, a former colleague of mine, Farzad Bazoft, then a freelance correspondent at *The Observer*, was executed in Iraq on Saddam Hussein's orders in 1990 after being accused of espionage. A relatively inexperienced reporter, Bazoft was an Iranian born journalist who was arrested by Iraqi authorities while on a reporting trip and hanged after being 'convicted' of spying for Israel. In a Reuters Institute report, Robert G. Picard and Hannah Storm made the point: 'A significant challenge for journalists in conflict zones is that some combatants or sides in the conflict may believe journalists are propagandists or spies for their enemies' (2016: 11). Suspicions that journalists are spies, they said, were not completely unwarranted. The same argument can apply to the UK. Frank Snepp, a CIA field officer in Vietnam in the 1970s, said he knew from first-hand experience that the British were using journalists as field operatives or that journalists were British field operatives: 'certain MI5 men were operating under deep cover as journalists and we using them to plant stories favourable to American interests in certain publications that we couldn't reach in the same way' (Snepp 1981). The CIA's recruitment of journalists or placing of agents undercover as journalists was purportedly banned in 1977, but CIA director John Deutch stated in 1996 that the agency had a waiver that gave it the right to continue to do so (Picard and Storm 2016: 11).

In 1999, I wrote a story based on inside sources for *The Independent* newspaper that British Intelligence officers working undercover abroad often claimed to be journalists, using forged National Union of Journalists (NUJ) press passes. The article also revealed that SIS officers had used 'deep cover' as reporters to work in Yugoslavia during the Bosnian War. The NUJ condemned the practice. 'If spies pose as journalists, some people will see journalists as legitimate targets', said John Foster, the then NUJ's general secretary. 'Every year, hundreds of legitimate journalists put their lives at risk while reporting overseas and many are killed. Other people using falsified documents would make journalism even more dangerous' (Lashmar 1999).

In my second article on this subject, former intelligence officers told me that British spies used their forged NUJ card to gain access to and interview officials (Lashmar 2000b). This would have been impossible or difficult for other foreigners. At the time, my sources close to the SIS also told me that their officers preferred to use journalistic cover when in the field, rather than posing as businesspersons or academics. The renegade SIS officer Richard Tomlinson admitted that he and other officers had frequently posed as reporters while on spying missions in hostile environments. Tomlinson claimed that SIS officers use journalistic cover on about four out of every ten spying missions. Tomlinson also confirmed that the SIS set up news agency 'fronts' to give cover for SIS operations and he told me in conversation that, in 1992, the SIS set up a surrogate news agency in central London as a front for cultivating and recruiting Russian journalists to spy for Britain and obtain military secrets. The Truefax news agency was established in Conduit Street in central London by Tomlinson and a KGB defector, to provide short-term cover (Tomlinson 2001: 103–6).[3]

There are sufficient examples of journalists working for US and UK news organisations being killed, having been accused of being a spy, to support the notion that there is a real and escalating danger. Terrorist groups, militias and authoritarian regimes have often justified the arrest, kidnapping, torture or murder of journalists, by claiming they were 'spies'. The abuse by intelligence agencies of the freedom of the press is a significant factor in endangering the lives of those journalists who operate in hostile environments. The sheer number of examples of US and UK intelligence using journalists over the years is so widely known that when supporters of terrorists, militias and authoritarian security forces make claims that a journalist is a spy they can believe it might be true.

There were those, in government and the intelligence community, who believed that covertly paying and using journalists, whether in the USA, in other democratic Western nations or elsewhere, was entirely justifiable. This position was firmly rebuffed by *The New York Times* in 1976, when it published a leader highly critical of the CIA's involvement with journalists.

> Practically as well as philosophically, this was wrong. American readers have a right to assurance that the journalists are not in any sense accountable to unseen paymasters. And foreign sources of news and the international consumers of American news have a right to expect that government purposes do not influence the process of reporting and editing. (*The New York Times* 1976)

Despite their protestations they are the victims, the spooks have helped to create a very dangerous climate in which to be a journalist. In 2015, I attended a panel where the former Director of GCHQ, Sir David Omand, made a welcomed, but at the time unreported, admission that UK intelligence agencies had used journalistic cover and that 'used to be the case in Britain' but that it 'stopped some years ago because it put the whole journalistic profession at risk' (Omand 2015). I am not aware of any other policy statement by a senior UK intelligence chief on this controversial issue. The suborning of journalists by intelligence agencies and using journalistic cover thus undermining the freedom of the press is an example of 'the paradoxical suspension of democracy as a means of saving democracy' (Agamben quoted in Melley 2012: 5).

Watchdogs or Lapdogs?

In addressing how intelligence and the media interact, it is important to consider the function of intelligence within the state and to examine the checks and balances that are in place to make sure intelligence powers are not abused. Intelligence academics Peter Gill and Mark Phythian have commented on the importance of the media in bringing accountability to the intelligence agencies:

> The media in general remain significant, if inconsistent, contributors to oversight. Certainly, the heightened public concern with security of the wake of 9/11 has increased greatly media attention to intelligence matters, and the media have played an important role in alerting the public to concerns among intelligence professionals at the politicization of their product. (2012: 169)

Dr Claudia Hillebrand suggested that the news media have three oversight roles:

1. Information Transmitter and Stimulator for Formal Scrutinisers.
2. Substitute Watchdog.
3. Legitimizing Institution.

She argued there are limitations especially when the news media act as 'lapdogs' where journalists fail to sufficiently question government policies or simply transmit unsubstantiated claims by government officials.

> Overall, the research has shown that the media's scrutiny functions are practised in an infrequent, ad hoc and informal manner. The media, thus, provide an uneven quality of intelligence oversight and, while contributing to the scrutiny of intelligence, do not easily fit into existing conceptual frameworks of intelligence oversight. (2012: 705)

Striking a Balance

Since 1996, all UK intelligence agencies have been able to state they operate in a legal framework. They also assure us from time to time that they tightly monitor legal and ethical frameworks. We have little actual idea because of the secrecy that surrounds their operations. When their operations do become public it is not always reassuring, as we will see in Chapter 17, when we actually find out, often many years after the event, that intelligence agencies lied and were granted exemptions from the rule of law. Vian Bakir has argued that intelligence agencies 'are increasingly central to policies that challenge and contravene human rights in fighting the Global War on Terror' (2018: 1). The current situation for the intelligence and media relationship is imperfect and I have discussed devising a framework for an ethical relationship that would allow accurate information to enter the public domain without jeopardising legitimate national security (see Lashmar 2015c).

Undercover with the Special Branch

Andrea (pseudonym) was introduced by a friend to a good-looking man in his thirties called Carlo Neri at an anti-war demonstration in London in 2002. At a public meeting some sixteen years later, Andrea reflected that while she was not what she would describe as a serious activist, she was well known and trusted by different groups of anti-fascist campaigners. This, she believes, is why Neri (whose real name has not been officially released) targeted her (Logan 2018). Neri struck up a relationship with her claiming to be an activist. As Andrea recalled, they, as she thought, fell in love, moved in together within months and, after a while, Neri proposed (Logan

2018). Andrea explained how Neri, who claimed to single and employed as a locksmith, presented a credible story of why she was never able to meet his family. He played on her sympathies for the trauma he claimed to have experienced:

> He arrived with a story of difficulties in the family, and he had talked about a difficult relationship with his father. He said his mother was dead and his father was still alive but there had been domestic abuse in the family life. (Logan 2018)

Well-regarded and ubiquitous within the activist and trade union community, nobody suspected that Carlo Neri and his elaborate backstory were a well-rehearsed fiction. After two years the relationship ended as he gave the impression he was having a nervous breakdown – apparently a standard exit strategy used by undercover cops. A decade later Andrea was shown documentation which proved Neri was a police officer, not as he claimed a locksmith, and that he was married with children at the time of their relationship.[4] Neri was a senior member of the SDS, part of the Metropolitan Police's Special Branch, and retrospectively it can be seen his targets were socialists and anti-fascist groups. Andrea recalled Carlo was a convincing in his part:

> If you can imagine a really good method actor, someone like Christian Bale, who can change the way he looks, or Robert DeNiro, and they become someone else and they live it, I think it's a little bit like that. A really sinister, state sponsored version of method acting. (Logan 2018)

There were two main units of undercover officers tasked with spying on political groups. The SDS ran from 1968 to 2008. The second unit was called the National Public Order Intelligence Unit (NPOIU). It was set up in 1999 and then merged into other units in 2011 after an undercover officer Mark Kennedy was exposed and the subsequent revelations about the undercover officers began. At the heart of this relationship, which is similar to many other SDS operations, is the abuse of power. Andrea was not the only victim. There were other women and a few men. In some cases the undercover officers even fathered children with the women they had targeted or used as cover for infiltration operations. This was an abuse of trust and some victims have argued – if unsuccessfully in court – rape. What can the state say to a woman, as happened in some cases, who has had a child with an undercover officer she thought was a soul mate but was in fact using her to infiltrate a political campaign?

Senior officers of the security forces assented to these relationships, presumably claiming it was in the wider public good. So undercover police officers like Neri have the power of knowledge, which they use to control and manipulate partners, knowing for instance that any relationship is going to end. Was an indication of an ethos that has to exist in the organisation to allow such abuses to occur a form of *jus in intelligentia* where some harm occurs to prevent a much greater harm?[5] However, in the case of Andrea – where is the proportionality? There is no evidence that she posed any serious threat. Nevertheless, given the abuses were unknown until investigated by campaigners and *The Guardian*, cases like these show why the media must be at the heart of accountability of the intelligence and security services and provide such a vital counterbalance.

Carlo Neri requested anonymity at the inquiry, expressing his concerns about a personal attack from the people he infiltrated – a left-wing anti-fascist group called No Platform:

> During my deployment, I became very close to a number of activists who were the main organisers of this group. During my operation I witnessed a number of assaults, public disorder and petty crime all of which was reported through my chain of command to the appropriate recipients. My deployment was instrumental in disrupting a lot of this group's activities as police resources were targeted accordingly to disrupt their intentions.[6]

There remain questions of whether officers acted as agent provocateurs, and even whether they were well targeted, given there is little evidence that the SDS or NPOIU engaged early enough with the rise of 'home grown' Islamist terrorism. *The Guardian* journalist, Rob Evans, raised with the author an interesting (and still unanswered) question: how many undercover officers were targeted at Islamist terrorists in July 2005 when such a number of them were infiltrating environmental/left-wing groups? (Evans 2018)

A third of the undercover police officers used identities taken from the register of births and deaths where the child had died young. The SDS they built up a false 'script' or life for the officer. Interestingly, in 2001, the former SIS officer Richard Tomlinson wrote; 'MI6 do not use the "dead baby" aliases, as described in Frederick Forsyth's book "The Day of the Jackal", for fear of legal action by angry relatives if an operation should go wrong and be publicly exposed' (2001: 108)

As one of the journalists who revealed the activities of the SDS, Rob Evans made another interesting point to the author about the nature of power when he observed that the women duped into relationships that were suddenly curtailed were 'for years isolated, if suspicious' and powerless but then there was a change in the power balance (Evans 2018). As their stories emerged they began to work together, researching their vanished partners and campaigning for justice. Together these women have reversed the power relationship and have triggered a public inquiry and have found, confronted and outed many of the officers who once manipulated them. The SDS scandal presents a remarkable failure of oversight and any sense of managerial moral compass and raises the question of what the other agencies were doing in the same period.

The history of intelligence tells us, if we care to note, that intelligence entities, screened as they are from public view, have a tendency to exceed their remit, in the same way the Victorian politician Lord Acton suggested 'power tends to corrupt, absolute power tends to corrupt absolutely'. I first heard this dictum when I was a student and thought it a bit glib, but forty years on I have seen it proved time after time. I have reported extensively on breaches of trust and note their persistent recurrence in slightly different permutations. The quest for the grail of an effective oversight mechanism remains frustrated, though many countries have tried.

Notes

1. For a detailed analysis of the evidence see Lashmar 2017a.
2. Before becoming a journalist, Tice was a US Marine officer. This highlights the danger of mixing careers and that being a former serviceman raises the risks if taken hostage. Many freelance journalists in the Middle East conflicts have had military backgrounds.
3. At the same time I was able to reveal that MI6 officers had been working undercover in Iraq as part of the part of the United Nations teams of arms inspectors looking for chemical and biological weapons. The disclosure followed admissions that US spies had worked in the United Nations Special Commission (UNSCOM) teams. Sources in Whitehall and at the UN in New York told us that MI6 first infiltrated the UN weapons inspectorate soon after it was set up in 1991: 'A number of officers were asked if they were interested in the posting.

One officer joined for a period', said a source. Some officers are thought to have been rotated through the teams (see Lashmar and Usborne 1999).

4. Like many of the SDS officers on operation, he only saw his wife and family sporadically.

5. See Bellaby 2012 for the full definition.

6. Neri's statement called be seen at <https://www.ucpi.org.uk/wp-content/uploads/2017/08/HN104-Open-personal-statement-from-Slater-Gordon.pdf> (last accessed 17 June 2019).

SIXTEEN

Ostriches, Cheerleaders, Lemonsuckers and Guardians

Before the 1990s, the UK executive oversight of the intelligence services was straightforward, if minimal and often ineffective. The Foreign Secretary oversaw the SIS and GCHQ. MI5 was answerable to the Home Secretary. In any organogram, it would be a straightforward chain of command up from the agencies through the Cabinet to the prime minister. Security and espionage scandals were investigated by ad hoc inquiries but only limited versions of the inquiry reports, concentrating on management issues, were published until Harold Macmillan set up the Security Commission in the 1960s to deal with such embarrassments. The long-standing convention that government did 'Not confirm nor deny' (NCND) anything to do with the intelligence agencies was still in place. So no one would admit to the existence of the constituent parts of the UK intelligence community, or comment on their activities. This approach resulted in some complex procedural acrobatics when trying to explain scandals that had occurred in government departments that officially did not exist.

In the UK, official accountability and oversight mechanisms for the intelligence agencies have developed over the last fifty years in response to external pressures.[1] Prime Minister Margaret Thatcher adhered to NCND whenever the issue of intelligence arose in Parliament. However, her government came under relentless pressure to put the agencies on a legal footing. The line of command is important. Who, it was asked, do intelligence officers ultimately have loyalty too? Left-wing critics argued that MI5 saw its primary allegiance to the Crown rather than the elected government of the day. Phythian noted: 'There were suspicions that this extended to undermining Labour governments, reinforced by the revelations contained in the former MI5 officer Peter Wright's memoir *Spycatcher*' (2007: 76).

Spy Watching

As a result of the many revelations in the 1980s of UK intelligence and security services' wrongdoing, regulation followed. In 1989 legislation was passed to constitute the Security Service, MI5, as a full legal entity. In November 1993 the government published its Intelligence Services Bill and simultaneously published, for the first time, the estimates for the intelligence services – then £900 million for the year (Gill 1996: 313). The Bill was enacted in 1994. Gill suggested that the Act came about, at least in part, because of the government's concern that the non-legal status of the intelligence services would leave them vulnerable to adverse court rulings, not least from the European Court of Human Rights (1996: 323). But which oversight system to use?[2] Gill noted the main innovation in the Act, and one which apparently provided some potential challenge to the executive's information control, was the creation of the Intelligence and Security Committee (ISC), a Parliamentary body, which is not quite a select Committee but an unique entity that could examine the expenditure, administration and policy of the Security Service, the SIS and GCHQ:

In their book, Gill and Phythian noted: 'Oversight of intelligence, whoever carries it out, is inescapably political' (2012: 194). To counter accusations of arbitrary power, democratic nations have sought to open up government information to public scrutiny after a certain, often quite long, period of time has elapsed. In his paper, Gill noted that oversight of security intelligence agencies is perhaps the most demanding of all parliamentary challenges and it has become harder in the wake of 9/11 and the declaration of the war on terror (2007: 15).

Even with ISC in place robust parliamentary oversight of the intelligence services was slow in coming. Former Labour MP and chairman of a select committee, Chris Mullin, stated the struggle to render the security and intelligence services accountable to Parliament has been a long one.

> When I first joined the home affairs committee 20 years ago, I asked the then Home Secretary, Ken Clarke, if we could interview the then head of MI5, Stella Rimington. Clarke refused. However, it was rumoured that Rimington, in an effort to improve the image of the service, had been privately briefing newspaper editors. I rang a couple who confirmed they had met her. How come, I asked Clarke, when he next came before the committee, the head of MI5 was permitted to meet with the unelected, but not with the elected? At which point he came out with his hands up. Half a dozen of us were invited to lunch with her. (Mullin 2013)

While Parliament's ISC is the most high profile of the UK's intelligence oversight mechanisms, there are a number of oversight organisations that intermesh with the intelligence agencies. The Investigatory Powers Act 2016 brought into being the Investigatory Powers Commissioner's Office (IPCO) that consolidated independent oversight of the use of investigatory powers by intelligence agencies, police forces and other public authorities. The IPCO also replaced the previous regime of three judicial commissioners. The Prime Minister approved the appointment of Sir Adrian Fulford as the first Investigatory Powers Commissioner in 2017.

In addition there is:

1. The Investigatory Powers Tribunal (IPT), a court that investigates and determines complaints of unlawful use of covert techniques by public authorities infringing our right to privacy and claims against intelligence or law enforcement agency conduct which breach a wider range of human rights.[3] In February 2015 for the first time in its fifteen year, existence the Tribunal issued a ruling that went against one of the security agencies. It ruled that GCHQ had acted unlawfully in accessing data on millions of people in Britain that had been collected by the NSA, because the arrangements were secret (Shirbon 2015).
2. The Independent Reviewer of Terrorism Legislation whose role is to inform public and political debate on anti-terrorism law in the United Kingdom, in particular through regular reports,

which are prepared for the Home Secretary or Treasury and then laid before Parliament. The uniqueness of the role lies in its complete independence from government, coupled with access based on a very high degree of clearance to secret and sensitive national security information. At the time of writing it was Max Hill QC.

Chesterman has observed: 'meaningful accountability of intelligence services depends on a level of public debate that may be opposed by the actors in question, proscribed by official secrets acts and constrained by the interests of elected officials' (2011: 80–1). From talking to people I know who have worked for the intelligence services, detailed ethical and legal guidelines have been built into the decision making process. It is a very different world from Peter Wright's generation. Gone are buccaneering old school approaches to intelligence gathering and covert action. Today, in Western intelligence agencies there are strict procedures to follow for any operation and in-house lawyers to consult as to the precise legality of any course of action.

The Performance of Oversight Mechanisms

Gill has made a compelling case that putting the intelligence agencies on a legal footing was not so much an enlightened move but damage limitation designed to minimise negativity from the media. He suggested that the exposure of illegality and incompetence in the 1980s by the news media was clearly likely to force major change to accountability and transparency.

> Some examples of 'resistance' to traditional state secrecy in the UK during the last 20 years have succeeded to the extent that the state has shifted its ground from traditional assertions of an absolute right to secrecy in any matter that can be labelled 'national security' to a more subtle strategy mixing secrecy and persuasion. (1996: 327)

Gill's persuasive case has led me to reconsider what I saw until recently as a retreat by the agencies and their political overseers to something more like a pragmatic repositioning and not in fact a change of ethos. The ISC was set up to reassure the public that there is cross-party parliamentary scrutiny, and while it had to some extent over the last twenty-five years provided better oversight than expected, the Snowden revelations had placed it in a poor light as reactive and complacent. In documents released by Snowden it was revealed that GCHQ promoted Britain's weaker surveillance laws and regulatory regime as a 'selling point' to win engagement with the NSA (Hopkins and Harding 2013). While the Snowden material had forced the Obama administration to review NSA operations, the British government has resolutely refused to admit there is any problem with GCHQ's activities and powers.

After Snowden the suspicion remained that UK intelligence accountability bodies have too often 'gone native', possibly mesmerised by the glamour or political significance of the task undertaken by intelligence agencies. Another element of accountability was the office of the UK Intelligence Services Commissioner appointed under Section 59 of the Regulation of Investigatory Powers Act 2000. In March 2014 the then incumbent Sir Mark Waller, a retired High Court Judge, was questioned by the Parliamentary Home Affairs Select Committee about the Snowden revelations as to whether GCHQ had acted unlawfully. The Committee seemed less than impressed when in his response he told them that he had been to see a senior official at GCHQ who had assured him it was not true. [4] In fairness, he had no resources; his office was staffed by two people (Sparrow 2014).

Perhaps the most respected of the oversight officials of recent years has been David Anderson QC who until 2017 was the independent reviewer of terrorism legislation; he was forensic and critical in his method. For example, he reported publicly that MI5 could have prevented the terrorist attack in Manchester, which killed twenty-two people, if it had not 'wrongly' interpreted intelligence on the bomber, Salman Abedi (Anderson 2017). Anderson stopped short of blaming MI5 and counter-terror police for failing to prevent four attacks in the UK since March, which resulted in the deaths of thirty-six people. However, his report highlighted shortcomings in the way the Security Service and the police work together and share intelligence with local police forces and local authorities.

244 / Spies, Spin and the Fourth Estate

The US academic Loch K. Johnson insightfully suggested that overseers fall into four categories: ostriches, cheerleaders, lemonsuckers and guardians:

> For example, some *cheerleaders* and *lemonsuckers* may be mild in their advocacy or criticism, respectively, while others may be zealous. In the case of the *ostriches*, some may poke their heads out of the sand at least once in a while, if only to cheer for the CIA. As for guardians, some may be better than others at keeping an even keel between offering praise and finding fault. (2011: 304; emphasis added)

Gill pointed out that we have learnt of highly controversial policies such as rendition and torture and mass communication surveillance, not from these formal institutional mechanisms of oversight in the UK, but rather as a result of whistle-blowers, legal action and investigative journalists (2013: 3). Official oversight in the UK, he stated, was insufficient:

> First, because of the inadequate legal basis for the authorisation and control of UK intelligence agencies and, second, institutions of oversight are overly-concerned with the legalities of intelligence practices compared with broader issues of ethics and public education. Effective oversight will always depend partly on an informal network of researchers, journalists and lawyers in civil society but a mature democracy must develop an oversight system with adequate powers and full-time research staff. (2013: 4)

The ISC has only recently developed the capability to monitor the programming and mathematical sides of its charge's work. Accountability lies at the heart of this book and I have sought to establish how effective are the raft of official oversight mechanisms in the UK. I have examined the reports and publications of these bodies, read the various key texts, and discussed these with some of the leading international experts on intelligence accountability, intelligence professionals and journalists.[3] I have not been able to find a compelling example of an institutional mechanism *proactively* identifying a serious intelligence failing. This not only covers the UK but also other Five Eyes countries and others.[6]

This supports the point made by Gill that revelations have come about as a result of whistle-blowers, legal action and investigative journalists working together. *The Guardian* in particular has consistently made the public aware of management and oversight failures in the UK security state.[7] The official oversight mechanisms are reactive and *post facto*. It has been argued that journalism has been the most effective means of holding the intelligence services to account in Britain and other Western democracies.

Intelligence and PR

The self-presentation of the intelligence community as benign is ever more systematic (Lashmar 2018b). Aldrich observed, 'the most common misperception concerning modern intelligence agencies is that they have attempted to live in the shadows. They are often interpreted as seeking to conceal themselves from the press.' He argued that those intelligence agencies and their former employees have been very active in shaping perceptions of their work. 'Much of what we know about modern intelligence agencies has in fact been placed in the domain deliberately by the agencies themselves' (2009: 17–18). The world of intelligence and the relationship between intelligence and the news media has changed a great deal over the last forty years. How damaging has the press been to the intelligence services since they became more open?

Praising the openness initiatives in both countries, Christopher Moran noted that UK and US intelligence agencies have opened up, that in the UK official authorised histories of MI5 and SIS have been published, and that we have seen a lot more public appearances by spy chiefs. He pointed out that one of the lessons from all of this is that the world has not caved in.

All of those concerns that the hardened Cold Warriors had in the 70s and 80s had about opening up a little bit, were: 'Wow! If we give the public a little bit, will their appetite grow with the eating and suddenly we be giving everything away? Agents' names will be all over the front page of *The Guardian*. Intelligence will cease to be.' Well that hasn't happened. Those truly cataclysmic predictions about 'end of the world' intelligence scenarios have not happened. Measured degrees of openness are important. (Stout and Moran 2018)

Moran suggested that part of the job of the modern spy chief is to market a positive view of intelligence.

> The spy chief in 2018 and 21st century has to be public, has to be visible, has to try and sell the intelligence mission to a sceptical Congress, to a sceptical Parliament, to a public that is often inherently distrustful of intelligence activity. (Stout and Moran 2018)

Moran proposed that that spy chiefs, 'play a huge role now in trying to shape and influence those, misunderstandings, in many cases, of the intelligence role and they have to play this role' (Stout and Moran 2018).

Robert Hannigan, who was Director of GCHQ from 2014 to 2017, was not a veteran intelligence senior official but a civil servant with expertise in PR who was adept at presentation and moved into the security arena when he was promoted to be the Prime Minister's Security Adviser, under Tony Blair in 2007. Given GCHQ remains the most secretive of all the agencies this was an interesting appointment (Stout and Moran 2018). As part of its presentational strategy it has started to let trusted journalists visit the famous 'doughnut' building. Former *Daily Telegraph* editor Max Hastings was given a tour, but more significantly Gordon Corera, the BBC's security correspondent, reported from GCHQ and was the first journalist to see the holy of holies, the inner sanctum – the central computer area (Corera 2017b). But was it just a piece of PR? Meanwhile the accredited reporter system with its attributable briefings continues to operate between MI5 and SIS and the major mainstream UK news media. Intelligence is power. It contributes to Britain's standing among its allies. The ability of nations like Israel and Saudi Arabia, that are widely perceived as pariah states, to enjoy support from the British government, comes in part from the quality of the intelligence on Islamist terror that they provide.

The Big Bang

The intelligence elite extend far beyond the well-known Whitehall agencies and committees. The police have been involved as the effective arm of anti-terrorism operations and Special Forces have a role as well as military intelligence. There is also a substantial and expanding private research and security industry, particularly in the USA, worth hundreds of millions of dollars per year. Aside from political connections, operational priorities since 9/11 have enabled intelligence elites to closely connect with military and corporate domains through symbiotic private consultancies (Walker 2014; Bakir 2018). According to a 2013 *New York Times* op-ed article, 70 per cent of America's intelligence budget is used to outsource to private contractors. The US intelligence budget for 2013 was about $80 billion, and the *NYT* suggested that made private intelligence a $56 billion-a-year industry (Shorrock 2013).

Outsourcing in the UK is not on the same scale as the US in terms of actual expenditure or percentage of budget, but there has not been an accurate estimate of the value of the sector. Nevertheless, outsourcing is expanding and this raises very serious and unaddressed questions about ethics, privacy and transparency. There are also major issues about private intelligence companies working for both the state and private clients at the same time. It is worth noting that Edward Snowden was working for the private contractor Booz Allen Hamilton of McLean, Virginia, at the time he decided to go public with his revelations. Booz Allen Hamilton is one of America's biggest security contractors that was worth at the time $6 billion and had 25,000 staff (Borger 2013). Former high-level intelligence officials and government trained surveillance specialists are turning up working for authoritarian governments. If private companies are handling intelligence data, what is the oversight to make sure it is not also provided to private sector clients? Bakir noted that intelligence elites extend into the private sector and that makes holding them accountable difficult (Bakir 2018: 23). There was the Project Raven team, which included former NSA officials who worked for the United Arab Emirates intelligence services against dissidents, and journalists (see Doctorow 2019). The Five Eyes governments, who claim such tight oversight, have articulated no response to this profoundly disturbing trend – a new generation of government trained techno spy mercenaries.

Rarely a week goes past in which some dramatic aspect of national security has not been news. Intelligence is becoming more, not less, important and it remains a powerful political tool on the global platform to have a highly effective intelligence agency. On the one hand, Mossad's intelligence omnipotence in the Middle East has protected Israel from greater sanctions over its policies. On the other hand, the GRU's blunderings over the Skripal poisonings and other failures have made Russia look mendacious, incompetent and guilty.

The repercussions from Russian involvement in the 2016 Brexit referendum and the US Presidential Election rumble on. When the British Prime Minister Theresa May was having a difficult time negotiating Brexit with the EU in June 2018, the highest card in her hand was to call on the reputation of British Intelligence. She accused the EU of putting European lives at risk if under the withdrawal deal, the mysterious all-pervasive surveillance powers of British Intelligence, and in particular GCHQ, were no longer available to the twenty-seven EU countries.

Notes

1. Accountability is a wider concept than oversight. 'Oversight ensures that the overall policies of intelligence agencies are consistent with their legal mandates' (Gill and Phythian 2012: 173). The aim is to ensure efficacy and propriety. By contrast, accountability requires giving an account or explanation of actions, and taking blame or undertaking to put matters right if errors are made. Gill stated that oversight refers to the review or scrutiny of intelligence activities so that those directing them can be held accountable: 'The main objective of the scrutiny is to secure public trust in the agencies through ensuring that their expenditure is efficient and effective and that their operations are legal with proper respect for human rights. This scrutiny will, ideally, be carried out both by specialist units *within* agencies and ministries as well as externally by parliamentary and/or extra-parliamentary bodies' (2013: 1).

2. As Bochel et al. noted there is no one model of intelligence oversight. 'It will, of necessity, vary from country to country, and may be affected and defined by a state's history, its constitutional and legal systems, and its political culture' (2013). The British system is very different from the US system and just about every other nation's system.

3. In February 2015 for the first time in its fifteen-year existence the Tribunal issued a ruling that went against one of the security agencies. It ruled that GCHQ had acted unlawfully in accessing data on millions of people in Britain that had been collected by the NSA, because the arrangements were secret (Shirbon 2015).

4. The report can be read at <http://www.publications.parliament.uk/pa/cm201314/cmselect/cmhaff/231/23108.htm> (last accessed 17 June 2019).

5. I raised this question with intelligence studies academics at the International Studies Conference, 2015.

6. The only example was a case in Canada where the commissioner identified a mismatch between what an agency had said and what their documentation actually stated.
7. A long-term police security operation to monitor environmentalists and other activists using undercover officers in the UK has been detailed. Undercover officers were often years undercover and engaged in long-term relationships, fathering children under their aliases and disappearing afterwards. It is also alleged that in some cases police officers acted as agent provocateurs in illegal actions. For a full account see Evans and Lewis 2013.

SEVENTEEN

Reflections on Forty Years of Spy Watching

Scepticism is a useful characteristic for some professionals, especially for the journalist or academic, but you must also be able to identify change when it occurs. A powerful motivation for writing this book was anger and despair that the UK official oversight and accountability system had failed to be inquisitive, robust and critical. I could only identify a handful of occasions in a quarter of a century when oversight bodies or officials had been in any way critical of the intelligence agencies and then only when the case was irrefutable.[1] However, change can occur, and my critique was partially confounded during writing, as in little over one week, in June 2018, a series of reports by oversight bodies appeared that were notable for their unprecedented criticism. Notably, there were two reports released by parliamentary oversight body, the ISC, whose past record had been notably supine. These new reports contained disturbing details about SIS involvement in the CIA's rendition and torture policy after 9/11 (Intelligence and Security Committee 2018a, 2018b). This involvement had been deliberately concealed for over a decade (Cobain and MacAskill 2018). In December 2005 the then Labour Foreign Secretary Jack Straw, the minister responsible for the SIS and GCHQ, issued a categorical denial of SIS involvement in rendition and torture when he told the Commons Foreign Affairs Committee:

> Unless we all start to believe in conspiracy theories and that the officials
> are lying, that I am lying, that behind this there is some kind of secret

state, which is in league with some dark forces in the United States . . .
there simply, is no truth in the claims that the United Kingdom has been
involved in rendition. (Cobain 2018c)

Straw was setting out the line for government and the intelligence
agencies to parrot for a decade. Significantly, some thirteen years
later the 'cheerleaders' (as Loch K. Johnson typology has it) at the
ISC had evolved into 'guardians' and it seemed that Jack Straw had
misled the media and public. ISC's full oversight of MI6's involvement in rendition and torture was constrained as they lacked the
key powers to investigate further. They note that the then Prime
Minister Theresa May had intervened to exempt SIS officers from
public accountability and the rule of law. The ISC were unable to
require the senior SIS officers who had overseen cooperation with
the US rendition programme and the junior SIS officers who took
part in these events to give evidence.

ISC's four-year inquiry found that the UK had planned, agreed
or financed some thirty-one rendition operations. Moreover, there
were fifteen occasions when British Intelligence officers consented
to or witnessed torture, and 232 occasions on which the intelligence agencies supplied questions put to detainees during interrogation, who they knew or suspected were being mistreated. MI5
had helped to finance a rendition operation in June 2003 (Cobain
and MacAskill 2018). In October 2004, the then foreign secretary,
Jack Straw, authorised the payment of a large share of the cost of
rendering two people from one country to another. The underlying
proposition is that national security trumps the rule of law and that
is a slippery slope. The ISC reports contradict what the government
and intelligence services had said publicly and forcefully from 2004
onwards about their involvement in torture and rendition (Cobain
and MacAskill 2018).

That the ISC had found some guts, if not teeth, maybe down
to the chairmanship of the ISC of Dominic Grieve, the maverick
Conservative politician who has been a very different chair from his
predecessor, Sir Malcolm Rifkind. That intelligence accountability
appears so dependent on the character of the chair is a concern. The
2018 reports reflected a more robust and critical tone than earlier
ISC reports, but were still constrained by the Committee's lack of

powers for subpoenaing officials. The Committee forcefully made the point it needed greater powers to undertake its work effectively.

The ISC reports were timely and came just a month after Theresa May issued a public apology to Abdel Hakim Belhaj, who was kidnapped in 2004 with the assistance of the SIS. He was rendered to one of Muammar Gaddafi's prisons, along with his pregnant wife Fatima Boudchar, and tortured. These reports are important landmarks for accountability, but a year later one of the first actions of Boris Johnson on taking office as prime minister, was to block the next stage of the inquiry, a decision *The Guardian* (2019) labels 'immoral'.

Two days before the ISC reported, an important independent tribunal judgment was delivered, officially confirming that the British government broke the law by allowing spy agencies to amass data on UK citizens without proper oversight from the Foreign Office.[2] GCHQ had been given greatly increased powers to obtain and analyse citizens' data after the 9/11 terrorist attacks in 2001, on the condition that it agreed to strict oversight from the Foreign Secretary. An independent court that was set up by the government to investigate unlawful intrusion by public bodies, the IPT, concluded that the Foreign Office has, on several occasions, given GCHQ 'carte blanche' to extract data from telecoms and internet companies. The judgment noted: 'In cases in which . . . the Foreign Secretary made a general direction which applied to all communications through the networks operated by the [communications service provider], there had been an unlawful delegation of the power.'[3] To my pleasant surprise two oversight mechanisms were seen to act as guardians rather than ostriches.

Lying Bastards?

There is a jokey dictum in journalism that when interviewing powerful figures you should always ask yourself. 'Why are the lying bastards lying to me?' It is not always funny as they do lie on key issues or are, as Robert Armstrong admitted in the *Spycatcher* court case, 'economical with the truth'. Jack Straw has never explained his 2005 denial that British Intelligence were involved in rendition and torture. Perhaps he did not know but in that case he has a responsibility to say so in public. In Chapter 14 I noted that the then Prime Minster David Cameron's response to the 2013 publication of the Snowden documents was that GCHQ operated within the law and was 'properly governed intelligence', and that was the main thrust of the government's counterattack. Nearly a decade later it became clear that was simply false and GCHQ was often operating outside the law, or if one is being very benign, covered its legal exposure with a threadbare patchwork of antiquated laws that were never drafted for the modern age.

'It was all a bloody lie'

The release of the scathing ISC reports in 2018 sparked one of the most powerful condemnations of the deceitful nature of the British Intelligence community I have seen in recent years by a journalist. It came from *The Observer*'s Peter Beaumont, who has been dealing with official intelligence contacts over many years. He notes that the denials are what readers get to see – the carefully formulated statements written in government press offices often after a period of to and fro with the journalist.

> What readers don't get to see is another kind of to-and-fro. The direct appeal to editors and reporters. The insistence that our secret services 'don't do this kind of thing', are bound by rules, by UK, EU and international law, are 'Crown Servants', and in any case are bound by a sense of decency.
>
> Except, as it is now quite clear, it was all a bloody lie. The answers given to journalists at *The Observer* over the years, as well as colleagues at *The Guardian* and those at other news organisations, as they investigated these allegations, were rotten with untruth and evasion. (Beaumont 2018)

More likely, the exasperated Beaumont fumed, as the reports suggest, it was worse than that: it was nothing short of a long-running cover-up that persisted for a decade and a half, that saw British officials tell lie after lie over the years for British public consumption, to sustain the impression that torture is something that only happens in other countries:

A fundamental test of a functioning democracy is that all of its citizens should be accountable to the same scrutiny and laws, yet it appears that the government continues to protect MI6 officers in particular who may be implicated in wrongdoing.

Most urgent of all is that Britain's intelligence agencies not only give a full account of their behaviour but that new safeguards are put in place to ensure that British officers stick to the letter of the laws they claim to uphold. (Beaumont 2018)

After these reports, the thinking media's trust in the intelligence services is at a low. In recent years, the agencies have given assurances that they are concerned with human rights. However, we have no way to check. It is very seductive to connect with the secret world of intelligence but these people, I am sad to say, do lie, dissemble and act outside the rule of law, all with the support of government.

Techniques of Deflection

As a journalist reporting on the intelligence world you are often working with limited data and the danger is the wrong conclusions are drawn. From forty years of covering intelligence, policing and other controversial areas as journalist I note certain recurring patterns: agencies exceeding their powers; national interest overriding morality; political bias; suborning freedom of speech; jobs for the boys; deception and lies. Intelligence is often exempted from the rule of law, when there is pressure on the national security state for results. There are also the tropes which those in authority use deflect censure for their failings. A major story breaks with embarrassing and detailed evidence but it is still the agencies instinct not to come clean but instead to use one of the deflecting techniques from those that are tested and tried:

Technique 1: It's All Right Now

Over the years of reporting stories that revealed illegality or incompetence, and not only in the areas of intelligence and organised crime, it is frequently followed by the refrain from that organisation's senior leadership that 'it's alright now'. The leadership always says that the situation has now been remedied and the rotten apples removed from the barrel. Typically, there will be a high profile press conference where the leaders feign shock at the revelations but claim wholesale changes had been implemented. Lo and behold – and almost guaranteed –it will happen again a few years down the line. Organisations tend to insert some new guidelines and after a 'decent interval', those who are determined will find their way round them. The buck does not stop at the top but the bottom. Bakir undertakes a telling case study of the Bush administration and shows it used a number of strategic political communication techniques to frame media exposés of administration abuses as isolated examples and therefore atypical, where in fact they were a product of secret, systemic policies.

> To reframe the depicted abuses as something other than torture, the Bush administration pursued three strategies: providing evidence that interrogation techniques, although harsh, were legal – evidencing that the Abu Ghraib incidents were examples of isolated abuse rather than policy. This was reinforced by depicting Guantánamo as a model prison; and destroying visual evidence of torture. (Bakir 2013: 140)

As Bakir noted with this approach 'The people caught on camera as the isolated abusers serve jail time – everyone else gets off scot free' (2013: 140).

Technique 2: Kick into the Long Grass

Some of these investigations and inquiries take years if not decades to conduct and meanwhile all those responsible have moved on. Alternatively, the documents are withheld for decades. The Chilcot Inquiry into the Iraq War report was released thirteen years after the events it investigated. The Intelligence and Security Committee's torture and rendition inquiry took a further four years after other inquiries failed to deliver – again reporting thirteen years after the events. At the time of writing there is a public inquiry into the activities of the Special Demonstration Squad a policing unit that was created in 1968. Some inquiries are never really completed, such as the investigation into the Stalker Affair. An inquiry into the circumstances around the policing and involvement of MI5 in the Miner's Strike has still to occur. We still have only a limited picture of the collusion between British security forces and loyalists in Northern Ireland during The Troubles, as recent documentaries on both the massacre at Ballymurphy in 1971 and the massacre at Loughinisland in 1994 show. The government has resisted pressure to hold an inquiry into the interference and covert funding of some of the Leave campaigns despite evidence of massive illegal manipulation of the democratic process.

Technique 3: Safe Pair of Hands

Try to assign to the inquiry a chairperson who will not cause the government or responsible authorities too much pain. Lord Denning's report into the Profumo case was a 'whitewash', and so they continue. Many felt the Hutton Inquiry into the BBC coverage of WMD, which reported in 2004, was one sided – highly critical of the BBC but soft on the government.

Technique 4: Nelson's Blind Eye

This was a technique long used by the ISC especially under Sir Malcolm Rifkind. They did not see what they did not want to see. Therefore the ISC put out a report shortly before Snowden's documents were published giving no indication of the massive global expansion of bulk collection, the agency's intrusions into all aspects of electronic communication and that the legal basis on which GCHQ operated was dubious.

Technique 5: Complete Denial

This is tricky one to use as Jack Straw discovered with SIS involvement in torture and rendition. Your version of events had better be true or history will come back to haunt you and destroy your reputation. Dissembling and denial are short-term fixes that fail in the long term, and just undermines trust in the democratic process.

Technique 6: Override the Rule of Law

When the intelligence services were placed on a legal footing from 1989 onwards, they were said to have developed and put into place rigorous legal and human rights frameworks. In reality we have little or no idea how these are implemented in practice. What we do know is that the agencies SIS, MI5, GCHQ and Special Branch have all acted outside the law yet have suffered no consequences. When there is any sign of intelligence agency staff being formally questioned by police over legal breaches in their work the attorney general or the prime minister steps in. There are also caveats.

In the case of the ISC Inquiry 2014–18, Grieve said that because it had been denied access to key intelligence staff by the prime minister, the committee had reluctantly decided to bring the inquiry to a premature end. He said the 2018 reports were being published because he felt the information gathered so far should be put into the public domain. Commenting on Prime Minister Theresa May's interventions, Lord Macdonald, a former Director of Public Prosecutions, noted that Theresa May had derailed the ISC's inquiry into rendition by refusing to allow it to interview more junior SIS and MI5 officers.

Her purported reason for refusing the ISC access to the officers actually involved in these events – that there was 'legal uncertainty over the protection that would be offered to officers appearing as witnesses before the committee' – is completely bogus, as she and her advisers must have known. (Cobain 2018a)

When it comes to illegality in the intelligence services government will act to prevent prosecution of officers on the basis that it endangers national security. So as with so many of the cases described in this book, the intelligence services operate outside the rule of law.

Historically, there is still much we do not know about how British Intelligence has operated. How was it that South African intelligence, the notorious Bureau of State Security (BOSS) that wreaked mayhem and murder in the interests of apartheid, seemed to have free rein on the streets in the UK during the 1980s? Did it have anything to do with Prime Minister Margaret Thatcher and other members of the Cabinet's known sympathies towards the apartheid regime (Cobain and MacAskill 2018)? We do not know. Neither do we know much about MI5 and Special Branch's involvement in the 1984/5 Miner's Strike. There is growing evidence that MI5 and Special Branch had secret two-way channels with the Economic League, a private blacklisting organisation used by a number of UK industries to keep out trade union activists. The League was closed down by 1993 as result of media exposure – I was one of the reporters – of their insidious, shadowy activities that destroyed many working people's lives. We know little of British Intelligence's relationship with Mossad – which does assassinate targets – except it is highly valued for its intelligence penetration of Arab regimes, and this tends to protect the Israeli government from criticism by the British government. The SIS and GCHQ's involvement with economic intelligence is little known despite the economic security of the nation being one of their three primary objectives.

There remain a plethora of historical intelligence operations to research and understand. What is now known of the activities of the Special Demonstration Squad is of concern and quite Orwellian in nature. As a Special Branch sub-species, they were outliers on the security forces spectrum, nearest to the MI5 constellation, but nonetheless their activities and lack of accountability are profoundly disturbing. We do not have much of an idea whether MI5 or (in a different mode) SIS did or still do these kind of highly unethical operations, taking advantage of innocent participants. We, of course, cannot know what we do not yet know, until the archives become available.

While this book mostly concerns itself with the main intelligence and security agencies, I am very aware of the multi-faceted expansion of the intelligence world post-9/11. One evolving and major oversight concern is the outsourcing of intelligence operations. Certainly, the direction of travel by the Five Eyes network means surveillance capability is subject to gradual integration with the private sector. The power of algorithm-based technology and artificial intelligence, focused on profit, where public and private sectors become indistinguishable, has the potential for mass behavioural modification. This presents a terrifying prospect.

Value Systems

The closed nature of the intelligence services makes it difficult for the public and the media to exercise an informed and coherent critique of the performance of the agencies. We do not know what the value systems of those who populate the intelligence services are and how their value systems guide the choice of targets. Within the intelligence agencies, it is impossible to test empirically as the UK intelligence community have successfully resisted any kind of external ethnographic study as far as I am aware. I only know of two such studies and both were in the United States.[4] I do not doubt that the agencies run psychometric tests of recruits to ascertain whether they have a suitable personality for the work. I have no idea if the agencies have commissioned value system studies of their own staff but in the unlikely event that such studies were published it would provide an anchor point to understanding what intelligence staff think is their job and who they think they protect.

There is no doubt that many of the MI5 staff had the racist and supremacist attitudes that were common in Britain in the twentieth century. Thankfully, MI5 officers I have met since 2000 have been sophisticated cosmopolitan characters with apparently enlightened values. However, all are men and white. SIS officers still have a tendency to be a bit *Boy's Own* and GCHQ staff are of a different ilk and are mostly analysts, technologists and linguists.

Understanding what the intelligence community does, how to think about what exactly it is there for and how we judge it is unresolved. Intelligence historian Christopher Andrew points out that the 'under-theorisation' of intelligence studies is not simply a problem for academic research:

> It also degrades much public discussion of the role of intelligence. Since September 11, 2001, the media and even some learned journals have been full of claims of 'intelligence failure'. However, the majority of those who use the phrase seem to have no coherent idea of what it means. Clearly, a lack of a 100 per cent success rate does not constitute failure. (Andrew 2004: 181)

Christopher Andrew is right as most of the news media are stuck in a 'success' or 'failure' binary that does not serve their audience well. It is a shame that public perceptions of intelligence are warped by fictional accounts of the spy world, which reduce and infantilise the serious problems faced by the intelligence community into simplistic binary concepts. In that dialectic, they can only win or lose. How do journalists get to understand how well the intelligence community functions and replace the binary narrative with a more nuanced approach to reporting? Brunatti argued that organisational histories of Australian intelligence should be published, to counter 'the skewed perception [of the agencies] as both all-seeing behemoths and dangerous bumblers'. '[T]he truth' he says, 'is in the middle.' While locating the truth is the middle needs empirical support, Brunatti makes a good point that can equally apply to the other Five Eyes countries (2018: 212).

As we have seen, spies and hacks do not merely interact but actually interchange, but that does not make it professional or ethical. Professor Richard Keeble examined a wide range of claims of inappropriate relationships between intelligence agencies and journalists. His article goes right up to the New Labour government at the time of the Iraq War.

> Thus from this evidence alone it is clear there has been a long history of links between hacks and spooks. But, as the secret state grows in power, through massive resourcing, through a whole raft of legislation – such as the Official Secrets Act, the anti-terrorism legislation, the Regulation of Investigatory Powers Act and so on – and as intelligence moves into the heart of ex-British leader Tony Blair and prime minister Gordon Brown's ruling clique so these links are even more significant. (Keeble 2008)

Some journalists have paid for such opaqueness with their lives. The problem with this interchange is that the media has a well-established watchdog duty, their fourth estate role. If there is inter-change then conflicts of interest arise. It should be deontological that once in one of the two professions you should not switch to the other. It might be understandable that the post-war generation took a more relaxed view but their deliberate opaqueness has left all journalists open to the allegation that they are spies. Journalists and spies should be separate. Suborning journalists and journalism undermines the very freedoms that intelligence agencies are meant to protect.

The Last Refuge

In the days when news organisations were regional or national and during international tensions, as in the Cold War, the notion of 'patriotic' journalists had some traction in the Western news indus-tries. Today, the patriotic tendency, whether in intelligence or the news media, is looking archaic in a world that is globalised and has multinational entities and agreements, like the Five Eyes network, where there are many different realities and cultural narratives. In a globalised world, journalists should be exceedingly careful about the ethics of 'patriotic' motives as their audience is global. The relationship between ethics and intelligence is still an unresolved ontological problem, in understanding what a modern state is. As this book documents, the intelligence services have purveyed fake news on behalf of the Crown for at least a century (see also Bellaby 2012). They have even bypassed the prime minister if they believe they have a higher motive, as with the Khokhlov case. Untroubled by journalistic ethics, IRD, funded by the taxpayer, pumped out highly selective facts – or as we know it now 'spin' – and pure fantasy for thirty years (Lashmar and Oliver 1998b: 176).

In Northern Ireland, the British propagandists produced concocted anti-IRA stories that verged on the surreal. These state propagandists argued they were engaged in an ideological war and theirs was a higher calling. Dispensing with notions of the truth is detrimental to democracy, full stop. A short-term piece of mischief has long-term negative consequences. Over the years, the evidence that has trick-led out of the intelligence community does not reassure, revealing instead a long history of ideological targeting, evidence of inter- and intra-agency turf wars, betrayals, lying and incompetence. A disregard for the truth or any sense that the public need to informed accurately. It is not reassuring. Yet there is a huge psychological need to feel the intelligence community are doing a good job and the nation wants to believe that the modern intelligence community is highly effective and has overcome the failings of the past. While I am delighted to have seen robust oversight reports in June 2018, it cannot be assumed that the oversight mechanism is now effective.

Mass Surveillance?

Currently, observers have very little idea of the length and breadth of the current capabilities of the Five Eyes intelligence community. The last substantive insight came in June 2013 with the Snowden documents, which revealed that technological capability was far more developed than even experts suspected, making Five Eyes surveillance capabilities global and hugely powerful, and further expansion was planned. Snowden's documents also showed that their global spread had widened as the Five Eyes network collaborated with around thirty-two other partner countries, though the degree of sharing is varied and partial. Since Snowden there has been little further insight. There have been a few top-secret Five Eyes documents released by WikiLeaks since then but nothing that gives us a clue to the contemporary bigger picture.

As a journalist, one hears allegations of far greater abuses of power and illegal activity by the agencies than those that have been publicly reported in the past. However, without hard evidence it is difficult to prove or disprove. This a challenging task as the intelligence world is even more protective of its secrets than in the past. We learnt from Snowden's documents that the government is prepared to massively expand the remit of the intelligence community and surveillance without wider debate. We cannot rely on whistle-blowers; there are few brave people like Katherine Gun or Cathy Massiter, but it is just a handful. Nor is the mantra that one hears from senior intelligence chiefs that the more people of intelligence would blow the whistle if anything untoward was occurring. Look at the decision of the Bush administration's post-9/11 instruction to allow the CIA to illegally wiretap targeted American citizens. It is estimated that up to 200,000 intelligence staff knew about this but no more than five were prepared to raise the issue either at the time or in the years that followed. Thomas Drake says he went through fourteen levels of whistle-blowing and then was persecuted and faced jail as a result (2015). It was only after a very hesitant effort by the US media that the illegality was brought to light.

Why bother with all of this? To understand enables change. The French philosopher Michel Foucault provides a possible answer when he identified that a key task of intellectual activity is to explain the present:

> What's effectively needed is a ramified, penetrative perception of the present, one that makes it possible to locate lines of weakness, strong points, positions where the instances of power have secured and implanted themselves by a system of organisation dating back over 150 years. (1980: 62)

To help understand the role of intelligence in the state, Vian Bakir developed the concept of the 'intelligence elites' from C. Wright

Mills's wider notion of the power elite (Mills 2000). Bakir sought 'to focus attention away from intelligence agencies and towards far less accountable elements in intelligence policy making' and has adopted the term for two reasons:

> Firstly, it highlights that they are a more restricted group of people than the power elite, but with close relationships and interconnections across military, political and corporate worlds, making fundamental decisions on policies concerning intelligence that affect all citizens. Second, it highlights the exclusion of the public from the intelligence elite's decision-making, including their oversight and accountability. (Bakir 2018: 10)

Foucault provided a historically based approach for re-evaluating popular constructions of the world, encouraging readers to think deeply about power and knowledge. His ideas provided a new way to look at surveillance but talked about the 'gaze' and 'interiorisation' to explain how we control our social behaviours. 'There is no need for arms, physical violence, material constraints', he noted. 'Just a gaze. An inspecting gaze, a gaze which each individual under its weight will end by interiorising to the point that he is his own overseer, each individual thus exercising this surveillance over, and against, himself' (1980: 155). Foucault applied such insight to his ideas where he tried to conceptualise the nature of the way government interacts with its citizens in governing them and what he called 'governmentality'. Two key parts of this approach examine:

- the way governments try to produce the citizen best suited to fulfil those governments' policies;
- the organised practices (mentalities, rationalities and techniques) through which subjects are governed.

Why is all this important? Intelligence agencies have the potential to exercise power through secrecy that, in certain circumstances, would not be just undemocratic but authoritarian. With his usual concision, John le Carré summed up the key question in 'Fifty Years later', a foreword to a new edition of his book, *The Spy Who Came in from the Cold*, as 'how far can we go in the rightful defence of our

Western values without abandoning them along the way?' (2013: x). Analysis of intelligence elites post-9/11 is vital at a point when they have more resources, more legal powers and more political influence than ever before.

Any discussion that may improve the practice of these professions in a democracy must be of value providing it serves the public interest. If philosophy and political theory have real application in statecraft, there are few more important tasks than to develop a normative and conceptual framework for the way intelligence agencies should serve democratic nations. This policy should be framed so that it does not undermine the very democracy they are there to serve. This is still unresolved. Some have suggested that the intelligence services becoming more open to the media was folly. In light of the WMD debacle, two intelligence academics proposed that the intelligence services should return to anonymity (Glees and Davies 2004). I would counter by proposing that Waldegrave's 1993 Initiative for Open Government was only a move in the right direction. Had complete anonymity still been the order of the day we would not have known of the politicisation of the SIS, involvement in the CIA's torture and rendition, and illegal GCHQ surveillance.

No Longer Fit for Purpose

Based on my own experience from 1978, the historic record and the evidence considered above, I argue that in the UK the news media became effective, if inconsistently so, in the period 1960 to 2000 in bringing intelligence to account. It was ad hoc, as there was no attempt at a long-term strategy of revelation, either across the media, or in individual news organisations. Media organisations do not act in deliberate concert. The combination of media ownership, the war on terror, tougher anti-whistle-blowing laws, consumer interest and technology has conspired to make it harder for journalists to perform this role. However, there is some light. Since 2014, the emergence of Open Source Intelligence (OSINT) as a tool for investigative journalism has been pioneered by Bellingcat,[5] a radical collective experiment set up by Eliot Higgins that has done extraordinary work in a number of important stories including the shooting down of the jet MH17 over Ukraine and revealing the identities of the GRU officers who were responsible for the botched assassination of Sergei Skipral in Salisbury. The example of the Skipral case shows that OSINT has the capability to bring accountability to intelligence agencies (Matthews 2018). As the name suggests Open Source Intelligence uses information that is in the public domain, occasionally following up with traditional investigative journalism methods but also using the power of international crowdsourcing to huge effect. The power of OSINT is such that intelligence agencies are wondering how to employ such techniques, although Bellingcat are the diametric opposite of the secret world of spying and eavesdropping.

The Legacy

Senior members of the intelligence services have told me in recent years that the agencies are packed full of decent people who would not allow illegal or undemocratic acts to take place. While not decrying the fact that the tasks these people do are often honourable and seek to protect the nation, we must also remember the wiretapping scandal of the Bush administration, the SDS, torture, rendition and many historical examples. Few insiders, and in some cases no insider, came forward to raise concerns. That, to me, reinforces the value of independent journalism. Like a number of journalists of the post-1970 school, I took the view that government, utilising the national security blanket of the Second World War, used secrecy to hide a range of anti-democratic actions, illegality and a good deal of incompetence. These we sought to expose and very much saw this as our fourth estate duty. I argue that the evidence demonstrates that intelligence did frequently exceed its remit. Many examples of Aldrich's concept of 'regulation by revelation' are set out above.

Incursions into the freedom of the press deepen. From the second half of 2014 it emerged that the police and other agencies in the UK had been making use of the provisions of the Regulation of Investigatory Powers Act (RIPA) to identify journalists' sources. Derbyshire Police's Chief Constable, Mick Creedon, who was also the Association of Chief Police Officer's national coordinator for serious and organised crime, said RIPA could 'absolutely' be used to secretly obtain journalists' phone records in a leak probe (Turvill 2014). By February 2015, RIPA has been used at least eighty-two times to identify journalists' sources (Turvill 2015).

Importantly, Snowden's disclosures present journalists, as in other professions like lawyers, doctors, and religious ministers, with a problem of source protection, as their professional ethics require, as appropriate, total confidentiality. Journalists have to ask whether they are any longer in a position to give a reasonable guarantee of protection. In a sense, it does not matter whether intelligence agencies do use data to track down confidential sources; it is the fact that they can do so much more easily than ever before that is significant. That such surveillance potentially creates a negative 'chilling effect' on the flow of information from confidential sources was, as we have seen, recognised at least as far back as the Watergate scandal in the early 1970s. Journalists will not give up their work but what are they to do? How will they protect sources? Without greater legal protection for sources, much of government and private sector organisations will no longer be subject to effective scrutiny by the fourth estate. The media remain vital. While official UK oversight bodies have recently been more robust, these accountability mechanisms are reactive, not proactive, and are usually triggered by media reports. What is needed is a proactive accountability investigative capability of these bodies.

A State of Exception

The UK and USA have changed greatly since 2001 and not necessarily for the better. Everywhere one travels in the UK – unlike other EU countries – one is constantly reminded of the threat of terrorism, and at the time of writing travellers are bombarded by the police campaign message, 'See It, Say It, Sorted', on public transport. The incessant repetition has been positively Orwellian. The threat of terrorism eats away at the national psyche. We accept restrictions, intrusions and draconian laws that would have been unthinkable twenty years ago. For nearly thirty years, from the 1970s, the UK had a civil war that occasionally spilled over from Northern Ireland to the mainland. During The Troubles repressive legislation was resisted and debated. The Prevention of Terrorism

(Temporary Provisions) Act (PTA) 1973 was temporary, requiring annual renewal by Parliament. The Home Secretary introducing it said, 'The powers ... are Draconian. In combination they are unprecedented in peacetime.'⁶ For many years the PTA was controversial but the provisions of all related legislation were consolidated into the permanent Prevention of Terrorism Act 2005.

The British have developed a capacity for exceptionalism born out of the supremacist nature of the Empire. We simply justify repressive actions against those whose actions we do not think are part of the normal by 'othering' them, whether they are 'natives', suffragettes, trade unionists, people of colour, lesbian, gay, bisexual or transgender (LGBT), Catholics, Jews or Muslims. These instincts lie uneasily next to the enlightened aspirations of British culture that include democracy, tolerance and aiding those in distress.

Historically, government has resisted enhancing oversight of the secret state unless it is forced to do so by revelation. However, in the war on terror, the UK government applied the brake to openness, detecting an increase in public sympathy or possibly an exhaustion of civil society by terrorism. The public response to the Snowden revelations has been muted compared with that of other developed nations, especially Germany. Foucault's ideas are useful to understanding why, as central to his concept of governmentality is the idea of 'government' that is not limited to state politics alone, but includes a wide range of control techniques, and that applies to a wide variety of objects, from one's control of the self to the 'biopolitical' control of populations (Lemke 2001). Any change in the method of government that affects how we behave and impacts on our concepts and practice of freedom warrants full discussion, rather than the power-holders sweeping aside such concerns as secondary to the imperative of national security. Britain is arguably the most surveilled democracy in the world, and Foucault saw surveillance as a 'discipline' that could be used to change public behaviour.

There is always the suspicion that fear of terrorism is a card UK politicians play in order to distract from other issues like austerity. Writer Cory Doctorow proposed that the UK war on terror is, in part, political theatre by the government, when he stated, 'I think they are throwing red meat to their base':

> It is all just theatre when they say, we are going to make sure everyone
> takes their shoes off or make sure that everyone isn't carrying more than
> three ounces of liquid or make sure people are not using crypto or what-
> ever, none of this has any nexis with stopping actual terror attacks . . . I
> certainly appreciate that terrorism is a danger but the total mortality from
> terrorism is infinitesimal. (Doctorow 2015)

Perhaps the BBC filmmaker Adam Curtis caught the post-9/11, post-Iraq War signal moment well in his 'Power of Nightmares' series that suggested that politicians now encourage citizens to believe that they are the only protection in an uncertain world (Curtis 2004). It is worth saying there are moments of light. In May 2019 a dogged consortium of civil society bodies lead by Privacy International won a significant court victory. After a five-year battle with the UK government, the UK Supreme Court ruled that the Investigatory Powers Tribunal's decisions are subject to judicial review in the High Court. Privacy International said: 'The Supreme Court's judgment is a major endorsement and affirmation of the rule of law in the UK. The decision guarantees that when the IPT gets the law wrong, its mistakes can be corrected.'[7]

How to encapsulate this changed world so we can better understand it? Agamben's concept of the 'state of exception' has resonance – what was once exceptional and temporary is now the new normal. Agamben's concept has been summarised as 'the par-adoxical suspension of democracy as a means of saving democracy' (Melley 2012: 5). Melley suggests the state of exception is now remarkably stable. We may or may not be in a state of exception, but there certainly has been a turn that has not yet been well artic-ulated or theorised. An enormously powerful mass surveillance machinery is now in place without adequate safeguards. It is one thing while a democratic state operates, but if we continue to move in an authoritarian or populist direction that is quite literally fright-ening. In the wrong hands, GCHQ can now make the Stasi in East Germany look like a surveillance cottage industry. Fact can be stranger than fiction. The election of President Trump who can direct the NSA's global surveillance programmes to target anyone, has been a very troubling development. There are politicians in the British Parliament whose authoritarian views, dislike of expertise and history, certainly make me as nervous as Trump. Distracted, perhaps we really are sleepwalking into the surveillance state.

Notes

1. As the independent reviewer of terrorism legislation, 2011–17, David Anderson QC was the most robust oversight official. When the BBC discovered that MI5 has secretly been collecting vast amounts of data about UK phone calls to search for terrorist connections, Anderson told them the legislation used to authorise the collection was 'so vague that anything could be done under it'. He added: 'It wasn't illegal in the sense that it was outside the law, it was just that the law was so broad and the information was so slight that nobody knew it was happening' (Corera 2015). On another occasion, in February 2015, the intelligence watchdog, the Investigatory Powers Tribunal, found GCHQ had breached human rights conventions in relation to the UK's access to the NSA's bulk data collection program.
2. The IPT judgment can be found at <https://www.ipt-uk.com/judgments. asp?id=45> (last accessed 17 June 2019).
3. The IPT judgment can be found at <https://www.ipt-uk.com/judgments. asp?id=45> (last accessed 17 June 2019).
4. There is the *Analytic Culture in the U.S. Intelligence Community: An Ethnographic Study* commissioned by the CIA to improve their analytical capability after the failure of weapons of mass destruction intelligence (Johnston 2005). There is also a PhD dissertation which is an ethnographic study of the National Counterterrorism Center (Nolan 2013).
5. <https://www.bellingcat.com/> (last accessed 24 September 2019).
6. Hansard col. 35, 25 November 1974, Mr Jenkins.
7. The judgment can be found at: <https://privacyinternational.org/press-rel ease/2897/privacy-international-wins-historic-victory-uk-supreme-courthttps:// privacyinternational.org/press-release/2897/privacy-international-wins-histor ic-victory-uk-supreme-court> (last accessed 17 June 2019).

REFERENCES

Agee, P. (1975), *Inside the Company, CIA Diary*, London: Penguin Books.

Aldrich, R. J. (2001), *The Hidden Hand: Britain, America and Cold War Secret Intelligence*, London: John Murray.

Aldrich, R. J. (2004), 'Policing the past: official history, secrecy and British intelligence since 1945', *English Historical Review*, 119: 483, 922–53.

Aldrich, R. J. (2009), 'Regulation by revelation? Intelligence, the media and transparency', in R. Dover and M. S. Goodman (eds), *Spinning Intelligence: Why Intelligence Needs the Media, Why the Media Needs Intelligence*, London: C. Hurst, pp. 13–36.

Aldrich, R. J. (2010), *GCHQ: The Uncensored Story of Britain's Most Secret Intelligence Agency*, London: HarperCollins.

Aldrich, R. J. (2015), 'American journalism and the landscape of secrecy: Tad Szulc, the CIA and Cuba', *Journal of the Historical Association*, 100: 340, 189–209.

Aldrich, R. J. and R. Cormac (2016), *The Black Door: Spies, Secret Intelligence and British Prime Ministers*, London: William Collins.

Allan, S. (2010), *News Culture*, 3rd edn, Maidenhead: McGraw-Hill/Open University Press.

Anderson, D. (2017), *Attacks in London and Manchester: March-June 2017: Independent assessment of MI5 and police internal reviews*, <https://assets.publishing.service. gov.uk/government/uploads/system/uploads/attachment_data/file/664682/ Attacks_in_London_and_Manchester_Open_Report.pdf> (last accessed 31 October 2019).

Andrew, C. (1985), *Secret Service: The Making of the British Intelligence Community*, London: Sceptre.

Andrew, C. (2004), 'Intelligence, international relations and "under-theorisation"', *Intelligence and National Security*, 19: 2, 170–84.

Andrew, C. (2009), *The Defence of the Realm: The Authorised History of MI5*, London: Penguin.

Asthana, A. (2017), 'Nine terrorist attacks prevented in UK in last year, says MI5 boss', *The Guardian*, 5 December

Bagdikian, B. H. (1977), 'Woodstein U: notes on the mass production and questionable education of journalists', *Atlantic*, March.

Bakir, V. (2013), *Torture, Intelligence and Sousveillance in the War on Terror: Agenda-Building Struggles*, Farnham: Ashgate

Bakir, V. (2015), 'News, agenda building, and intelligence agencies: a systematic review of the field from the discipline of journalism, media and communications', *The International Journal of Press/Politics*, 1: 1, online first, 30 January.

Bakir, V. (2018), *Intelligence Elites and Public Accountability: Relationships of Influence with Civil Society*, Abingdon: Routledge.

Ball, J. (2014), 'Government admits NSA data is viewed with no warrant', *The Guardian*, 29 October.

Ball, J. (2015), 'GCHQ captured emails of journalists from top international media', *The Guardian*, 20 January.

BBC (2015), 'Frederick Forsyth reveals MI6 spying past', *BBC News*, 30 August, <http://www.bbc.co.uk/news/entertainment-arts-34101822> (last accessed 5 June 2016).

BBC *Radio 4 News* (1988), 10.00am, 7 March.

Beaumont, P. (2018), 'I tried to expose the truth about MI6 and torture – but was lied to', *The Observer*, 1 July.

Bellaby, R. (2012), 'What's the harm? The ethics of intelligence collection', *Intelligence and National Security*, 27: 1, 93–117.

Bennett, G. (1999), '"A most extraordinary and mysterious business": the Zinoviev Letter of 1924', FCO History Note no. 14, London: FCO.

Bennett, G. (2006), *Churchill's Man of Mystery: Desmond Morton and the World of Intelligence.* London and New York: Routledge.

Berg, S. (2019), '"Fake news" sent out by government department', *BBC News*, 18 March, <https://www.bbc.com/news/uk-politics-47571253> (last accessed 11 May 2019).

Bernstein, C. (1977) The CIA and the Media, Rolling Stone, 22 October, <http://www.carlbernstein.com/magazine_cia_and_media.php> (last accessed 29 July 2019).

Bird, K. (1992), *The Chairman: John J. McCloy & the Making of the American Establishment*, New York: Simon & Schuster.

Bloch, J. and P. Fitzgerald (1983), *British Intelligence and Covert Action: Africa, Middle East and Europe since 1945*, London: Brandon Press.

Bochel, H., A. Defty and J. Kirkpatrick (2013), 'New mechanisms of independent accountability', *Parliamentary Affairs*, 13 November.

Bolton, R. (2018), 'Shooting the messengers', *British Journalism Review*, 29: 2.

Borger, J. (2013), 'Booz Allen Hamilton: Edward Snowden's US contracting firm', *The Guardian*, 6 June, <http://www.theguardian.com/world/2013/jun/09/booz-allen-hamilton-edward-snowden> (last accessed 16 February 2019).

Bower, T. (1995), *Perfect English Spy: Sir Dick White and the Secret War 1935–90*, London: St. Martin's Press.

Boyce, G. (1978), 'The fourth estate: the reappraisal of a concept', in G. Boyce, J. Curran and P. Wingate (eds), *Newspaper History from the Seventeenth Century to the Present Day*, London: Constable.

Brandt, D. (1997), 'Journalism and the CIA: The Mighty Wurlitzer', *NameBase News Line*, 17, April–June.

Bridges, E. (1956), 'The report of an enquiry on an intelligence operation against Russian warships', 18 May.

Bright, M. (2002a), 'Look back in anger', *The Observer*, 2 February.

Bright, M. (2002b), 'Terror, security and the media', *The Observer*, 21 July.

Brunatti, A. (2018), 'Managing reputational risk', in D. Baldino and R. Crawley (eds), *Intelligence and the Function of Government*, Melbourne: Melbourne University Press, pp. 209–39.

Calder, R. (2004), *Beware the British Serpent: The Role of Writers in British Propaganda in the United States, 1939–1945*, Montreal: McGill–Queen's University Press.

Campbell, D. (1993), 'The Hill', Channel 4 *Dispatches*, 6 October.

Campbell, D. (2010), 'GCHQ: the uncensored story of Britain's most secret intelligence agency', *The New Statesman*, 28 June.

Campbell, D. (2014), Interview with the author and follow-up communications, 2 January.

Campbell, D. (2017), Interview with the author, 8 April.

Campbell, D. and M. Hosenball (1976), 'The eavesdroppers', *Time Out*, 21 May.

Campbell, D. and P. Lashmar (1999), 'How Britain eavesdropped on Dublin', *The Independent*, 16 July.

Campbell, D. and P. Lashmar (2000), 'Revealed: 30 more nations with spy stations', *The Independent*, 9 July.

Carlyle, T. (1840), *On Heroes, Hero-Worship, and the Heroic in History*, <http://www.gutenberg.org/files/1091/1091-h/1091-h.htm> (last accessed 17 June 2019).

Cavendish, A. (1997), *Inside Intelligence*, London: HarperCollins.

Chesterman, S. (2011), *One Nation under Surveillance: A New Social Contract to Defend Freedom without Sacrificing Liberty*, Oxford: Oxford University Press.

Church, F. (1975), *Alleged Assassination Plots Involving Foreign Leaders*. Interim Report. Washington, DC: US Government Printing Office.

Church, F. (1976), *The Final Report of the Select Committee to Study Governmental Operations with Respect to Intelligence Activities*, Washington, DC: US Government Publishing House.

CNN (2019), September 11 Terror Attacks Fast Facts, CNN Library, 22 October.

Cobain, I. (2012), *Cruel Britannia: A Secret History of Torture*, London: Portobello Books.

Cobain, I. (2013), 'Foreign Office hoarding 1m historic files in secret archive', *The Guardian*, 18 October.

Cobain, I. (2016), *The History Thieves*, London: Portobello Books.

Cobain, I. (2018a), 'Wilson government used secret unit to smear union leaders', *The Guardian*, <https://www.theguardian.com/politics/2018/jul/24/wilson-government-used-secret-unit-to-smear-union-leaders> (last accessed 24 July 2018).

Cobain, I. (2018b), '"Subversive" civil servants secretly blacklisted under Thatcher', *The Guardian*, 24 July, <https://www.theguardian.com/uk-news/2018/jul/24/subversive-civil-servants-secretly-blacklisted-under-thatcher> (last accessed 24 July 2018)

Cobain, I. (2018c), 'What did Jack Straw know about the UK's role in torture and rendition?', *The Guardian*, 28 June.

Cobain, I. and J. Doward, (2018), 'MI6 put questions to prisoner waterboarded 83 times by CIA', *The Guardian*. 30 June.

Cobain, I. and E. MacAskill (2018), 'True scale of UK role in torture and rendition after 9/11 revealed', *The Guardian*, 28 June.

Cobain, I., A. Ross, R. Evans and M. Mahmood (2016), 'Revealed: UK's covert propaganda bid to stop Muslims joining Isis', *The Guardian*, 2 May.

Cockburn, P. and P. Lashmar (2001), 'Spy tells of MI6 smear of UN boss', *New Zealand Herald*, 21 January.

Cole, M., R. Esposito, M. Schone and G. Greenwald (2014), 'Snowden docs show British spies used sex and "dirty tricks"', *NBC News*, <http://www.nbcnews.com/feature/edward-snowden-interview/exclusive-snowden-docs-show-british-spies-used-sex-dirty-tricks-n23091> (last accessed 30 July 2019).

Conant, J. (2009), *The Irregulars: Roald Dahl and the British Spy Ring in Wartime Washington*, New York: Simon & Schuster.

Cook, J. (2016) Explore Cuban leader Fidel Castro's controversial life in photos, *Huffington Post*, <https://www.huffingtonpost.co.uk/entry/fidel-castro-life-in-photos_n_5839a286e4b000af95ee4e34?guccounter=1&guce_referrer=aHR0cHM6Ly93d3cuZ29vZ2xlLmNvbS88&guce_referrer_sig=AQAAAIZYO3mFxsxPIF_5k8XqaaVmw1IPdeyJLoUaxEtyZtRNxkaN998CdVLFGJX-JphnfQhXX8OQmNSIf67pFVKbhKkOXpp5vY7lyvgCMsoi5Hub0RuCeHlBK_YMQivpiYa9H-Z6GoQG6qAM4g-KBCc9cmge83pfcYBYli3kGd54ddhX> (last accessed 16 September 2019).

Cookridge, E. H. (1965), *Inside SOE*, London: Arthur Barker.

Corera, G. (2015), 'MI5 "secretly collected phone data" for decades', *BBC News*, 5 November.

Corera, G. (2017a), *The Art of Betrayal: The Secret History of MI6: Life and Death in the British Secret Service*, London: Pegasus Books.

Corera, G. (2017b), 'Inside GCHQ', *BBC News*, 5 April, <http://www.bbc.co.uk/news/uk-39508983> (last accessed 29 August 2018).

Cormac, R. (2018), *Disrupt and Deny*, Oxford: Oxford University Press.

Crewdson, M. J. (1977), 'Worldwide propaganda network built by the C.I.A.', *The New York Times*, 26 December.

Cromwell, O. (1842), *The Very Interesting Life of the Famous Oliver Cromwell Lord Protector of the Commonwealth of England, Scotland, and Ireland*, London: Thomas Allmann.

Cronkite, Walter (1984) article in Society of Professional Journalists, *Leading Journalists Tell What a Free Press Means to America*, Chicago: SPJ.

Crozier, B. (1994), *Free Agent*, London: HarperCollins.

Cruickshank, C. (1981), *Fourth Arm: Psychological Warfare, 1938–45*, Oxford: Oxford University Press.

Cull, N. J. (1995), *Selling War*, Oxford: Oxford University Press.

Cull, N. J., D. Culbert and D. Welch (eds) (2003), *Propaganda and Mass Persuasion*, Santa Barbara, CA: ABC-CLIO.

Curran, J. and Seaton, J. (2010), *Power without Responsibility: The Press, Broadcasting, and Internet in Britain*, 7th edn, London and New York: Routledge.

Curtis, A. (2004), 'The Power of Nightmares', three-part TV series. UK: BBC.

Curtis, L. (1984), *Ireland: The Propaganda War*, London: Pluto Press.

Daily Telegraph (1995), Obituary of Peter Wright, 28 April.

Daily Telegraph (2009), Obituary of David Smiley, 9 January.

Davies, N. (2008), *Flat Earth News: An Award-Winning Reporter Exposes Falsehood, Distortion and Propaganda in the Global Media*, London: Chatto & Windus.

Davies, N. and D. Leigh (1984), 'Spyhunter threat to expose MI5', *The Observer*, 22 July.

Davies, P. H. J. (2009), 'Theory and intelligence reconsidered', in P. Gill, S. Marrin and M. Phythian (eds), *Intelligence Theory: Key Questions and Debates*, Abingdon: Routledge, pp. 186–207.

Dearden, L. (2018), 'Parliament car crash is sixth attempted terror attack targeting Westminster in 17 months', *The Independent*, 14 August.

de Burgh, H. (ed.) (2008), *Investigative Journalism*, Oxford: Routledge.

Deery, P. (1997), 'Confronting the Cominform: George Orwell and the Cold War offensive of the Information Research Department, 1948–50', *Labour History*, 73 (November), 219–25.

Defty, A. (2002), '"Close and continuous liaison": British anti-communist propaganda and cooperation with the United States, 1950–51', *Intelligence and National Security*, 17: 4, 100–30.

Delmer, S. (1961), *Trail Sinister*, London: Secker & Warburg.

Delmer, S. (1962), *Black Boomerang*, London: Secker & Warburg.

Der Derian, J. (2000), 'Virtuous war/virtual theory', *International Affairs*, 76: 4, 771–80.

Der Spiegel (2013), 'Snowden document: NSA spied on Al Jazeera communications', *Der Spiegel*, 31 August, <http://www.spiegel.de/international/world/nsa-spied-on-al-jazeera-communications-snowden-document-a-919681.html> (last accessed 17 June 2019).

de Vries, T. (2012), 'The 1967 Central Intelligence Agency scandal: catalyst in a transforming relationship between state and people', *The Journal of American History*, 98: 4 (March), 1075–92.

Doctorow, C. (2015), *Start the Week*, Radio programme, BBC Radio 4, 20 January.

Doctorow, C. (2019), 'Ex-NSA whistleblower says she and other US ex-spooks targeted Americans on behalf of UAE', *Boing Boing*, 14 February, <https://boingboing.net/2019/02/14/literal-american-exceptionalis.html> (last accessed 15 February 2019).

Dodds-Parker, A. (1997), Interviewed by James Oliver, 25 July.

Donnelly, P. (2012), *Assassinations*, London: Dataday Publishing.

Dorling, P. (2013), 'Living in a state of surveillance', *The Melbourne Age*, 13 June, <http://www.theage.com.au/it-pro/security-it/living-in-a-state-of-surveillance-20130612-2o4au.html> (last accessed 17 June 2019).

Dorril, S. (2002), *MI6: Inside the World of Her Majesty's Secret Intelligence Service*, London: Simon & Schuster.

Dorril, S. (2015), 'Russia accuses Fleet Street: journalists and MI6 during the Cold War', *The International Journal of Press/Politics*, 20: 2 (April), 204–27.

Dorril, S. and R. Ramsay (1992), *Smear! Wilson and the Secret State*, London: HarperCollins.

Dover, R. and M. S. Goodman (eds) (2009), *Spinning Intelligence: Why Intelligence Needs the Media, Why the Media Needs Intelligence*, London: C. Hurst.

Doward, J. (2019), 'Sex, ska and Malcolm X: MI6's covert 1960s mission to woo West Indians', *The Observer*, 26 January.

Drake, T. (2015), 'The whistleblower: an interview with Thomas Drake', Spycast, <https://www.spymuseum.org/exhibition-experiences/online-exhibits/agent-

storm/listen-to-the-audio/episode/the-whistleblower-an-interview-with-thom as-drake/> (last accessed 31 October 2019).

Drogin, B. (2007), *Curveball: Spies, Lies, and the Con Man Who Caused a War*, New York: Random House.

Dylan, H. (2015), 'Operation Tigress: deception for counterintelligence and Britain's 1952 atomic test', *Journal of Intelligence History*, 14: 1, 1–15.

Egawhary, E. (2010), 'Your next scoop is hiding in a spreadsheet', *Television* (May), 26–7.

Ellsberg, D. (2017), Skype talk to War, Journalism and Whistle-blowers panel, Birkbeck University, 2 March.

Ellsworth-Jones, W. (1984), 'How the KGB fools the West's press', *The Sunday Times*, 8 January.

Evans, H. (1983) *Good Times, Bad Times*, London: Atheneum

Evans, H. (2006), 'Journalism under pressure', speech on reporting terrorism by Sir Harold Evans, IPI World Congress, Edinburgh.

Evans, R. (2018), Interview with *The Guardian* journalist Rob Evans by the author.

Evans, H. (2019), Correspondence with the author.

Evans, R. and P. Lewis (2013), *Undercover: The True Story of Britain's Secret Police*, London: Guardian Books.

Fitzpatrick, S. (2019), 'People and Martians', *London Review of Books*, 41: 2 (24 January), 13–15.

Fletcher, R. (1972), *Who Were They Travelling With?* Privately published. There is a copy in the Lashmar Archive.

Fletcher, R. (1982), 'British propaganda since WWII – a case study', *Media, Culture and Society*, 4, 97–109.

Fletcher, R., G. Brock, P. Kelly, P. Lashmar, T. Smart and R. Oliver (1978), 'How the FO waged a secret propaganda war in Britain', *The Observer*, 29 January.

Foot, M. R. D. (1984), *SOE: the Special Operations Executive, 1940-46*, London: BBC.

Foot, P. (1990), *Who Framed Colin Wallace?*, London: Pan Books.

Forsyth, F. (2015), *The Outsider, My Life in Intrigue*, London: G. P. Putnam & Sons.

Foucault, M. (1980), *Power/Knowledge: Selected Interviews and Other Writings 1977–1984*, New York: Pantheon.

Franks, O. (1983), *Falkland Islands Review Report of a Committee of Privy Counsellors*. London: Her Majesty's Stationery Office.

Frost, C. (2011), *Journalism, Ethics and Regulation*, 3rd edn, Harlow: Longman.

Gall, S. (1994), *News from the Front: The Life of a Television Reporter*, London: William Heinemann.

Gellman, B. (2013), 'Code name "Verax": Snowden, in exchanges with Post reporter, made clear he knew risks', *Washington Post*, 9 June.

Gill, P. (1996), 'Reasserting control: recent changes in the oversight of the UK intelligence community', *Intelligence and National Security*, 11: 2, 313–31.

Gill, P. (2007), 'Evaluating intelligence oversight committees: the UK Intelligence and Security Committee and the "War on Terror"', *Intelligence and National Security*, 22: 1 (February), 14–37.

Gill, P. (2013), 'Obstacles to the oversight of the UK intelligence community', *E-International Relations*, 19 July, <http://www.e-ir.info/2013/07/19/obstacles-

to-the-oversight-of-the-uk-intelligence-community/> (last accessed 4 February 2015).

Gill, P. and M. Phythian (2012), *Intelligence in an Insecure World*, 2nd edn, Cambridge: Polity.

Gill, P., S. Marrin and M. Phythian (2009), *Intelligence Studies: Key Questions and Debates*, Abingdon: Routledge.

Glees, A. and P. Davies (2004), *Spinning the Spies: Intelligence, Open Government and the Hutton Inquiry*, London: Social Affairs Unit.

Graham, B. (1987), *Break-In*, London: Bodley Head.

Greenwald, G. (2014), 'Snowden docs show British spies used sex and "dirty tricks"', NBC News, <http://www.nbcnews.com/feature/edward-snowden-interview/exclusive-snowden-docs-show-british-spies-used-sex-dirty-tricks-n23091> (last accessed 26 October 2019).

Greenwald, G. (2017), 'The surveillance state', in E. Bell and O. Taylor (eds), *Journalism after Snowden*, New York: Columbia Journalism Review Books, pp. 34–52

Grey, S. (2004), 'US accused of "torture flights"', *Sunday Times*, 14 November.

Grey, S. (2006), *Ghost Plane: The Inside Story of the CIA's Secret Rendition Programme*, London: Hurst.

Griffith, R. (2010), *Patriotism Perverted: Captain Ramsay, the Right Club and British Anti-Semitism 1939–40*, London: Faber & Faber.

The Guardian (2019), 'The Guardian view on rendition and torture: a shame that Britain cannot erase', *The Guardian* (editorial), 28 July.

Guardian correspondent (1956), 'No retreat by Col Nasser?' *The Manchester Guardian*, 7 September.

Habermas, J. (1962), *The Structural Transformation of the Public Sphere: An Inquiry into a Category of Bourgeois Society*, Cambridge, MA: MIT Press.

Hall, S., C. Critcher, T. Jefferson, B. Roberts and J. Clarke (1978), *Policing the Crisis: Mugging, the State, and Law and Order*, London: Palgrave Macmillan.

Hampton, M. (2010), 'The fourth estate ideal in journalism history', in S. Allan (ed.), *The Routledge Companion to News and Journalism*, London: Routledge, pp. 3–12.

Hastings, C. (2006), 'Revealed: how the BBC used MI5 to vet thousands of staff', *The Telegraph*, 2 July.

Henderson, D. (1904), *Field Intelligence, Its Principles and Practice*, Pretoria: Government Printer.

Hiley, N. (2006), 'Entering the lists: MI5's great spy round-up of August 1914', *Intelligence and National Security*, 21: 1 (February), 46–76.

Hiley, N. (2010), 'Re-entering the lists: MI5's authorized history and the August 1914 arrests', *Intelligence and National Security*, 25: 4, 415–52.

Hillebrand, C. (2012), 'The role of news media in intelligence oversight', *Intelligence and National Security*, 27: 5, 689–706.

Hope, C. and B. Waterfield (2013), 'David Cameron: newspapers which publish Snowden secrets help terrorists who want to "blow up" families', *Daily Telegraph*, 25 October.

Hopkins, N. and L. Harding (2013), 'GCHQ accused of selling its services after revelations of funding by NSA', *The Guardian*, 2 August.

Huhne C. (2013), 'Prism and Tempora: the cabinet was told nothing of the surveillance state's excesses', *The Observer*, 6 October.

Hulnick, A. and D. W. Mattausch (1989), 'Ethics and morality in United States secret intelligence', *Harvard Journal of Law & Public Policy*, 12: 2 (Spring), 509–22.

Intelligence and Security Committee (2018a), Detainee Mistreatment and Rendition 2001-2018. HC1113.

Intelligence and Security Committee (2018b), Detainee Mistreatment and Rendition Current Issues. HC1114.

ITN News (1988) 9.00 pm, 6 March.

Jack, I. (2018), 'Time for several whiskies', *London Review of Books*, 40: 16 (30 August), 3–8.

Jeffery, K. (2010), *MI6: The History of the Secret Intelligence Service, 1909–1949*, London: Bloomsbury.

Jeffreys-Jones, R. (2018), 'The sensitivity of SIGINT: Sir Alfred Ewing's lecture on room 40 in 1927', *Journal of Intelligence History*, 17: 1, 18–29.

Jenkins, S. (2013), 'The days of believing spy chiefs who say "Trust us" are over', *The Guardian*, 20 November.

Jenks, J. (2006), *British Propaganda and News Media in the Cold War*, Edinburgh: Edinburgh University Press.

Johnson, L. K. (1988), *A Season of Inquiry: Congress and Intelligence*, Chicago: Dorsey Press.

Johnson, L. K. (2011), *The Threat on the Horizon: An Inside Account of America's Search for Security After the Cold War*, Oxford: Oxford University Press.

Johnson, L. K. (2013), 'Intelligence shocks, media coverage and Congressional accountability 1946–2012', *Journal of Intelligence History*, 13: 1, 1–21.

Johnson, L. K. (2015), Correspondence with the author, 23 February.

Johnson, L. K. (2018a), Interview with Vince Houghton, *Spycast*, 6 February.

Johnson, L. K. (2018b) *Spy Watching*, Oxford: Oxford University Press.

Johnston, R. (2005), *Analytic Culture in the U.S. Intelligence Community: An Ethnographic Study*, Washington, DC: Central Intelligence Agency.

Keeble, R. (1997), *Secret State, Silent Press*, Luton: John Libbey Media.

Keeble, R. L. (2008), 'Uncovered: British reporters who are spooks', *The-Latest.com*, 2 July, <http://www.the-latest.com/uncovered-british-reporters-who-are-spooks> (last accessed 8 August 2018).

King, C. (1971), *Without Fear or Favour*, London: Sidgwick and Jackson.

Kington, T. (2009), 'Recruited by MI5: the name's Mussolini. Benito Mussolini', *The Guardian*, 13 October.

Knight, F. H. (1921), *Risk, Uncertainty and Profit. Hart, Schaffner, and Marx Prize Essays, No. 31*. Boston and New York: Houghton Mifflin.

Knightley, P. (1986), *The Second Oldest Profession: Spies and Spying in the Twentieth Century*, London: André Deutsch.

Knightley, P. (2006), 'Journalists and spies: an unhealthy relationship', *Ethical Space*, 3: 2/3, 7–11.

Laqueur, W. (ed.) (1977), *The Guerrilla Reader: A Historical Anthology*, Philadelphia: Temple University Press.

Laqueur, W. (ed.) (1978), *The Terrorism Reader: A Historical Anthology*, Philadelphia: Temple University Press.

Lashmar, P. (1992), 'Walking a tightrope', *West Africa Magazine*, 24 February–1 March, p. 326.

Lashmar, P. (1994), 'Mr. Waldegrave's need to know', *History Today*, 44: 8 (August), 5–9.

Lashmar, P. (1996), 'Baiting the bear – how the real life Dr Strangelove generals brought us close to Armageddon', *Timewatch*, television programme, BBC, 8 October.

Lashmar, P. (1998), 'US air strike: how a phoney passport led the FBI to the lair of the embassy bombers', *The Independent*, 21 August.

Lashmar, P. (1999), 'MI6 officers use forged press passes', *The Independent*, 14 June.

Lashmar, P. (2000a), 'The who's who of British Nazis', *The Independent*, 9 January, p. 1.

Lashmar, P. (2000b), 'Is a good story worth a prison sentence?', *The Independent*, 28 March, p. 8.

Lashmar, P. (2000c), 'Europe sound alarm as Britain backs US cyber-spies', *The Independent*, 14 May, p. 6.

Lashmar, P. (2001), 'Infamous casement "black diaries" to be tested for veracity', *The Independent*, 16 January.

Lashmar, P. (2003), 'Iraq & the WMD fiasco: Saddam destroyed weapons in 1990s', *Independent on Sunday*, 6 July.

Lashmar, P. (2004), 'Special report: War on Terror – terror – they say it changed the world for ever. But how?', *Independent on Sunday*, 12 September.

Lashmar, P. (2007a), 'Victory to the traffickers Britain's drugs debâcle; heroin and cocaine prices on the street are at record lows as seizures plummet', *Independent on Sunday*, 25 November.

Lashmar, P. (2007b), 'Record £125m in assets recovered from criminals', *The Guardian*, 24 May.

Lashmar, P. (2008a), 'From shadow boxing to ghost plane: English journalism and the war on terror', in H. de Burgh (ed.), *Investigative Journalism: Theory & Practice*, 2nd edn, Abingdon: Routledge, pp. 191–214.

Lashmar, P. (2008b), 'The great class A drugs sale; how prices have tumbled under Labour', *The Independent on Sunday*, 9 March, 1.

Lashmar, P. (2013), 'Urinal or open channel? Institutional information flow between the UK intelligence services and news media', *Journalism: Theory, Practice and Criticism*, 14: 8 (November), 1024–40.

Lashmar, P. (2015a), 'Investigating the "Empire of Secrecy" – Three Decades of Reporting on the Secret State', PhD thesis, Brunel University.

Lashmar, P. (2015b), 'Spies at *The Observer*', *British Journalism Review*, 26: 3 (September), 60–5.

Lashmar, P. (2015c), 'Spies and journalists: towards an ethical framework?', *Ethical Space, The International Journal of Communication Ethics*, 12: 3/4, 4–14.

Lashmar, P. (2015d), 'Review of Jean Seaton's Pinkoes and Traitors,' *British Journal of Film and TV*, 12: 4, 595–98.

Lashmar, P. (2017a), 'Putting lives in danger? Tinker, tailor, journalist, spy: the use of journalistic cover', *Journalism: Theory, Practice and Criticism*, online first, 13 September.

Lashmar, P. (2017b), 'No more sources? The impact of Snowden's revelations on journalists and their confidential sources', *Journalism Practice*, 11: 6, 665–88, online first 2016.

Lashmar, P. (2018a), 'Nest of spies', *British Journalism Review*, 29: 1 (March), 53–9.

Lashmar, P. (2018b), 'Journalistic freedom and surveillance of journalists post-Snowden', in B. Franklin and S. A. Eldridge (eds), *The Routledge Handbook of Developments in Digital Journalism Studies*, Abingdon: Routledge, pp. 360–72.

Lashmar, P. and A. Mullins (1998), 'Churchill protected Scottish peer suspected of spying for Japan; Second World War: government papers show prominent aristocrat was believed to be leaking naval secrets to Tokyo', *The Independent*, 24 August.

Lashmar, P. and J. Oliver (1998a), 'How we destroyed Sukarno; Foreign Office "dirty tricks" helped overthrow Indonesia's President Sukarno in 1966', *The Independent*, 1 December.

Lashmar, P. and J. Oliver (1998b), *Britain's Secret Propaganda War: A History of the Foreign Office's Information Research Department 1948–77*, Stroud: Sutton.

Lashmar, P. and J. Oliver (2000), 'MI6 spread lies to put killer in power', *Independent on Sunday*, 16 April.

Lashmar, P. and R. Oliver (1996), 'How well does your local council really do its job?', *The Observer*, 3 May.

Lashmar, P. and D. Usborne (1999), 'MI6 officers worked in Iraq as UN inspectors', *The Independent*, 25 January, p. 1.

Lashmar, P. and R. Whitaker (2003), 'On the brink of war: the spies' revolt MI6 and CIA: the new enemy within', *Independent on Sunday*, 9 February.

le Carré, J. [1963] (2013), *The Spy Who Came in from the Cold*, Harmondsworth: Penguin.

Leigh, D. (1978), 'Death of the department that never was', *The Guardian*, 27 January.

Leigh, D. (1984), 'Belgrano case man revealed', *The Observer*, 22 August.

Leigh, D. (1986), 'MI5 fails to gag *The Observer*', *The Observer*, 27 July.

Leigh, D. (1987), 'MI5 secrets kept from Armstrong', *The Observer*, 29 November.

Leigh, D. (1988), *The Wilson Plot: How the Spycatchers and Their American Allies Tried to Overthrow the British Government*, London: Pantheon Books.

Leigh, D. (1989), 'Smiley's people secured Oman airbase', *The Observer*, 1 January.

Leigh, D. (1990), 'MI5 on trial', Thames TV *This Week* programme, 26 April.

Leigh, D. (2000), 'Tinker, tailor, soldier, journalist', *The Guardian*, 12 June.

Leigh, D. (2009), 'Review of The Defence of the Realm: The Authorized History of MI5 by Christopher Andrew', *The Guardian*, 10 October.

Leigh, D. and P. Lashmar (1982), 'The well paid art of conning the media', *The Observer*, 3 January.

Leigh, D. and P. Lashmar (1983), 'Double-glazer put MI6 on trail of Russian agents', *The Observer*, 20 February.

Leigh, D. and P. Lashmar (1984a), 'Mark Thatcher and a £300m Arab deal', *The Observer*, 15 January.

Leigh, D. and P. Lashmar (1984b), 'MI5 double agent defects to *The Observer*', *The Observer*, 7 October.

Leigh, D. and P. Lashmar (1984c), 'MI5 on legal moves to stop agents telling all', *The Observer*, 16 December.

Leigh, D. and P. Lashmar (1984d), '"Soviet" faked tape is rock group hoax', *The Observer*, 22 January.

Leigh, D. and P. Lashmar (1985a), 'Secret service cash soars in secret', *The Observer*, 3 March.

Leigh, D. and P. Lashmar (1985b), 'Revealed: how MI5 vets BBC staff', *The Observer*, 18 August, pp. 1, 9.

Leigh, D. and P. Lashmar (1986), 'MI5 memoirs to be revealed in courtroom', *The Observer*, 22 June.

Leigh, D. and P. Lashmar (1987a), 'Tests back MI5 "dirty tricks plot" allegations', *The Observer*, 5 July.

Leigh, D. and P. Lashmar (1987b), 'MI5 bid to blacklist Anna Ford', *The Observer*, 27 September.

Leigh, D. and P. Lashmar (1988a), 'MI6 "blew up Jewish ships"', *The Observer*, 22 June.

Leigh, D. and P. Lashmar (1988b), 'Right-wing job blacklist revealed', *The Observer*, 4 September.

Leigh, D. and P. Lashmar (1989), 'Insight into distortion', *The Observer*, 15 January, p. 6.

Lemke, T. (2001), 'The birth of bio-politics: Michel Foucault's lectures at the Collège de France on neo-liberal governmentality', *Economy and Society*, 30: 2, 190–207.

Lippmann, W. (1922), *Public Opinion*, <http://image.sciencenet.cn/olddata/kexue.com.cn/upload/blog/file/2010/11/20101113143833504463.pdf> (last accessed 7 November 2014).

Lloyd, J. (2017), *Journalism in the Age of Terror*, London: I. B. Tauris.

Lofgren, M. (2016), *The Deep State: The Fall of the Constitution and the Rise of a Shadow Government*, New York: Penguin.

Logan, C. (2018), 'Woman duped into relationship by undercover cop tells how he used tales of childhood abuse and mental trauma as part of his act', *Commonspace*, 23 June, <https://www.commonspace.scot/articles/12929/woman-duped-relationship-undercover-cop-tells-how-he-used-tales-childhood-abuse-and> (last accessed 5 August).

Lownie, A. (2015), *Stalin's Englishman*, London: Hodder & Stoughton.

Lycett, A. (1996), *Ian Fleming*. London Weidenfeld and Nicholson.

McCrisken, T. and C. Moran (2018), 'James Bond, Ian Fleming and intelligence: breaking down the boundary between the "real" and the "imagined"', *Intelligence and National Security*, 33: 6, 804–21.

McFadden, C., W. M. Arkin and T. Uehlinger (2017), 'How the Trump team's first military raid in Yemen went wrong', *NBC News*, 2 October.

McSmith, A., P. Lashmar and J. Bennetto (2004), 'This is the tower at Canary Wharf. Was it the target of an al-Qa'ida plot of a cynical exercise in fear-mongering?', *Independent on Sunday*, 28 November.

Mahl, T. E. (1998), *Desperate Deception: British Covert Operations in the United States, 1939–44*, New York: Brassey's.

Mantel, H. (2009), *Wolf Hall*, London: HarperColllns.

Matthews, O. (2018), 'How Bellingcat outfoxes the world's spy agencies', *The Spectator*, 20 October.

Meek, J. G. (2018), Interview with Vince Houghton, *Spycast*, 10 July.

Melley, T. (2012), *The Covert Sphere*, London: Cornell University Press.

Meyer, C. (1982), *Facing Reality*, Lanham, MD: University Press of America.

MI5 (1993), *MI5: The Security Service*, London: HMSO.

Miller, D. (1993), 'Official sources and "primary definition": the case of Northern Ireland', *Media, Culture & Society*, 15: 3, 385–406.

Miller, J. (1986), *One Girl's War: Personal Exploits in MI5's Most Secret Station*, Dublin: Brandon.

Mills, C. W. [1956] (2000), *The Power Elite*, new edn, Oxford: Oxford University Press.

Montgomery Hyde, H. (1989), *The Quiet Canadian: The Secret Service Story of Sir William Stephenson*, London: Constable.

Montgomery Hyde, H. [1963] (2001), *Room 3603*, Guilford: The Lyons Press

Moore, C. (2013), 'Edward Snowden is a traitor, just as surely as George Blake was', *Daily Telegraph*, 5 July.

Moran, C. (2011), 'Intelligence and the media: the press, government secrecy and "Buster" Crabb Affair', *Intelligence and National Security*, 26: 5, 676–700.

Moran, C. (2013), *Classified: Secrecy and the State in Modern Britain*, Cambridge: Cambridge University Press.

Muggeridge, M. (1973), *The Infernal Grove: Chronicles of Wasted Time: Number 2*, London: HarperCollins.

Mullin, C. (2013), 'Can the security and intelligence services answer the accountability question?', *The Guardian*, 16 December.

Naftali, T. (1993), 'Intrepid's last deception: documenting the career of Sir William Stephenson', *Intelligence and National Security*, 8: 3, 72–99.

Nasrawi, S. (2007), 'Egyptian kidnap victim "was tortured"', *Independent News*, 13 February.

The New York Times (1976), 'The reporter and the spy', *The New York Times* (editorial), 3 January.

Nichols, P. (1978), 'Assault on Britain's "lie factory" by Jesuit', *The Times*, Thursday, 19 January.

Nolan, B. (2013), 'Information Sharing and Collaboration in the United States Intelligence Community: An Ethnographic Study of the National Counterterrorism Center', PhD dissertation, University of Pennsylvania.

Northcott, C. (2015), *MI5 at War 1909–1918: How MI5 Foiled the Spies of the Kaiser in the First World War*, London: Tattered Flag Press.

Norton-Taylor, R. (2000), 'Papers win Shayler case', *The Guardian*, 22 July.

Norton-Taylor, R. (2001), 'MI5 detained Trotsky on way to revolution', *The Guardian*, 5 July.

Norton-Taylor, R. and M. White (2004), 'Blair misused intelligence, says ex-spy officer', *The Guardian*, 29 October.

Observer Reporters (1984), 'Bettaney spy case reveals MI5's bungles', *The Observer*, 22 April.

O'Carroll, L. (2013), 'Seymour Hersh on Obama, NSA and the "pathetic" American media', *The Guardian*, 27 September.

Omand, D. (2009), 'Intelligence secret and media spotlights: balancing illumination and dark corners', in R. Dover and M. S. Goodman (eds), *Spinning Intelligence: Why Intelligence Needs the Media, Why Media Needs Intelligence*, London: C. Hurst.

Omand, D. (2015), 'Journalists, surveillance and the police: how can the secret state learn to live with the fourth estate?', Discussion panel at City, University of London, 30 March.

PA Mediapoint (2007), 'MI5 director addresses Society of Editors conference', *Press Gazette*, 7 November.

Page, B., Leitch, D. and Knightley, P. (1968), *Philby: The Spy who Betrayed a Generation*, Harmondsworth: Penguin Books.

Philby, K. (1969), *My Silent War*, London: Panther.

Phythian, M. (2005), 'Still a matter of trust', *International Journal of Intelligence and CounterIntelligence*, 18, 653–81.

Phythian, M. (2007), 'The British experience with intelligence accountability', *Intelligence and National Security*, 22: 1 (February), 75–9.

Picard, R. and H. Storm (2016), *The Kidnapping of Journalists: Reporting from High-Risk Conflict Zones*, Oxford: Reuters Institute.

Pike, O. (1977), *CIA: The Pike Report (Extracts)*, Nottingham: Spokesman Books.

Pincher, C. (1981), *Their Trade is Treachery*, London: Sidgwick and Jackson.

Pincher, P. (1987), *A Web of Deception: The Spycatcher Affair*, London: Sidgwick and Jackson.

Pincher, C. (2009), 'Reflections of a lifetime of reporting on intelligence affairs', in R. Dover and M. S. Goodman (eds), *Spinning Intelligence: Why Intelligence Needs the Media, Why the Media Needs Intelligence*, London: C. Hurst, pp. 149–64.

Ponting, C. (1985), *The Right to Know: The Inside Story of the Belgrano Affair*, London: Sphere Books.

Porter, B. (1989), *Plots and Paranoia: A History of Political Espionage in Britain 1790–1988*, London: Unwin Hyman.

Poulantzas, N. (1975), *Classes in Contemporary Capitalism*, London: New Left Books.

Purvis, S. and J. Hulbert (2013), *When Reporters Cross the Line*, London: Biteback.

Ransom, H. H. (1975), 'Secret intelligence agencies and Congress', *Society*, 12: 3, 33–8.

Rawls, J. (1971), *A Theory of Justice*, Cambridge, MA: Harvard University Press.

Reese, S and Lewis, S. (2009), 'Framing the war on terror: the internalization of policy in the US press', *Journalism*. 10: 6, 777–97.

Reynolds, P. (2018), 'The vetting files', *BBC*, 22 April, <https://www.bbc.co.uk/news/ampstories/the-vetting-files/index.html> (last accessed 30 July 2019).

Richardson, P. (2009), *A Bomb in Every Issue*, New York: The New Press.

Richelson, J. (1995), *A Century of Spies: Intelligence in the Twentieth Century*, Oxford: Oxford University Press.

Robertson, J. (1997), Interviewed for 'Gentleman Spies', *Timewatch*, television programme, BBC, 18 November.

Rose, D. (1994), 'First the Cold War ended. Now the IRA ceasefire spells big changes for MI5', *The Observer*, 18 September.

Rooo, D. (2007), 'Spies and their lies', *New Statesman*, 27 September, <https://www.newstatesman.com/politics/2007/09/mi6-mi5-intelligence-briefings> (last accessed 29 July 2019).

Rusbridger, A. (2011), 'Hacking away at the truth: Alan Rusbridger's Orwell Lecture', *The Guardian*, 10 November.

Rusbridger, A. (2013), '*Guardian* will not be intimidated over NSA leaks, Alan Rusbridger tells MPs', *The Guardian*, 3 December.

Schlesinger, P. (1991), *Media, State and Nation: Political Violence and Collective Identities*, London: Sage.

Schlosberg, J. (2013), *Power beyond Scrutiny: Media, Justice and Accountability*, London: Pluto Press.

Scott, L. and P. Jackson (2004), 'The study of intelligence in theory and practice', *Intelligence and National Security*, 19: 2, 146–9.

Shorrock, T. (2013), 'Put spies back under one roof', *The New York Times* 17 June, <http://www.nytimes.com/2013/06/18/opinion/put-the-spies-back-under-one-roof.html?_r=0> (last accessed 28 October 2019).

Sweet-Escott, B. (1965) *Baker Street Irregular*, London: Methuen.

Shirbon, E. (2015), 'UK tribunal says intelligence-sharing with U.S. was unlawful', *Reuters*, 6 February.

Shpiro, S. (2001), 'The media strategies of intelligence services', *International Journal of Intelligence and CounterIntelligence*, 14: 485–502.

Skinner, Q. and R. Marshall (2013), 'Liberty, liberalism and surveillance: a historic overview', *Open Democracy*, 26 July.

Smiley, D. (1984), *Albanian Assignment*, London: Chatto & Windus.

Smith, J. (2012), *British Writers and MI5 Surveillance, 1930–1960*, Cambridge: Cambridge University Press.

Smith, L. (1980), 'Covert British propaganda: the Information Research Department: 1947-1977', *Millennium*, 9: 1, 67–83.

Smith, M. (2003), *The Spying Game*, London: Politicos.

Smith, M. (2006), 'The great MI5 spy coup that wasn't', *New Statesman*, 3 April.

Smith, M. (2007), *The Spying Game*, London: Politicos.

Smith, M. (2010), *Six: The Real James Bonds 1909–1939*, London: Biteback.

Snepp, F. (1981), Interview on BBC TV's *Panorama* programme, 23 February.

Sobel, L. A. (1975), *Political Terrorism*, New York: Facts on File.

Sparrow, A. (2014), 'MPs question intelligence services commissioner: politics live blog', *The Guardian*, 18 March.

Stafford, D. (1986), *Camp X: SOE and the American Connection*, London: Viking.

Stevenson, W. (1976), *A Man Called Intrepid: The Secret War 1939–1945*, London: Book Club Associates.

Stonor Saunders, F. (1999), *Who Paid the Piper?*, Cambridge: Granta.

Stout, M. and C. Moran (2018), 'Spy chiefs: a conversation with Mark Stout and Chris Moran with Vince Houghton', *Spycast*, 5 June.

Thomas, E. (1996), *The Very Best Men: Four Who Dared: The Early Years of the CIA*, New York: Simon & Schuster.

Thompson, E. P. (1980), *Writing by Candlelight*, London: Merlin.

Thomson, G. P. (1947), *Blue Pencil Admiral – Secrets of the Press Censorship by the Chief Censor*, London: Sampson Low, Marston & Co.

Today (2003), BBC Radio 4, 4 June, transcript, <http://www.guardian.co.uk/politics/2003/jun/04/iraq.iraq> (last accessed 7 February 2015).

Tomlinson, R. (2001), *The Big Breach: From Top Secret to Maximum Security*, London: Mainstream Publishing.

Trelford, D. (ed.) (1980), *Siege: Seven Days at the Iranian Embassy*, London: Macmillan.

Trelford, D. (2018), *Shouting in the Street*, London: Biteback.

Tugwell, M. (1971), Public Opinion and the Northern Ireland Situation, A Note by the Colonel GS (Information Policy, HQ Northern Ireland), 9 November

Turvill, W. (2014), 'Police chief constable: RIPA should "absolutely" be used to investigate press leaks', *Press Gazette*, 4 November.

Turvill, W. (2015), 'Interception commissioner: 82 journalists' phone records grabbed by police in three years, judicial oversight needed', *Press Gazette*, 4 February.

Tzu, S. (2007), *The Art of War*, Minneapolis: Filiquarian Publishing.

USCNS/21 (2001), *Roadmap for National Security: Imperative for Change*, Washington, DC: US Government Printing Office.

Vincent, D. (1991), 'The origins of public secrecy in Britain', *Transactions of the Royal Historical Society*, 1, 229–48.

Walker, H. (2014), 'These 7 men owned the company linked to CIA torture', *Business Insider*, 11 December, <http://uk.businessinsider.com/the-company-behind-cia-torture-2014-12> (last accessed 17 June 2019).

Walters, J. (2013), 'NSA "hacking unit" infiltrates computers around the world – report', *The Guardian*, 29 December.

Ware, J. (2013), 'Britain's secret terror force', *Panorama*, television programme, BBC, 21 November.

Warner, M. (2009), 'Intelligence and risk shifting', in P. Gill, S. Marrin and M. Phythian (eds), *Intelligence Theory: Key Questions and Debates*, Abingdon: Routledge.

Webb, A. (2014), *London Calling: Britain, the BBC World Service and the Cold War*, London: Bloomsbury.

Whitaker, R. and P. Lashmar (2005), 'Franchise terrorism: "trying to hit al-Qa'ida is like trying to hit jelly"', *Independent on Sunday*, 10 July.

Whitaker, R., P. Lashmar, S. Goodchild, S. Carrell, J. Huggler and L. Veevers (2006), 'The fight against terror: Surveillance UK', *Independent on Sunday*, 20 August.

Wilford, H. (1998), 'The Information Research Department: Britain's secret Cold War weapon revealed', *Review of International Studies*, 24: 3, 353–69.

Wilford, H. (2008), *The Mighty Wurlitzer: How the CIA Played America*, London: Harvard University Press.

Wilkinson, N. (2009), *Secrecy and the Media: The Official History of the United Kingdom's D-Notice System*, London: Routledge.

Wilkinson, P. (1986), *Terrorism and the Liberal State*, 2nd edn, New York: New York University Press.

Wood, V. (2016), 'GOT HIM: Taliban leader WIPED OUT by furious firepower of multiple drones', *Daily Express*, 22 May.

Wright, P. with P. Greengrass (1987), *Spycatcher*, London: Viking.

294 / Spies, Spin and the Fourth Estate

FI I Authoriood Representative: Easy Access System Europe Mustamäe tee 5
0, 10621 Tallinn, Estonia gpsr.requests@easproject.com

Printed and bound by CPI Group (UK) Ltd, Croydon, CR0 4YY

16/04/2025

01846994-0001